THE BRASS BELL

The Legacy of Marion Parsons

By Nancy "Camille" Cole

SAHALIE PUBLISHING • EUGENE, OREGON

Copyright © 2013, Nancy "Camille" Cole

Published in the United States

All rights reserved. No part of this book may be used or reproduced in any manner, without the written permission of the publisher, Sahalie Publishing, except where brief excerpts are reprinted for review purposes only.

Manufactured in the United States of America

Edited by Ali McCart and Holly Franko

Cover and interior design by James Kiehle / www.jameskiehle.com

Printed by United Graphics, Incorporated

For the chicken-coop kids who lived to share their story:
Mildred Mitchell Dunk, Betty Templar Jerome (Van Jerome),
and Leland Mitchell

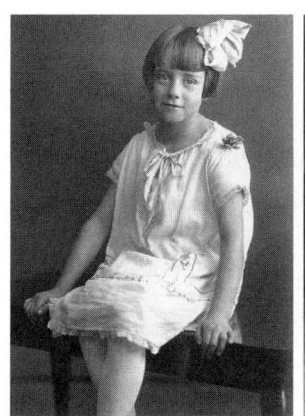  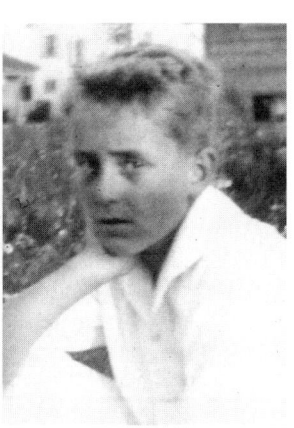

Millie Mitchell   **Betty Templar Jerome**   **Leland Mitchell**

Contents

Introduction
Prologue
Chapter One—Marion Parsons —1
Chapter Two—Her Great Adventure—7
Chapter Three—Lemon Trees—19
Chapter Four—Going Home—32
Chapter Five—The Fire—42
Chapter Six—Terry Road School, End of an Era—57
Chapter Seven—The Brass Bell—72
Chapter Eight—The New School—82
Chapter Nine—A Red Brick Schoolhouse—88
Chapter Ten—The Mothers' Club—96
Chapter Eleven—Our Miss Parsons—108
Chapter Twelve—The Great Depression—117
Chapter Thirteen—The Discipline—131
Chapter Fourteen—The Circus—135
Chapter Fifteen—Cherry Road School—144
Chapter Sixteen—A Time to Remember—153
Chapter Seventeen—The Class Trip—156
Chapter Eighteen—Our Miss Parsons—161
Chapter Nineteen—World War II—168
Chapter Twenty—A Life of Dreams—181
Chapter Twenty-One—Farms, Families, and Baby Booms—190
Chapter Twenty-Two—Good-bye, Miss Parsons—199
Chapter Twenty-Three—My Aunt Marion—214
Chapter Twenty-Four—Marion —221
Epilogue—228
Afterword—234
Maps—237, 238
Appendix A— What became of the Cherry Road Alumni?—240
Appendix B—Parsons Family Tree—243
References/Permissions—254
Photographic Credits—256
About the Author—261

Acknowledgments

Though it's not possible to name all the friends, family, former Cherry Road School students and neighbors who contributed to The Brass Bell for fear of leaving someone out, there are a few I must acknowledge. The Solvay-Geddes Historical Society gave me unfailing support throughout the years: Susan Millet, Jim Jerome and Joe Barnello.

Through this project, I reunited with cousins I haven't seen since childhood and some I have never met. Cousin Charles "Chuck" Parsons, his wife, Elfriede, sister, Martha Parsons Paine, and son, John C. Parsons II, were there every step of the long way, sharing stories about their arm of the family. Their abiding belief in the project drove me onward when I couldn't go on. Sally Parsons Stewart shared letters written by her father and grandfather, providing a glimpse into a time and place and people whose lives came to a conclusion a long time ago. Cousin Anna Gordon imparted her magnificent Parsons database—she has lovingly and energetically tracked our family for thirty years. Many thanks to all the Cole, Jerome, and Parsons cousins, including, but not limited to, Aunt Betty Jerome, Jim Jerome, Patty Jerome, Ruth Springer, Bob Burford; my Cole cousins, Jay, Barb, Dave, John Peter.

Thanks also to the remaining Cherry Road neighbors who endure in their loyalty to Miss Parsons—the Owen brothers, Dennis and Joe, Bob and Joan Coulter, Marilyn Lewis Marcy, Alexandra Terziev and her daughter, Katherine Greenleaf, and all the others, too many to name.

The administration and staff at Cherry Road School opened their doors to me, smiles on their faces. They all demonstrate a level of excellence at the school for which my Aunt Marion would be proud.

I have deep gratitude for every Cherry Road School graduate who spent untold hours sharing their stories, information about the history of the school, and their love for Miss Parsons—thank you. Many are featured here in The Brass Bell. I would especially like to thank Jack Mitchell and the entire Mitchell Family, and Martha Ballard Lacy and her husband, Dick. Without their loyal support there would be no book.

I am grateful for my friends and colleagues who contributed their expertise, making sure *The Brass Bell* would meet my Aunt Marion's standards of excellence. Thanks to Indigo Editing, MyWord Editing, Mary Kitchel, John Anthony, James Kiehle, and of course, Sahalie Publishing, my dear friends, Nicki, Sheila, and Lois.

Thanks to my daughter Iris for her abiding interest in family history; you were my inspiration to pick up where I had left off.

Many cheers to my beloved Aunt Marion for sharing those stories about the Olden Days with a little girl who would remember them with appreciation sixty years later.

Introduction

In everyone's life there is one person, one event, or one experience that stands out, affects who they become and the road they will take. For me, that person was my aunt Marion. Once I began work on her story, I discovered she was also that one person for the children of a small farm community in Central New York. She was the principal of their school during the days of the Great Depression, World War II, and the years that followed. I discovered that she was not just my Aunt Marion; she was everyone's Miss Parsons. I always saw her as a woman with no children of her own—auntie to her sister's children and their children. But the truth is, she was a role model, a mentor, and sometimes even a mother figure to hundreds of people now in their seventies, eighties, and nineties. Those who are still alive contributed to this story, this legend of a woman who once longed for children of her own but relented to destiny's alternate plan for Miss Parsons.

Marion Parsons was born July 8, 1888, in the upstairs bedroom of a farmhouse along the Genesee Turnpike, where a string of family farms would one day become a suburb on the western edge of Syracuse, New York. She lived during some of the most difficult times in our country's history, when the sociological and economic shifts that followed both the Great Wars shook farm communities across the country.

The middle daughter of three girls, Marion was profoundly influenced by her beloved father, her papa, Willis Parsons. The youngest son of Edwin and Julia Armstrong Parsons, Willis raised a cherry orchard where Marion and her sisters, cousins, and friends played amongst the squat, lush fruit trees, part of a sixty-some-acre farm Willis purchased from Burritt Chaffee in 1890. Willis was well-known throughout the state for his orchards, and for many years, handsome profits from these orchards supported the family. In 1917, he was elected president of the New York State Fruit Growers Association.

He owned more than two hundred acres of prime farmland along the turnpike—the first road that ran the length of New York State. Here, Marion grew up. She enjoyed an idyllic childhood on the farm, learned how to behave according to the statutes of Victorian society and learned how to bear loss at an early age.

Her early education in a one-room schoolhouse set the stage for a life of studying and teaching. She relished what she saw as her mission to guide youngsters in the ways of learning and living a proper and happy life, of upholding honesty and integrity. Her vivacity and a curiosity for what lay beyond the farm motivated and inspired her throughout her life.

As a single woman in her thirties in 1923, she traveled west and took a teaching post in a frontier town in Washington state, on the Canadian border.

As the twentieth century began to unfold, the industrial age took its toll on family farms throughout the country. By 1924, Willis saw no solution other than the sale of what he referred to as the Lower Farm. He imagined in its place a modern neighborhood with a new school that met certain social and moral standards. He envisioned a new kind of economy based on the stock market and real estate.

Terry Road School, 1897
Front Row (seated): Guy Terry Parsons, unknown, unknown
Second Row: Mable Vinton, Marion Parsons, Will Andrews, George Jerome, Gertrude Allen (teacher), Martha Parsons, Grace Parsons, Louise Hubbell, Hazel Andrews
Back Row: Roy Vinton and Herbert Parsons. Standing: Guy Terry, Trustee

Just two years after Marion struck out on her own to teach school in our nation's Northwestern frontier, her father wrote to her about his plans. An obedient daughter who honored duty and a sense of responsibility for her family and community, Marion responded to her father's wishes and returned home in 1925 to take the helm of a new school for the growing community. The school would replace the worn-out Terry Road School that had served the community of cousins and neighbors since 1847.

The one-room schoolhouse where Marion and her sisters, cousins, and friends had learned lessons to the snap of a switch sat atop a tiny knoll just up the turnpike from the Parsons farm. By 1925 it had become unusable and outdated—too drafty and too small. Children once trudged through deep snow and frigid wind to spend the day sitting on hard wooden benches or small wooden desks dotted with inkwells. At the Terry Road School, they wrote with quill pens, then fountain pens, or on chalk slates; they all learned together in one big room.

By the mid-1920s, before the market crashed, before farming became obsolete as a way to support growing families, before two world wars put in people's minds that they might not be safe, this tight-knit community already knew times were changing. But the new school wasn't ready to replace the Terry Road School by the end of summer. So Marion and the children made do in a tiny henhouse across the lane from Willis's cherry orchard. As the new school took shape—indeed for many years after that—Miss Parsons, as she became known and is still lovingly called, oversaw the business of the school under the guidance of a board of trustees, neighbors, and community members who joined forces to raise money for the new school that would become known as Cherry Road School. The school became the heart of a budding neighborhood that would become one of thousands of postwar suburbs in the 1950s.

Because of the wisdom and courage of the woman who was born and died on the farm where the school still stands and thrives, Cherry Road School has become a landmark in the lives of generations. This woman and community joined forces and called upon a body of common-sense values to prepare their children for an uncertain future. No country bumpkins, they knew the world would be irrevocably changed as a result of the onslaught of the Great Depression and a looming Second World War. While no one could have known the specifics, the people of the community that came to be known as Westvale knew their way of life would be changed by the time their children were adults. They stuck together and prepared their children for a new economy based on machinery, industry, and wide-scale consumption of natural resources. They relied on Marion Parsons for leadership. They entrusted her with their children.

As we age, many of us look back and judge our lives. Have we made a difference? If we have children, are they happy? Are they successful? One of Marion's dreams as a young woman was to have a family. She may have thought that she failed. But I can testify that without my great-aunt Marion's input, I would not be who I am today. In writing her story, I see that she touched many others in the same way. Marion chose duty to her family and community over her own personal desires. I invite you to read her story and judge for yourself.

Why I Wrote This Book

Throughout my childhood I was enraptured by stories of the olden days. I don't know if my fascination was because of the way the stories were told or because of their content, but to this day I'd give a finger to take one ride in that horse and buggy I heard about so often. Someone once said that grandmothers tell us about the past and lead us into the future—and when I heard the sentiment, I wrote it down.

When I was about three years old, my parents and I moved into the old family farmhouse. When I played in the third-floor attic, I could evoke the voices of the Parsons girls giggling in the garret in long skirts and high-buttoned boots. I became fascinated with that time and place and the people who inhabited those days. The stories Aunt Marion told me were my link to the past.

I remember simple details about that time—the sound of Marion's car keys jingling in the hallway or outside the dining room window. Off we'd go in her car, the two of us. Sometimes she would let me sit on her lap and steer the car while we sang "I'm a Lonely Little Petunia." I remember sitting on her kitchen counter eating cream cheese and Ritz crackers. After we moved out, I recall my father sliding me through the little kitchen milk door to run and find Marion if she didn't hear us knocking. I remember cozy fires in her great stone fireplace. We'd have popcorn and I'd ask her, one more time, to tell me a story. She was always happy to oblige.

Now I'm as old as she was when I was born. A few years ago I visited Cherry Road School and conjured up the feeling I'd had there on my first day of kindergarten. That would have been the year Marion retired. During my visit I realized Marion and the Parsons family had been all but forgotten except for the brass bell sitting on the current principal's desk. Without a second thought, I knew, as a writer and an educator, it was my job to put the story to paper—the legend of a woman who sacrificed so much to build an award-winning school from a henhouse. It's a gift to one day discover what you were born to do; for me, the mission is to chronicle the life of the woman who did so much for me and for others, the legacy of the family farm, and the history of the community that became a suburb but never lost its heart (the school) or its soul (the people). To tell the story, I've talked to many people, read letters, journals, and even walked the streets of the old neighborhood in hopes of discovering who Aunt Marion really was.

Hundreds of people—some who attended the first year in the chicken coop—have come forward to share their stories and offer encouragement for the book, all while expressing their love and admiration for Miss Parsons. Most are now retired from their own successful careers. They've sent pictures, written letters and talked with me on the phone or in person for untold hours. They've attended meetings at the historical society; all have offered unconditional support and enthusiasm for this project. Some died while I was writing the book; some have gone to live in nursing homes or assisted living facilities. None has tired of anticipating this book. Their stories have provided a firsthand insight into the amazing woman, the unique school, and the productive people that shaped their youth.

I wrote the book because I, like so many, carry a debt of gratitude to Marion Parsons. I wrote the book for all of us. I believe in the importance of the past in shaping the present and navigating an uncertain future, and I believe Miss Parsons gave us all the tools to do that.

Voices in The Brass Bell

Though Miss Parsons has been gone too long for today's Cherry Road students to remember her, they still strive to do their best each year in hopes of winning the Marion Parsons Award. Surviving alumni from the early days of the school, no matter where they live or how long they've been gone, still get together when they can to remember the diminutive yet powerful woman. They are in their seventies and eighties, and some travel great distances to get together with old friends. Some still have lunch together once a month. They reminisce about their days at Cherry Road School, marveling at their luck to have known the amazing team of teachers who shaped their lives during the hardest of times.

First-Person Accounts

Many of the old-timers have come forward to help tell the story of Cherry Road School, as I realized early on that the stories of the woman I knew as Aunt Marion and those of her school and students are deeply entwined. To find out more about the woman I knew, I've spent the past several years talking with other people who knew her: former students, teachers, staff, family members, and neighbors. Some have reached their nineties and remember the simpler time I've sought to uncover. I've included input from these generous people in details in the main narrative and in their own words, which appear in boxes throughout the book.

Author as Family Member

When I was a girl, I would go to Aunt Marion and her sisters—Aunt Martha and my grandmother Grace—pleading, "Tell me a story out of your think." This was code for: tell me a story about the olden days, and Aunt Marion had many such tales to tell. Those stories about her years on the farm and in the little one-room schoolhouse are shared here, to the best of my ability.

Author as Storyteller

I've had the good fortune of inheriting the diary Aunt Marion kept during her travels before settling down to lead Cherry Road School. My extended family has generously shared other primary source documents including letters and notes written to and by Marion, my great-grandfather, and other relatives. They've shared their own stories orally. From these I've woven a narrative, taking generous literary liberties about Marion's life for the sake of the story.

It should be noted at least one more time that the narrative pieces of the story have been embellished, but all are based on primary sources: letters, journals, remembrances of stories told to me by my aunts and grandmother, and the recollections of those who were there and have generously shared their experiences. All such liberties have been taken for the sake of storytelling, as Aunt Marion and the many people who remember her are storytellers. Please enjoy.

Prologue

My parents and I lived with my great-aunt Marion until I was three years old. I remember her coming home from school in the afternoons, always jolly, always happy to see me. She would sit in her padded rocking chair, and I'd climb onto her lap, nestle my head on her shoulder, and listen to the hum of her hearing aid. The creak of the rocker marked a constant rhythm to her stories about the olden days, the ones I would beg her to tell me just one more time. She'd begin with "Papa hitched up the horse and buggy."

These stories came to be known to the two of us as "stories out of your think." I must have slept. She must have too during those afternoons, the chair lulling us both into a dream state. I'd see myself riding with Marion and my great-grandfather Willis in a rumbling black buggy down a dusty and rutted dirt road through the potato field and on to the cherry orchard. Men and women, shirtsleeves rolled above their elbows, were working throughout the orchard, ladders extended into trees, wagons filled with boxes of fruit. In these dream stories, fruit pickers plucked faster and foremen hollered louder when they caught sight of Willis Parsons' silver beard.

As we come to a halt along a cut bank of apple trees at the edge of the orchard, a young boy runs up to the buggy. On this day, the cherries have long since been harvested and sold at market. Autumn setting in, the Parsons' apple orchards are abuzz in preparation for market and for the upcoming state fair.

The boy's chest heaves from running. I can see my great-grandfather standing tall next to the buggy in his suit and tie. He smiles down at the youngster. Dressed in a floppy woolen cap, short pants, worn stockings crumpling around his lace-up boots, the boy is beaming as he holds up an apple, offering the prize to the towering man. "Mr. Parsons, sir, I believe this fancy McIntosh could take a prize at the fair." My great-grandfather takes the plump red apple and turns it around in one hand, placing his other hand on the boy's head.

"Young man, you are very observant and already have a keen eye for business. The next time I see you, I hope it is in the Terry Road School classroom."

"My father disapproved of children working in the orchards instead of attending school." Aunt Marion's eyes were open. I was awake now too, rested from our slumber and drift through the olden days. Marion let me ride on her foot—a pretend ride on a horse to Banbury Cross. Our days played out like this, and I never had an inkling they would end—that I would grow up and live a life, that she would retire from a life lived, for the most part, within the confines of a few square miles of farmland turned suburban community, orchards swallowed by neighborhoods of houses and streets.

Only once do I remember her ever being cross with me. Whenever she came into a room, I would run to her and she would hold me and give me the love I craved, until one day.

At some point I came to understand that the school was just up the street, visible from the yard. I'd watch until she was out of sight, my world empty without her. On this particular day when I must have been about three years old, I decided to follow her. I trailed her to the school and found my way to her office.

Expecting her to be thrilled to see me and proud of my resourcefulness, I ran straight into her office, stopping just short of her lofty desk. A dark cloud I had never seen or imagined descended across her face. Her voice roared across the desk in a tone I had never heard. She seemed to grow and grow, taking up all the space in the room like Alice after she eats the magic cake in Wonderland.

"What in heaven's name are you doing? How did you get here?" She grabbed my hand, pulling me toward the door, gently, yet firmly, in an unfamiliar gesture.

By the time we got back to the house, it was my mother for whom Marion had words. I stood back and listened to the rebuke, terrified. Then in an instant as quick and surprising as the onslaught of the storm cloud had been, Aunt Marion turned to me on her way out the door, bent down, and gave me a hug and a kiss I will never forget. The smell of a certain talcum powder still evokes that feeling. The sound of a creaking chair brings to mind a girl in a cherry orchard.

Chapter 1
Marion Parsons

Everything has been figured out, except how to live.
—Jean-Paul Sartre

The echo of a train's whistle resounded from the far end of the valley. It was the edge of winter in the year 1924. It was bitter cold. Marion Parsons raced across the station platform. She would be waiting, tall and straight and neat as a pin when her father and stepmother arrived. Taking extra time to dress that morning, she'd had to cover her best dress with a heavy wrap coat. She was a short woman, so the coat came all the way to her ankles. Pulling the fur collar closer around her, she covered her copper-colored curls at the nape of her neck, grateful for the coat's softness and warmth.

The train would appear soon, off in the distance where there was a slight bend in the tree line. What might her parents think of this place—cowboys, people dressed so casually, as if on a picnic every day of the week? Ladies wore gloves only when it was cold. Men wore hats all the time, even indoors, big felt hats with beaded hatbands. She paced in a small circle, pulling at her leather gloves, straightening her hat, its floppy felt brim falling over her eyes. Her breath hung in the air like tiny puffs of smoke. Why had her parents made such a huge detour on their way home from the Panama Canal tour? Omak, Washington, was, after all, the opposite direction from Syracuse, New York.

Marion had moved here last summer, to this tiny frontier town on the Canadian border nestled at the bottom of the Okanogan Highlands, to fulfill an agreement to teach for two years at the grade school. She had traveled alone from Syracuse first by train, then on a Great Lakes Steamer, and then by train again. Along the way, she stopped and made a side tour of the new national park called Yellowstone.

A man who lived on a ranch up the road had come to Omak from Saskatchewan in a covered wagon. One night the two of them shared traveling stories. She declared that, compared with his account of his family's rugged and terrifying passage, her story about her open-air car trip from Cody, Wyoming, to Yellowstone Park paled.

Yellowstone Park, 1923–the caravan of open-air cars drew up at Dragon's Mouth

Now, as she stood in the morning light on the slick wooden platform at the Omak train station, shifting from foot to foot to keep warm, her mind drifted back to that day riding into Yellowstone. A switchback road wound up and down and around the side of the mountain—more of a trail than a road. She had peeked over the side of the car at the Shoshone River, way down below. The water—blue, green, and shallow in places—ran too fast through the deep ravine to be clear. The long line of cars passed through at least five tunnels of stone, cut to make the drive possible. She felt the flush of fear on her face but kept her eyes on all there was to take in: the narrow, winding road, the tops of great fir trees, the sheer drop—no guardrails. That night she wrote in her diary: *At first I had to school myself not to be afraid and try to help the driver, but I got over it.* At nearly nine thousand feet, they finally stopped for lunch at Buffalo Bill's lodge, where they ate lunch at a rustic camp. Served like at church supper, Marion recalled falling upon the pear salad like a savage who couldn't wait for dinner. Farther on they traversed a spiral bridge, making perfect circles around and around the newly excavated mountainside. Soon after, they were rewarded by the sight of a glistening mountain lake that held the reflection of towering Mud Volcano. *We walked back and up some stairs to see a pool of muddy boiling water. It looked angry, like a dragon's mouth belching hot, clear water and clouds of steam. Having covered more than one hundred miles, the day ended mercifully at a magnificent Yellowstone Park hotel, built next to the Great Falls. The hotel was a huge and beautiful building, constructed to accommodate more than five hundred people. The lounge looks down from the lobby and is two stories high … the largest room I ever saw.*

The stationmaster hollered at an errant child running across the platform, interrupting Marion's reverie. She turned and continued to pace, wondered—not for the first time—why her father had so suddenly decided to make this great journey when in his letters he had let on that he was worried about the plummeting price of fruit, that the orchard was not profitable enough, and that he was investigating new pursuits in the real estate business. Now it seemed to her that out of the blue, Papa and Mother—she long ago settled on calling her stepmother, Allain, "Mother" when addressing her—were taking an extravagant trip. She wondered if it had to do with the plans for the new school her father had talked about in his last few letters. It was clear he expected her to participate. She would go home next year, even though she loved this place—so different from the farm back east—and her new western friends. There were real Indians who came into town from the Colville Reservation. Her friend Tom rode bulls in the rodeo, for which the town had become famous.

A louder and closer blast of a train whistle brought Marion to attention again. Steam rose from above Douglas firs on the horizon. Her heart raced, and she felt a sense of relief knowing that the school superintendent and his wife, Mr. and Mrs. Ivenson, had planned a dinner party for her parents that evening. Otherwise, how would she entertain them? How could she manage to fill the time until they boarded the train again in two days to head back to New York?

She had not seen Papa in over a year—though they had kept in contact by letters—and what of these plans that would commit her to the new school in the cherry orchard? Of course, there was no question as to her duty, and she missed her sisters terribly, her niece and nephew, and her Parsons cousins—Laura and Bess, Bertha and Jim, Herbert, Harry and Ned Jerome, and Charles F. There were so many repeated family names through the generations and among the cousins that they had to use middle initials sometimes, especially with the Charleses. How they had all loved to play in the haylofts and horse around in the cherry orchards so long ago. When family got together for Sunday picnics, it seemed as though there were a hundred Parsons and Jerome relatives. Now with all the new houses going up in and around the farm, everything would be different.

While Marion was gone, her father had hired a surveyor to divide the Lower Farm into parcels to put up for sale. The Terzievs had purchased the property on the north side of the cherry orchard next to Marion's sister and brother in-law, Grace and Claude Cole. She was glad they would have neighbors, that her sister wouldn't be so isolated with her young twins, David and Helen, only three and a half years old. Grace would never recover from the loss of young John, her beloved firstborn who had died of complications from smallpox only five years ago. Just thinking about that day made Marion's stomach clench. She wished she had some salts, always good for an upset stomach. Marion chided herself for being gone so long. How selfish she had been.

She heard the chugging of the train's engine, the screech of metal on metal. She thought about the students here in Omak she loved so dearly—little Howard with his popgun and cowboy gear—about Sunday dinners with the Holmeses out on the ranch, the afternoon Mrs. Eary, the janitor's wife, had all the teachers to tea. What a rare character Mrs. Eary was, full of fun and the grace and ease of a queen in meager surroundings. The tiny woman with salt-and-pepper hair had read Marion's fortune in the tea leaves. Marion would not tell Papa about this; he would pooh-pooh such a thing, but Mrs. Eary

The Kinneys, 1924

had given her something to look forward to. Perhaps this year she would meet someone special and one day have the family she always dreamed of.

She hated to leave Amy, a fellow teacher she had grown close to, and Amy's parents, Mr. and Mrs. Kinney. They had been lovely to her, inviting her to their house at Thanksgiving and Easter. She had gotten to know and love them—Mr. Kinney, such a hardworking man, and Mrs. Kinney, who confided in Marion how she enjoyed a person who could be true to her own nature, to her own dreams.

One afternoon Mrs. Kinney had asked Marion about those dreams. When Marion began to tell her about the new school back home, Mrs. Kinney interrupted her saying, "No, no, young woman, that is your duty—what are your dreams?" Marion gasped at this thought but kept silent. Even now, she put this conversation out of her mind, made use of the short time left before the train came around the bend to anticipate what might lie ahead. She would take her time on the trip back home, and she would return to Omak for a visit one day.

When finally the train shot from around the trees, roaring into the tiny station, Marion could not contain her tears; she scurried from one end of the platform to the other trying to get a glimpse of Papa.

Above: A page in Marion's diary

Papa and Mother visit Omak, March 1924

Omak teachers, last day of school, 1924, Marion far right

Chapter 2

Her Great Adventure

The purpose of life, after all, is to live it, to taste experience to the utmost, to reach out eagerly and without fear for newer and richer experience.

—Eleanor Roosevelt

It was nearing the end of May 1925 when Marion set off from Omak, heading west to Seattle on the Great Northern Railway. From there, she'd go south to California to visit cousins before journeying back home to New York. It was a glorious day, the sky so blue and clear, it looked like glass, like it could break if you touched it. Temperatures had already neared the nineties, normal for this time of year. She and her friend Penny had taken a hike along the Okanogan River last week. Yesterday, after she finished packing, they borrowed Penny's father's car and drove around, visiting some of the local sights Marion had not seen in her two years in Omak. They went to St. Mary's Mission, where they visited the mission school and the newly constructed church; then they walked along the creek and found a place for their picnic lunch. Marion did not want to leave without seeing some of the old Indian gravesites, but they were pressed to return the car.

Now the train was climbing into the clouds, cedar trees and rocky cliffs passing on one side of the train, infinite sky on the other. She had forgotten about the majesty of the western mountains. She could see rivers and creeks churning through the rocks and crags of the Cascade Range. On the other side of the mountains, she knew, were endless miles of scorched plains and high desert. She tried to imagine how life had been for those who had crossed these mountains and plains before trains, before automobiles. It wasn't that long ago that people had come in wagons and on foot, some falling ill, their families burying children along the way, never to see their gravesites again.

The train ride across the towering Cascades thrilled and scared Marion. Sometimes teetering along mountain passes, sometimes inside darkened tunnels, her journey through Okanogan County north to Canada, and then southwest to the main line at Wenatchee, Washington, was thick with grandeur and, at times, terrifying. Not long after the train left Wenatchee, heading farther west to Puget Sound, Marion felt stiff and nervous and dared not look out the window. She gripped the edge of her seat until her knuckles turned white as the train's engine strained at the onset of the passage over Stevens Pass. Endless minutes passed, and then the splendor of the fir-covered mountains captivated her as trepidation turned to wonder. Her heart filled with the same sense of awe she'd felt when she first glimpsed the Rockies almost two years ago. She wondered what Papa would say if he knew she was traveling at such heights and peril. The train crept around switchbacks and sometimes felt as though it might be suspended in midair. She made a quick notation in her journal: The engineering feats to build the rail line are out of this world.

She slept, and when she woke, she daydreamed about her imminent voyage to Los Angeles. From Seattle she would board a ship traveling down the West Coast to San Francisco, and then go on to Los Angeles a few days later. This would be her first sighting of the Pacific Ocean. She had vowed to her Omak friends she would return one day, but what if this was her last chance to see this part of the world?

She dozed again and dreamed about Papa, about their recent conversation. When she woke, she took a crumpled letter out of the inside pocket of her traveling bag. Dear, dear Papa. He meant well, but she wasn't at all sure if his words were intended to manipulate her or merely to keep her close to heart. It had been almost a year since he'd written the letter.

Syracuse, NY
September 13, 1924

My Dear Marion,

A letter from you this morning dated Sunday Sept. six impressed one that Omak is some distance from Syracuse. The distance by radio would not seem so far.

I have noted that you have mentioned in recent letters, namely that happiness is far from being entirely dependent on material things, in this I quite agree with your conclusions.

Your idea of writing family and neighborhood letters is quite all right as Nellie would say. You ask about the apples? Everything points to a large crop of choice fruit, the season for their ripening is about two weeks late as it has been with everything else this year. In regard to prices, they will be some less than last year, around two dollars for A-grade, although we may get three dollars for fancy Macintosh. Potatoes are selling for ninety cents at present. I am selling some cobblers they are yielding from one hundred fifty per acre to two hundred.

This has been a week of almost continuous rain, bad for the State Fair as well as for farming. Sowed six acres of winter wheat yesterday and have five more to sow when the ground gets dry. Got the seed wheat (Junior No. 6) from a Mr. Jeroleman who lives on the Weedsport-Cato road. This wheat took first prize at the State Fair. When I went to look at it, I took Mother, Grace, and the babies for a ride.

It is the middle of September; the days are getting noticeably shorter. I represented the family at church this morning. We went with the Coles for a ride this afternoon, I am sorry to report that Miss Helen developed quite a bad display of temper because she could not monopolize a seat on Grandma's lap. I wonder which side of the house she gets her spunk from.

Real estate business like other kinds is very quiet, I fear it does not argue well for a trip to California. Julia and family were home for the week-end. Charles F. and Bessie returned from the woods Thursday. Bessie is to take a trip west soon. Compton has not worked for me in over a week, don't think he has another job yet. We are badly in need of your hot weather, as I have said we are two weeks late in maturing, especially corn. Is the heat oppressive? Mr. and Mrs. Stilwell and the Salisburys have returned from their trips abroad.

Mother and I with Uncle Charles and Aunt Allie took another trip to Mr. Hitchings' this afternoon and I got some very valuable information in regard to picking, busheling, and marketing. I think we will put a part of our A-grade in cold storage to hold for better prices. Mr. Hitchings thinks the price will be two dollars for A-grade and three for Spies and Macintosh. It will be much easier I think to handle them in this way. You will note that the prices I quoted in the first part of this letter are identical with those of Mr. Hitchings. Raymond is buyer for a Chicago firm who want 100,000 bushels. Mr. H told of some English buyers that want a like amount. You see that argues well for a good future price.

A screw got loose and dropped down in the typewriter and interfered with the working of some of the keys which accounts for some of the lettering

As it is retiring time, I will close with love from all.

Your affectionate,

Dad

She put the letter aside and took enjoyment in the rest of the train ride to Seattle. By late morning she had befriended a young woman from St. Paul, and they whiled the time away playing rummy five hundred in the dining car.

Getting off the train in Seattle, she was grateful to feel the ground beneath her feet and took her time strolling through the Seattle business district on her way to the boat, the S. S. Ruth. She heard the sounds of the harbor, smelled the faint scent of dead fish. She was a million miles from Omak. There were fishmongers and farmers' markets all along the piers. She hadn't seen anything like this since her time in Boston right after Normal School. All this time in the northern frontier, she had forgotten what it felt like to walk city streets. When an unshaven man with twine for shoelaces and a dirty, wrinkled jacket began to follow her, she ducked into a bakery. Shaken, she ordered a fry cake and a cup of tea, sat at a little table by the window and watched the line of cars coming and going along the wharf. She had never seen anything like it, even in Boston.

The sea was smooth and we were near enough to the coast to be in sight of land some of the time. She put her journal aside and slept. When she woke in the morning, they were in San Francisco. Marion left the boat as soon as she dressed. Warm air washed across her face. She pulled off the long fur-trimmed coat that had provided a shield from the cold in Omak and flung it over her arm. Her calf-length dress flared at the bottom and fluttered in the breeze around her legs as she made her way carefully down the gangplank and onto the dock. The cloche she had purchased last week at the only ladies' dress store in Omak covered the back of her neck, and she felt pleased with herself for the indulgence. She hung on to the railing, aware of the sounds of the sea—sharp cries of seagulls and the deep moan of an ocean-going vessel in the distance. It sounded like the ship was crying softly, the way she did for her mama sometimes. It had been over twenty years since Mama had gone. Mama would have been proud of Marion's daring, her independence, she was sure of it.

The ship remained docked in the San Francisco Bay that night. Nestled in her stateroom, Marion made more notes in her journal about the day: *Golden Gate was the most wonderful park I was ever in. It was built on sand dunes, and there are eight artificial lakes for boating. There is a museum, an aquarium, amphitheater, and many historic artifices. Most notably, everything dates from since the great earthquake.*

She heard murmurings and mumblings from the adjoining berth; then a shout from the pier pierced the open porthole. Earlier in the evening she had pried the tiny window open in order to smell the sea air. A strange place, unknown voices and sounds, strangers. She felt

Omak School

exhilarated and frightened all at once.

    Closing her leather-bound journal, she mentally replayed her last hours with Papa. It was the morning he and Allain were to board the train and return to Syracuse. The sun had just risen, thawing frost-laden meadows along the road where father and daughter took an early morning walk past the school and beyond the edge of the little town of Omak. Papa wore a bowler hat. Ready for travel, his shirt collar was starched and stiff, and his tie looked to choke him. Marion was used to seeing him in more informal attire; the thought of his pin-striped pants made Marion grin. Ever respectful, she had looked up in admiration when he put his arm around her shoulders, and they strode this way in silence, the only sound their feet crunching on the gravel. Snow-covered mountain peaks loomed above the distant horizon at the edge of a vast swath of prairie. A small herd of cattle watched as they passed. The cloudless sky was blue all the way to the white peaks tinged with pink from the sun. She had wondered then if her father felt the same sense of being closer to heaven than they had ever been on this earth. She forgot about the weight of his arm across her shoulders as they strolled together in a kind of peace she rarely felt in his presence. She loved her Papa and longed to please him, make him proud of her.

A breeze—strong enough to pick up her hair and swirl it across her face—smelled of the sage and spring flowers covering the plain across the road. Papa asked her the names of some of the flowers he didn't recognize and squeezed her shoulder when she confessed she did not know. Then she did something she couldn't remember ever doing before: she rested her head on his chest, keeping it lowered so he wouldn't see her tears.

She wanted to tell him what she had discovered so far away from home, about the people who once ventured here in covered wagons and on horses. They had become ranchers and loggers, doing whatever they could to make a living in this wild land. They had come to carve a life for themselves out of the wilderness. They were fiercely independent.

Father and daughter stumbled along the rutted dirt road, musing about the gorgeous countryside—a place, Marion wanted to tell her father, where people could become spiritually whole if they had lost their way. She wanted to tell him about this and about a man by the name of Sam Hill who had come to Omak several weeks back to talk about building roads. He'd made a presentation to the students, and Marion had been impressed with his way of including young people in the conversations about society, about progress. After all, it would be their world one day—didn't they need to understand why they were forced to study subjects like mathematics and science? Mr. Hill had hosted a European queen at his new experimental community over in Oregon. The children had been enrapt with his stories and ideas.

"I want you to know that I've adjusted my will." Her father broke the silence, then bent to wipe the mud from his oxfords.

"Papa! Don't talk about such things." They both thrust their hands into their pockets and picked up their pace.

"Just a matter of business, Marion. I'll be leaving the Upper Farm to Mother. You and your sisters and Claude, eventually the twins, will continue in the way you see fit with the Lower Farm and the changes that will most likely happen there. Several more parcels have sold since I last wrote." Her father went on in this way, describing his dreams for the Lower Farm and the school until they were all the way back to the house where Marion had boarded these past two years. He told her there was no doubt they would go forward with the plans for the school. If they weren't successful, soon the whole area would be taken over by Syracuse, those wild people up on Tipperary Hill.

"No doubt they are bootleggers and worse," he'd said. "Do you know that Delaney fellow who picks our peaches had the gall to tell me that poison was good for his health?"

Alone in her stateroom, Marion smiled at the memory of her father all riled up.

"I've made a clause in every deed I sign over that there will be no consumption of alcoholic beverage on the premises." He had

Willis and his grandchildren, the twins, David and Helen, circa 1922

pulled his torso up, straightened his lapels, and at that moment, to Marion, he felt like a giant of a man. She was noticing the straight lines along the edge of his beard, his meticulous face, when he continued in his booming voice. "Not a one has refused to sign. I know I can count on you to see this through, Marion. You know," his expression softening, "a community is only as good as its school, and the school only as good as the people who run it and the neighbors who surround it."

"Yes, Papa, I agree." She had seen this coming, the school, the neighborhood in the potato fields and the orchards, but now it was inevitable. And it was exciting too, once she got used to it. With all the new houses going up, well, her father was right to slow down and sell off the Lower Farm. Papa was getting too old to manage two farms anyway, and the cherries were too much work for too little return. He would put most of the money back into his prize apple orchards at the Upper Farm. He had talked to her about investing some of this money in stocks. Many of his friends were doing this, and with banks failing right and left since the Great War, maybe this wasn't such a bad idea.

The new neighborhood would be as spectacular as the cherry orchards that would come down and the corn fields that would be dug up to make it possible—just different. Marion was beginning to understand what Mr. Hill meant in his conversation about progress, about the future for which they must prepare.

"Will you be home for the start of school next fall?"

"Yes, Papa."

As they approached the house, Allain flung open the front door, arms loaded with travel bags. Her long woolen coat reached to the tops of her lace-up boots; her face was pale and her hair a dull salt-and-pepper gray. Marion often felt that if the woman would smile more, her appearance would be more pleasant, might even take on some color. Her accent was a mixture of the British blend of her own mother's and what Allain had picked up during her years as a child in Scotland, Ceylon, and Nyasaland.

"Mother makes no attempt to dress in the fashion of the day," Marion had replied to Mrs. Kinney when she inquired if Marion's stepmother was a city woman or a country woman. "She would never be seen in a flapper-style dress."

Marion languished in the dark of her stateroom, lulled by the steady bellow and groan of a foghorn, a sound she had never heard before and would remember for the rest of her life. It was the sound that marked her resolve to take on the responsibility of the new school, to make it like no other. For now she would forget about her dream to meet someone, to have a family of her own.

Instead, she thought about her return to the farm. She could take over the teaching post at the old school on Terry Road while her father and the other trustees, Judge Farnham and Mr. Terziev, raised the money to break ground. For now, Papa had said he would donate the cherry orchard on the east side of the property, next to McArdle's farm. Over there, he pointed out, the school would be but a stone's throw for the twins, Helen and David, and they would be starting school next fall. Grace wouldn't have to worry about them walking along the turnpike—they would be right where she would know they were safe.

Papa had wanted to know whether he could count on Marion, and she answered in the only way she could—she would go home. She would make him proud. She would look after Helen and David and make sure they were out of harm's way. Losing John had been more than any of them could bear. No one should have to bury a six-year-old boy.

When she got home, maybe she'd move in with Papa and Allain, or maybe with Uncle Charles and Aunt Allie; their house was right next to the old schoolhouse where she would hold classes for now.

The school was at once real, no longer a dream of her father's. She took off her robe and crawled under the covers in the enormous stateroom bed. She had been surprised at how large the room was, how comfortable the bed. She lay on her back and folded her hands across her stomach, listening to the lament of foghorns. Through the porthole she caught a glimpse of the moon hanging in the sky. The Pacific Ocean smelled strange, unfamiliar; she had never smelled or tasted an ocean before. During their trip, Papa and Mother had just ridden on a vessel through the Panama Canal and could speak of little else during their visit. Now she understood the magnificence of it. The back of her throat ached with the emotion it evoked.

"My students will get to see the world, if it's all I can do for them. They will have moments like this. They will hold their breath at the beauty and mystery of a faraway place, of different worlds and uncommon sights." She stated these convictions aloud, even though no one was there to hear her. She'd help her students understand people far away from Central New York, ideas that were anything but run-of-the-mill. Wasn't that the purpose of teaching?

Some of her own classmates from the Terry Road School had never gone anywhere but the cow pasture behind the one-room schoolhouse. She would change that when she took charge. Just last year the Supreme Court passed legislation to strike down child labor. Imagine, children being forced to work instead of having the benefit of an education. That would never happen in her community, or in all the city of Syracuse, not if she had anything to do with it. She would organize the mothers; they would organize all over the city …

Marion fell into a deep sleep and didn't open her eyes until the butler knocked. She heard the thump as he left the morning newspaper outside the door.

Each day in San Francisco presented a new adventure. Marion visited the Palace Hotel where President Harding had died, the site of the great fire of 1906. She toured the historic Presidio at the San Francisco port three times… *We had a view of Golden Gate 7/8 mile widening to two miles and opening into the largest land-bound body of water in the world… San Francisco is the most wonderful town in the world.*

Lost in the kind of reverie only the solitary tourist understands, Marion Parsons walked around the boat, poking through merchandise shops and watching other tourists from a safe distance. She enjoyed exploring ship life. She spied on a gang of young men loading and unloading at the docks—lifting cars out of the hull with one turn of a pulley.

On her final day in San Francisco, Marion noticed a newspaper article on the stock market, about its rise and how that bore little resemblance to the rest of the economy. There had been an explosion in manufacturing of all kinds. Men who owned the factories were getting rich—buying up smaller companies—and the men and women who worked in the factories were earning less now than they were at this time last year. She hoped her father was right about the stock market.

She would concern herself about those details later. In the meantime, there were festivities to be enjoyed.

Later that night, she languished in her stateroom, dismissing the worries she had struggled with off and on during the day, thoughts of Tom and other Omak friends. Instead, she wrote about the boat and the adventure at hand:

It was a lovely boat. The meals were wonderfully good and did not get tiresome. We had the grand march every morning and dancing in the evening—a masquerade dinner and dance second night out. Paper cups, horns, and squeakers were at each place, and everyone tried to vie with the other to make more noise. The costumes at the dance were very funny. We kept in touch with the world by radio. A newspaper was published each a.m. One paper reported a very bad storm at Syracuse N.Y., but that's all I ever heard of the storm.

Then a movie outfit got on the boat, and the crowd changed. I greatly enjoyed the sensation they produced by coming to the dining room in costume. They were picturing a rough sea and produced it by waving a mirror in front of the film. It seemed very very tiresome work to me.

Chapter Three
Lemon Trees

*Though we travel the world over to find the beautiful,
we must carry it with us or we find it not.*

—Ralph Waldo Emerson

A FEW DAYS LATER, on May 28, Marion's ship docked safely at San Pedro Harbor at five o'clock in the afternoon. The waters had been rougher on the way to Los Angeles than they had been from Seattle to San Francisco. Gripping the rail running along the inside of the upper deck, Marion had wandered outside and inside the boat, even in the dark, determined not to miss anything.

She would spend the next few months with her cousins in the young city of Pasadena where the sun shone brighter than anywhere else she had ever been. The West Coast Parsons cousins had come here to visit when it was a resort, staying at the Raymond Hotel, riding through the mountains on the Mount Lowe Railway, visiting with friends on Grand Avenue, and they decided to stay. Now they all chipped in for Marion's visit, wanting to make it memorable.

When she arrived, they took her to see the brand-new train station. Cousins Mabel and Esther who had both been her close childhood friend, visiting in the summers, hosted a luncheon in her honor. They played croquet and lawn tennis, made party hats and aprons for prizes. She met cousins she had never seen before and made new friends right off. Everyone seemed eager to show her the sights in this wonderful paradise. They all went along, touring the cities and sights of Southern California, pointing out the highlights and the small details. Imagine the stories she would take home to New York. People she met who had been born in California pictured New York state as one giant metropolis instead of the pristine agricultural country that made up most of the state. Wasn't New York the largest city in the world? They couldn't see the cow pastures and apple orchards, rolling hills and lakes that comprised the New York where Marion and their other cousins lived, the place some had left behind for this land called California.

Marion's visit lasted several months, and as the season wore on, delicate blooms turned to fruit. For the first time in her life, Marion saw oranges and lemons growing on trees. On one of their rides through the valley, Marion called out to the driver to pull over. They all spilled out of the car onto the side of the road, and Marion took off running into the orange grove, carefully plucking one big orange fruit and sinking her teeth into its skin. Ripe or not, it didn't matter. She grasped the blooms of the exotic flowers she could never have imagined growing on this earth in the palms of her hands, inhaling their fragrance. It never occurred to her she might be trespassing. One time she had to sit right down on the ground or else swoon at the strangeness and wonder of the aroma, so delicate and wild. In July, they all pitched in and planted a vegetable garden and an enormous flower garden. Marion had never had so much fun in her life, not even in the haylofts or the beloved orchards of her youth.

At night, she struggled to put it into words. She wrote letters to Papa, trying to capture and replay the sights and smells of night-blooming jasmine, honeysuckle, and mysterious lilies. There were days when the best thing to do was stand with her eyes shut and smell the air. Onshore breezes carried whiffs of the Pacific Ocean. When the wind shifted, she could smell the Mojave Desert just over the mountains. Syracuse felt like a faraway place on the other side of daylight, her life there ten thousand midnights past.

After a while, she forgot about Papa and her sisters; not every day, but often, she felt more like a hummingbird at sea than an obligated young woman. She wrote to her father of her adventures and her garden, and he wrote back, reminding her of family, the farm, and the Parsons Estate:

Sunday, August 9, 1925
R.D.-4, Syracuse, N.Y.

My Dear Marion,

You may feel neglected but I assure you, you are not forgotten. The cherry picking lasted just four weeks, a rather long time, but picking with the stems on and several rainy days were responsible for some of the time. Most of the time the weather was cool so that we lost very few from spoiling. We surely had a wonderful market. The last customer that came after we were through said they had driven twenty miles out of their way to get them, sorry to disappoint them.

We harvested fifty-seven ton, about forty-five ton from the upper orchard. We have a standing offer of six cents a pound for next year's crop. It looks as if we might get on without the factory. Commenced to pick Red-Astricans the day following the cherry picking, "no peace for the wicked." The apple crop and quality look very promising. Would some New York state apples taste good?

The Terziev house is progressing quite rapidly and will be a credit to the tract. Have not sold any more lots as yet, but real estate business seems to be more active.

The Parsons clan are to have a reunion at Boonville the 19 of this month and we may go and hope others of the Syracuse relatives may go and make a bus load. We think that would be quite enjoyable.

With best of wishes and much love, as ever
Your Affectionate,
Dad

Marion managed to tuck her obligations aside for now and enjoy this summer more than any other. Traveling in open cars with Esther, Nellie, and Mabel along the California coastline, she was spellbound by the ocean, the mountains, and the miles and miles of freshly planted fruit orchards throughout the valley. One day she and Mabel and Esther who were sisters, and other cousins, Jim and Frances, drove the coastline to Santa Barbara and stayed at the Samarkand Hotel. She was astonished at the accommodations of eighteen dollars a day and up, could hardly admit even to herself that the experience would be worth the steep price. Brought up to be frugal, she had watched her father put every extra dime back into the farm business. Pleasure was a foreign country. She wouldn't mention it to Papa. To him, she wrote: *Oranges and lemons are about ready to pick—apricots are turning and walnuts are setting.* He would appreciate these observations. She and the cousins also toured the city and the missions, but the highlight was the Samarkand Hotel.

Just ten years earlier, the building had housed a school for boys, Boyland. Smitten by its grandeur, Marion questioned the staff and her companions. She learned that Samarkand means "the land of heart's desire," but that the founder's heart's desire was not fulfilled. Being a vocal pacifist during World War I—a time when pacifism was seen as disloyalty to country—the owner was consequently jailed and fined, and he eventually fled to Europe where he lived out his days as an expatriate. His school for boys shut down. Rechristened the Samarkand Persian Hotel by his mother, it was opened to the public in 1920. The hotel's immense and opulent grounds were surrounded by eighty white concrete pillars; a reflection pool stocked with goldfish sparkled in the rich California sunlight. Marion could not tear herself from the pond's edge, bounded by a rose pergola. She gazed into its mirror-like surface and saw a reflection of the sky and the deep green of the surrounding foliage. A strange bird called to her, and she sank down into the grass, lay back to feel its softness, and barely noticed that she and Mabel were the only group members who hadn't moved on. They ran to catch up with the others who had disappeared through the hotel doors. Inside, the Persian reds, golds, and oranges covering the walls almost hurt her eyes.

Once you adjusted to the light and the bright colors, every inch of wall space was buried in murals and paintings. There was a library, lounge, restaurant, and countless public and private rooms throughout the giant estate built on a hill overlooking Santa Barbara.

Another day they went to Long Beach, passing rows and rows of towering oil wells. They continued on past signs for San Pedro, Los Alamitos, and Seal Beach. When they arrived they parked first alongside the newly built Marine Stadium, where they would watch the regatta, which, they told her, was becoming an annual event. They stumbled through crowds of people, and Marion reached out to hold on to her cousins. Mabel told her this was the only manmade rowing venue in the world, and Marion was enthralled with the rowing and the thrill of the competition.

Later they went to the Pike amusement park and strolled along the boardwalk that wound along the shore. There were food stands, gift shops, and even a grand bathhouse. Marion declined both the bathhouse and the rides, but watching people laugh and scream and hang on for dear life as they flew over the water on the roller coaster was thrill enough for her. Her cousin Mabel begged her to get on the Dual Ferris Wheel and go for a spin. She would not. Instead she settled herself in the backseat of the open-air auto and quietly observed the oil fields again as they returned home. By the time they left the Pike, Marion was so tired she could've slept on her feet.

As they drove back toward home, she saw bathers walking alongside the road. Someone shouted for her to catch a look at the gusher at the Los Alamitos oil field. She looked but could not discern it—the strange world passed, and eventually her eyes closed and she was asleep, faintly aware of the murmuring conversation as they wound their way back home.

As her summer idyll neared its inevitable end, Marion and three companions took a final excursion to San Diego. She, Mabel, Esther, and Jim left home before sunrise, squeezed into Jim's Packard coupe, his baby by his own admission. Jim had been a medical doctor since before the war and had brought his family from New York to southern California where he set up his practice in what he considered paradise. They maneuvered by moonlight beneath a great bowl of stars, then through a thick, pasty fog. Jim piloted his fancy driving machine through a curtain of vapor.

He spotted the phantom of a farm wagon on the road in time to slow to a crawl. He hung back, creeping along the narrow curvy road. Everyone was focused on the dim lantern light in front, rising up in the middle of the mist like a beacon to the heavens. They rode in silence, trusting their pilot and sensing his fear of what might be ahead or hurtling toward them from behind should they strike a rut. Suddenly the car lurched and stopped. The small party huddled by the side of the road, waiting for Jim's prognosis of the broken automobile.

Jim emerged from beneath the coupe. "Looks like it's a broken spring."

Back in the car, spirits were dashed, but the Parsons cousins managed to keep one another bolstered and calm as they crept through the murky haze the rest of the way to Santa Ana. The first promising glow in the dark turned out to be a service station light turning on as they reached the edge of town. The owner had just pulled the switch. Their luck held, and the coupe was put back in shape in short order so the small band of adventurers could continue through the fog-laden sunrise.

As day broke, they decided to make one more unplanned stop to explore the Mission San Juan Capistrano, a chance to calm their nerves and keep their feet on the ground for a while. Jim steered the roadster around the Sunset Cliffs, a cove where the ocean had worn the rocks into distinctive shapes and, in one place, a natural bridge.

By nightfall they had arrived at Mission Beach, another resort community built on a sandbar between the Pacific Ocean and Mission Bay. The beach was nearly two miles of oceanfront bounded by the San Diego River on the south and Mission Bay Park on the east. To the north, there were more little beach communities and another boardwalk. Marion's companions warned her that there would be another amusement park, including a giant roller coaster, a Flow-Rider, and a Wave House. The big attraction was the dance hall and the Plunge indoor swimming pool, which had just opened and was drawing people from all over. Later on, Marion described it in a letter to Amy as the finest dance hall and plunge on the southern coast, the pool the largest saltwater pool in the world inside a building of breathtaking Spanish-style architecture.

Parsons cousins frolic at welcome luncheon, Marion far right

At daybreak they shoved out to Point Loma—a rugged setting guarded by soldiers. By noon they had made their way into Tijuana where, Marion wrote to her sister Martha, people went by the hundreds to fill their cars with beer. *This is desolate country, the only other reason for visiting would be curiosity.*

Once when they were in San Diego, they visited Balboa Park, a site that had been a branch of the World's Fair at San Diego. The Panama-California Exposition had been held there from 1915 to 1917, designed to coincide with and to celebrate the opening of the Panama Canal. Marion couldn't wait to write to Papa, to tell him what she had seen. He and Mother had loved their visit to the canal, and even Mother bubbled over with stories about their adventure.

There was so much to see and do at the park, and Marion was sorry they didn't spend more time at the remnants of the Exposition, La Laguna de Las Flores, but the others wanted to push on.

She was glad for once for her sensible shoes. They walked for miles, it seemed, visiting the botanical building, garden after garden, and endless pavilions and displays. At the end of one long promenade, Marion realized she was separated from Mabel. She looked around, turned back, but saw no one familiar. She stood still, waiting. Then she took refuge on a wooden bench where she could gaze out over the landscape. She had never seen so many unfamiliar trees, groves of trees, and birds that looked as though they had flown out of one of her fairy tale books—bright blue and green, red and fuchsia birds with long pointed wings. There were more Spanish-style buildings up ahead. Perhaps she should walk on up there and see if she could find Jim. Mabel would be worried. Maybe she should go back to the botanical building, or maybe the large lath house filled with plants from out of this world. She felt dizzy. What if she was really lost? She spotted a large grassy field, possibly a ballpark, over a rise in the hills to the east. Maybe they had gone over there. Jim had talked about catching a ballgame.

Marion decided to walk back to the Exposition. She could see more of the Casa del Prado Theater, and if she was going to be lost, she might as well be very lost. She crossed the Cabrillo Bridge and made her way past the California state building, where she noticed a sign that said Administration Building. Maybe they would have something like a lost and found for people in a place like this.

Then she heard someone call her name from above. It sounded like it was coming out of the sky. Marion covered her eyes, looked up, and turned around, and then all the way around again. The sun was too bright to see anything.

A man standing next to her touched her arm. "Excuse me," he said and pointed up at a bell tower next to a row of palm trees.

"We're up here," the voice drifted down. Her cousin waved her arm back and forth, and Marion recognized the hat—the big hat and the big flower—her cousin Mabel.

The next day they drove across the hills into Los Angeles so Marion could buy her train ticket back home, but they got caught in a snowstorm. It was pelting down in a thick curtain of giant wet flakes. These full-sized floppy snowflakes seemed out of place in California. They reminded Marion of the white paper cutouts she and her sisters used to make on winter days in front of the fire. Mixed with rain, the snow was so wet it melted as soon as it made contact with anything warm—someone's face, the hood of the car, the road—making for slick and scary driving. Marion patted Jim on the shoulder as he clung to the steering wheel.

None of them had brought along warm clothes—or even a change of clothes. Marion and Mabel huddled in the backseat, pulling their flimsy wraps as tightly as they would go across their chests. Dr. Jim and Cousin Esther talked softly in the front seat, but Marion heard only the slush of tires on wet snow and pavement. Mabel shook Marion's arm and pointed straight ahead where the sun was shining across the plain, cities and cultivated land laid out in the distance like checkerboard squares.

The color and odor of pine and bay trees filled the car. Forgetting about the cold, Marion leaned forward and tapped Jim on the shoulder again. "Please, pull over to the side," she pleaded, and in the midst of the storm, she and Mabel, hand in hand, made their way toward a stand of bay trees. "I'll take some of these leaves to Mother," Marion mused. "She will love these."

She left Mabel plucking leaves and small branches from the aromatic trees, pungent against the crisp morning air, and plodded through wet snow across a trail off the side of the pass. There she found a narrow lookout point and a view of the mountains. Most interesting, there was a small, gnarly tree where people had left cards and papers with their names to show they'd been there too.

Marion wished she had paper and something to write with, but she forgot about it when she was overtaken with worry. *What would Papa say about this wanton behavior, running around in the cold and wet without so much as a wool wrap or a hat?* She stood at the edge of the bluff, her sensible shoes firmly planted against the igneous rock, a stiff wind blowing up from the canyon and whipping around the kick pleat of her brown gabardine skirt.

She couldn't stop thinking about Papa and the way he had looked at her at the train station in Omak. It had been an odd look, unfamiliar and confusing to her then and now. Later that night she jotted a quick note in her journal, perhaps hoping to absolve herself of her joie de vivre. Despite her self-chastisement, neither she nor Mabel suffered any bad effect from exposure that day, even though they'd worn no boots, hats, or mittens.

Shortly before she embarked on her final cross-country journey, Marion and an eleven-year-old cousin, young Jim Parsons, hopped a trolley from Pasadena to Long Beach. From there, they found their way down to San Pedro Harbor where they boarded a glass-bottomed boat to Catalina Island. On this day Marion could hardly contain her own childlike glee, sharing eagerly in the boy's excitement, his thrill with the subterranean gardens, the colored fish darting about, and the plethora of colored fernery:

> *The band was playing as we boarded the ship for our two-hour ride across to the Island ... A fair-size boat with seats around the glass through which you gaze at the gardens below. After seeing the garden the boat goes out into clear water and a native diver goes over and swims under all the windows.*

Later on, Marion and Jimmy, tired from the boat ride, the choppy sea, and the excitement, were still in the mood for fun and adventure. Marion's well was deep, and the young boy's excitement to be along on this adventure was contagious. They took a bus to a hotel on the island, where they dined on a *poor meal for a good price.* In the morning Marion and her young charge toured the island. They visited the Wrigley Mansion and took in all the sights on Catalina Island.

On the boat ride back to the mainland, the captain steered the crowded, side-wheeled vessel through Avalon Bay. Passengers danced and clapped their hands to the gaiety, and Marion and Jim joined in by clapping and tapping their feet. Marion had never felt so gay. She didn't want to leave, to go back home. At that moment she indulged a desire to rebel, to stay in paradise with her friends.

When the boat propeller got tangled in the weeds, a diver had to go down and untangle the mess. For Marion and young Jim, it was all thrilling. When they returned home around nine o'clock, Marion could barely keep her eyes open as she wrote in her journal: *We have arrived home, tired but happy couple of children.*

A few days after the trip to Catalina Island, as summer waned, Marion was taken aback by a daring display of skin on a flat, white sandy beach when a local bather trotted past their lounge scantily dressed in the latest beach garb, bare midriff, bare arms. Marion had seen bare midriffs more than once at the California beaches, though, and she always cringed as she imagined how shocked her parents would be. She often felt a sense of relief that they were not there to see what she had just seen. She thought about summer days back in Syracuse—wonderful weekend holidays when they'd all take the trolley up to Oneida Lake. There, women bathers were covered in full, though they did dare an occasional sleeveless bathing top.

Marion had never worn a bathing suit—she preferred to lie back in the beach chairs and share conversation with her cousins and aunts. Marion had discovered that there was more than a separation of three thousand physical miles between the East Coast and the West Coast. Life back east on the farm was predictable and built on generations of Victorian ways of thinking, a lifestyle that had endured in both sides of her family for generations. Her mother's family, the Clowes from Burslem in Stafford, England, had crossed the Atlantic in the mid-1800s in bustles and top hats, their bags filled with dogma and attitude and convictions upon which they would build new lives in the New World.

The Parsons had escaped the rule of the crown in 1630 and risked their lives to make their way to the rocky shores of what would become New England. They came to live a Puritan lifestyle. Marion's father and his father had both served on the Board of the Plymouth Congregational Church in Syracuse. Back in Massachusetts there were as many Parsons pastors as there were Parsons schoolteachers. Out West—well this was, she learned, a destination for explorers and adventurers. One could go downtown without wearing gloves or a hat. One could disrobe at the beach, wear suits that exposed one's knees and one's midriff. Marion was ready to go home.

A letter came from her friend Tom in Omak. He revealed more than she felt comfortable telling Esther, or even Mabel. She destroyed the missive at once to make certain her father would never lay eyes on it. Papa had hopes for her, and she couldn't let him down.

She stayed in Pasadena until the garden she had helped plant and tend had been harvested and put up for winter. She loved the garden, and during the planting she had longed to stay in the fertile valleys of Southern California. She knelt in the rich loam, the California dirt, dug in her hands, and dreamed of the possibilities. She could have an orchard and a vegetable farm just like her father, only in a climate where winter storms were almost unheard of, where you could eat oranges off a tree, where you could sunbathe and no one would scorn. Maybe, just maybe, she could pursue life as an adventure. But in the end, she had to do what was right by her parents, her family, and her neighbors, who were more family than friend.

The garden turned out to be a huge success. Now there were rows of jars on the pantry shelves filled with larder for the winter, for the neighbors, for the memory of what she was certain would be the best summer of her life. She took one last look into the cold room before she left for the train station.

"Marion, please let me pack a basket with some of these jars of green beans," Mabel begged Marion one more time.

"No, no, I just can't be burdened for the train ride, and besides, Mother will have put up more than enough for all the Parsons in Geddes and beyond."

The cousins hugged and held on to each other for longer than they might otherwise have felt comfortable. They had shared a room, confidences, dreams, and even the worst of their fears. From now on, they would only have letters and a dream of seeing each other in the future.

Chapter Four

Going Home

How often have I lain beneath rain on a strange roof, thinking of home.
—William Faulkner

MARION BOARDED THE TRAIN for Chicago on October 15, 1925. She would be home in five days. Emerging from her sleeping berth, several times she made her way through the train to eat in the dining car. Occasionally she sat in the club car and watched the endless plains and fields of wheat pass by. It all looked the same—dry, dusty, empty. She saw men strapped to horses in barren fields, together pulling and guiding plows across the dry soil of summer's end—stalks of spent corn bent to the ground; then they would be gone from her sight as fast as they had appeared. She saw snippets of lives she would imagine later in the dark of night, to the sound of the train clacking across the prairie.

As they approached Chicago, there were more farms and then houses, lines of cars, and backsides of broken-down neighborhoods. Young boys ran alongside the train, mouthing words to her, waving sticks. It made her cry for reasons she didn't understand. She wanted to be home. She wanted to see something familiar.

After the train pulled away from the huge, thunderous station in Chicago, Marion found an empty seat in the coach car where she surveyed the crowded car in hopes of seeing someone she knew; after all, she was close enough to home that there might be someone onboard she would recognize, who knew her family. But there was not one person she could identify, and soon she was captivated by the familiar terrain of the northeastern landscape.

By the time the train passed Auburn, where she and her family had ridden the electric train and taken picnics to the amusement park on Owasco Lake, her heart was rattling like the click-clack of the giant engine. The surroundings took on more and more of a familiar feeling. She twisted her head back and forth as she tried to absorb the attractions on both sides of the car. Was that some of the remains of the Erie Canal? Maybe Geres Lock? Had they just passed the village of Camillus? She strained to catch a glimpse of Papa's Upper Farm, but she wasn't sure.

She was flooded with scenes from her childhood. It was an idyllic childhood. Marion Parsons and her sisters and cousins had frolicked in the orchards and haylofts with an abundance of neighbors whose families were so close they might as well have been blood relatives. They ran through open fields where horses were hitched to plows in the summertime, giant mounds of hay raked into hayracks in the springtime. They did chores along with the hired help, picked corn,

Terry Road School, 1908

dug potatoes. Piano and pump organ music filled parlors in the evenings and on stormy days, and during the long, dark nights of winter.

Aunts and uncles lived and farmed up and down the turnpike and were part of one another's everyday lives. There were cattle barns and pastures, tenant houses, vegetable gardens, crops of potatoes and corn, orchards filled with rows and rows of apples, peaches, cherries, and pears. Giant oak trees provided shelter from the sun for livestock, kept them cool in the summer and warm in the winter. Marion's sister, Grace, was well-known for her tree-climbing abilities—she would shinny up a tree and call down to the rest of the girls. Aunt Sarah or Aunt Mary would implore the young girl in the high-buttoned shoes to come down and act like a lady.

No child, male or female, was excused from farmwork or daily chores. When the duties were done, they played hard; they played together. One summer a group of the cousins built a pretend school in the carriage house at Francis and Sarah Parsons' farm. Marion loved the big old structure with heavy plank floors. All one summer, she and her cousins played school in the carriage house, Marion acting as the headmistress.

A gang of Parsons and Jerome cousins could almost always be spotted walking up and down the turnpike on a summer's afternoon. The girls went from household to household, helping with harvest undertakings, making jam, canning, or washing spring wool to be used for new school clothes in the fall. Every

Martha, Grace, Marion Parsons, 1909

house had a treadle sewing machine, but it was Aunt Mary who loved to sew and could turn any piece of cloth into a fine-looking garment.

The boys fancied themselves as their fathers' right-hand men—

Terry Road School Building

working in the barns and driving farm wagons pulled by a couple of old mares and filled with produce and newly baled straw. Sometimes they played down in the swamp, sometimes along the stream flowing through the meadow across the road from the Jerome's cow pasture. Seemingly endless land provided a vast territory for daylong tournaments of soldier, or games of hide-and-seek, riding the range or covered wagon. No one held back when it was time to swing on the rope in the hayloft or climb one of the oak trees at the top of the hill out behind Uncle Jim and Aunt Mary's place.

    A summer drive along the turnpike in the horse-drawn buggy was a social event as well as a day's journey if you happened to be traveling as far as Elbridge and back. Maple, elm, and oak trees lined the road. Fresh green leaves provided ample canopies of shade against the sweltering sun. Bouncing along to the clip-clop of the horses, you'd feel the light breezes carrying the sweet aroma of mowed grass and the not-so-sweet scent of a barnyard; broad, fan-shaped leaves danced overhead like green satin dresses sashaying in the sunlight. More than likely you'd come across cousins or friends—maybe an old friend you hadn't seen since the summer before—and this would delay the journey for as much as an hour. There were no phones, and the only way to keep up with the news was by word of mouth or letters. At county fair time, or later on during the state fair in the fall, the road would be busier, bustling with families in buggies and wagons heading to the exposition, prepared to spend the week.

At last the train had slowed to a crawl, and Marion spotted smokestacks from the Iroquois China factory. She remembered the night Papa took her there. He'd had a meeting with a night foreman. The seat across the train aisle was empty now, and she flew to the abandoned bench in time to see the backside of the grandstand as they passed the New York State Fairgrounds. She was home! She kept her face pressed to the window until she spotted Willis, Allain, Martha, and Grace standing in a row near the edge of the station platform. She leaped from her seat without waiting for the train to stop, forgetting her hat and the gloves she had carefully folded and laid out as they were passing through Palmyra a short ways back.

She was home. Marion woke in the morning to smells of bonfires in the wind, the scent of apples turned to cider, the chill of an early morning frost, and the sound of axes splitting rounds of fresh-cut cordwood. Later in the afternoon, strolling down the old farm road, she could hear the familiar clattering of the last dried leaves clinging to tips of tree limbs, clacking in the soft breeze of a warm autumn afternoon.

There would be few remaining days of summer; a chill wind filled the darkening afternoon. Brittle blackberry vines drooped along fencerows as though the summers Marion missed had never bloomed. Walking along, tracing the footsteps of her childhood, she tried to imagine what it had been like while she was gone so far away. How could life have gone on without her? Though difficult to imagine, it seemed silly to think anything to the contrary. Two summers and two winters came and went while she was on the other side of the world.

Signs of winter finally couldn't be ignored, and Marion's memo-

Willis Parsons, Grace (standing), Marion, Anna, Martha (seated)

ries of the bright sun and brilliant white California beaches dwindled into occasional dreams that would wake her in the middle of the night. She would lie in bed wondering about her friends in Omak, her cousins in California.

Her life back on the farm set in like a newly sprouting spring garden. Marion and Willis, the board of trustees, and other neighbors set about the business of raising money to build the new school. Marion took charge of afternoon classes at the old schoolhouse, the one built in 1847 where she'd first learned the magic of books, where she fell in love with Miss Allen's sharp tone and take-no-prisoners style that drew her into stories about other worlds. Like Jane Austen's characters, Marion sought to improve herself with reading. Miss Austen was one of her favorite writers. As a young girl, she had also loved the seemingly endless stories penned by Charles Dickens, and like the heroes in his tales, she was becoming the hero of her own life.

It soon became clear to Marion that the decrepit schoolhouse of her childhood and her father's childhood had been so well used that it could not weather another winter, not even another storm. Something had to be done before the imminent snowstorms left them stranded.

It would be a shame to say goodbye to the place. She and her sisters, cousins, and neighbors had played in the old schoolyard in nice weather. When bitter cold and pounding, relentless snow took hold, they'd trudged five mornings a week to the tiny school through mountains of snow and ice. They'd sat on benches while Miss Allen perched on a tall stool wielding a long pointer stick—a sure threat to any pupils who allowed their attention to wander from the wood-framed slate board at the front of the room.

In the mornings, if the brass bell could already be heard chiming across the Babcocks' field as the Parsons girls were leaving their mother's kitchen, there was a dreadful chance they would be late. At the sound of the brass bell, they would run, even in the snow.

Judge Farnham, George Terziev, and Willis Parsons searched for a suitable temporary installment for Marion and the children at the Terry Road School. Nothing came together. The rooms at the grange were in use. Church facilities were needed for other activities and couldn't be committed. They needed to find something in walking distance for the children in the vicinity of the tumbling and

Willis Parsons' farm (would become the Lower Farm)
From left to right: Unknown lady, unknown man, Marion Parsons, Grace Parsons, Martha Parsons, Mary Anna Clowes Parsons, unknown man, Emily Jerome. In carriage: Jerome (Jim) Parsons (with broken leg), Sarah Jerome Parsons (Jim's mother and Emily's sister)
In the window: Julia Armstrong Parsons (Grandmother)

crumbling Terry Road School.

As the winter of 1926 took hold, snowflakes swirled and beat at the windowpanes. Children shivered at their desks. The roof leaked, and the woodstove had all but worn out, belching wretched smoke into the classroom. There were days the children had to be marched out onto the front porch so Marion could air out the classroom.

Standing before the crowded schoolroom one frosty morning, beholding the children's breath hanging in the air, she was reminded again of bitter mornings long past, her own legs wrapped in woolen leggings, her neck in tightly knit scarves to keep ice off her face, keep her tears from freezing on her cheeks. She thought about the day she tried falsely to stay at home with mama in front of the fire instead of facing the winter storm, instead of traipsing through snow up to her waist.

That morning an icy wind, thick as pudding and laced with sleet and snow, had pounded against the kitchen window. Mama came into her room and headed for the curtains.

"Oh, Mama, I am so sick. Please may I stay home?" she had cried out from under the covers before Mama had a chance to open the drapery and let in the chill and light, before she had a chance to see the dishonesty in Marion's young eyes.

Mama rushed to her bedside and placed her cool palm on Marion's forehead. The memory of this gesture made her throat tighten, and she hoped the children, busy with their new readers, would not notice her tears. Mama had prepared a hot cup of tea and wrapped her in a blanket next to the kitchen fire. Marion had jumped when she heard Papa stomping his boots free of snow out on the back porch—had not expected him to return until later in the day—and was terrified. She feared the worst; she feared exposure.

She could still see that kitchen door opening, her father blowing in with a sharp gust of wind and snow.

Martha Parsons, 1897

She had thought he was meeting with some of the other farmers that morning to talk about safeguarding the peach orchard, but instead of continuing on down the turnpike after taking Grace and Martha to school in the sleigh, he had turned around and come back.

"Why didn't you show up in the barn this morning?" he wanted to know.

Marion was out of the chair and buttoning up her coat, pulling on her gloves before the question was even out of his mouth. But there would be no ride. She would have to walk. She could see that her mother felt sorry for her but could not say a word. Papa's word was law. If he saw Marion cry, he would remind her that she had brought this misery upon herself with her lies. He was right, but she didn't understand the depth of this fact until years later.

She could still feel his hand patting her back as she brushed past him on her way out the door. Even when Papa was angry, he wanted his girls to know he loved them. She had escaped his wrath, but she still had to face the long walk to school, had to inch her way through the snow and pelting ice. When the wind blew, the snow would drift in front of her before she could take another step. Any paths that might have been made by the horses and the sleigh earlier that morning were long buried.

Trudging past the open barn door, Marion was tempted to sneak in and ask one of the farmhands for a ride in the sleigh, but she knew better. Though she might be buried alive in the snow—they would find her later when Papa hitched up the horse and sleigh again—she had to walk. She tried not to cry because her tears would freeze on her face. She pressed on, and by the time she arrived at the schoolhouse, she was frozen all the way through; her lips and her face chafed from the icy wind, from the sharp snow on her scarf rubbing against her chin and her cheeks. Her ears were frozen. She worried that her nose would be bright red, and she stood by the door, not wanting to go inside and face humiliation. As she reached for an icicle hanging from the edge of the schoolhouse roof, the door flew open.

Claude Cole, 1909

What a sight she must have been. She had to spend the whole day on a bench by the potbellied stove so her stockings and skirt would dry out for the trip home after school. Marion never tried to get out of school again, or anything else for that matter.

Chapter Five
The Fire

The bluebird carries the sky on his back.
—Henry David Thoreau

MARION HAD BEEN ABOUT FOUR or five when her father purchased sixty-six acres of prime farmland from Burritt Chaffee—it must have been 1892—just up the road from Grandma and Grandpa Parsons. Before that they had lived on a smaller farm over on Onondaga Road, where both she and Grace had been born in a little farmhouse. With the purchase of the farm, the family moved into the big old farmhouse on the Genesee Turnpike, and Papa set to the business of farming.

Marion remembered him strapped into a harness behind a huge plow pulled by his father's best workhorses. He plowed acres and acres and rows and rows of loamy soil, planted potatoes, corn, and vegetables. Her mother would have New England boiled dinners and pies on the table when he finally came back inside at dusk. He would talk about the young cherry orchard already thriving on the eastern side of the property—he would nurse it into full production, and he planned to plant more fruit trees—apple, peach, and pear.

"I'm going to turn this into one of the best orchards in the state, Anna." Papa would make these sorts of pronouncements, and Mama and the girls would all nod and smile to cheer him on. He was their hero.

Marion and her sisters were almost late for school on September 10, 1897. A crew of men with a gigantic steam engine had shown up at the Parsons farm just after sunrise. They'd come to fill the silo with ensilage from the cornfield, and the two younger girls were eager to watch. Grace, the eldest, wanted to stay home with their mother, who was sick. But Willis Parsons was a stickler for being on time, and after his fruit trees, his daughters' education was his priority.

The girls ran down the farm road, long skirts flowing behind in a swirl of dust as they bounded across the potato field. The last dried leaves clung to Willis's apple trees. The brass bell's clanging resounded. Miss Allen would be closing the door soon, so they ran faster, panting as they reached the schoolhouse lawn; the teacher lowered the bell for one final warning.

Marion Parsons

Sometime around nine o'clock, Marion was helping the younger kids with their grammar lesson in the back of the classroom. Grace held a watercolor session in the mornings for middle grade girls; Martha was helping her pass out what was left of the paintbrushes. Already a hot, dry September day, Miss Allen propped open the door to let the breeze circulate. On their way to the county fair, people passed by in democrat wagons—open-air, two-seater wagons used for farmwork, trips to town, and everyday getting about. Some rode in buggies, which usually had covers and were used for more formal occasions or in the rain.

A shout rose from the front of the room. Several of the older boys had gathered by the window to watch passersby when one of them noticed the flames over the hill. As the boys clambered onto the porch, flames shot into the sky to the east, clearly visible now. One of the Jerome cousins hollered that it looked like the fire was coming from the Babcocks' barn—the only building between the school and the Parsons farm.

The girls ran out onto the porch where the boys were begging Miss Allen for permission to go to the fire. Cousin Herbert broke from the crowd to tell the teacher it was Willis Parsons' farm on fire; Louise Hubbell and Hazel Andrews gathered young Martha into their arms. Herbert, Roy Vinton, and other boys had already taken off across the field before Miss Allen could say, "The boys may go." She signaled the younger children back inside.

With Marion at her side, Grace confronted the teacher. "I'm going home to comfort my mother." The young teacher hesitated but realized there would be no arguing with the elder Parsons girl. Grace, Marion close behind, ran after the boys who had already disappeared into the orchard. Gasping and crying, the two girls held hands as they tore through the field, flames and black smoke cutting a giant swath across the once-blue morning sky—their farm was in blazes, maybe their house too.

There had been a long, dry spell that year, so when the steam engine blew that morning for lack of water and the flames shot into the hay-filled barn, the flames spread like tinder aflame in a storm. Soon the house caught fire, and in about half an hour, the barn had burned to the ground and the backside of the house was lost. Marion and Grace clung to their mother as they huddled at the edge of the dirt road. Willis shouted at them to get back, to go to the Babcocks', but they held firm. They wouldn't leave Papa. He had fallen to the ground with the explosion.

When the day was finally over, Martha had been carried back in the arms of Miss Allen. They all wandered around the property, eyes glazed, hearts heavy. It was clear that little had been saved from the barn or the rear of the house. Marion found her mother on her knees in the front yard, clutching the family photo album, all the precious portraits of her parents and the rest of her family who had come from England when Anna was a girl. The pictures were safe, as were most of the furniture and family items from the front of the house, but it was little comfort.

Neighbors and passersby on their way to the county fair had hitched their mounts and teams to the roadside fences and rushed to help. Had it not been for the coincidence of the fair, people would not have been nearby at that time of day to help save the house. There were no telephones to summon help, no fire houses, and no water except what could be pumped from the well by hand or the scant amount that had accumulated in cisterns from rain running off the roofs.

Mary Anna Clowes Parsons

At the time of the fire, Grandmother Julia Parsons' brick house a quarter mile to the west was vacant. After Grandpa Edwin died in 1893, Grandma Julia's brick house often sat empty as she spent most of her time at Aunt Mary's or at the farm with Willis, Anna, and the girls. The old homestead that had once bustled with aunts and uncles and cousins, farmhands, housekeepers, and friends had suddenly become as empty as a dance hall on a Sunday morning. So Marion and her family moved into the old place where their father had lived as a boy. They stayed for the winter and spring while the new house and barn were built on the same foundations as the buildings that had burned down.

The Terry Road schoolhouse was just over the knoll from the Parsons' farmhouse, and when the giant red barn was rebuilt, children would come by after school to explore this mysterious place—its dark corners, its musty odors of leather, grease, straw, and saddle soap. There were buggies and wagons to climb on; sometimes the children pretended they were driving the team to market. Farm implements and machinery could be examined but not touched.

The schoolhouse had been donated by Guy Terry, whose daughter Alice, or Allie, later married Willis's older brother, Charles H. Parsons. The building was covered with white clapboard siding; tall lead glass windows let rays of sunlight wash over the children's faces as they sat side-by-side on long, hard wooden benches. The students wrote their lessons with slates and chalk. Later on, the benches were replaced by wooden desks with inkwells. Paper was scarce, if available at all—lined paper unheard of.

All grades met in one room. There was an outhouse out back. During the frigid Central New York winters, the classroom was heated with a box stove that had to be fed all day long. A breezeway-like structure held stacks of firewood. In the depths of winter, snowdrifts covered the wagon roads and farm roads, and the ringing of the brass bell could be heard for miles, no cushion of leafy orchards to muffle the clang.

Julia Armstrong Parsons
(Grandmother)
Wife of Edwin Clark Parsons

Marion and her sisters may have peered out the window at day's end in hopes of catching a glimpse of Willis's sleigh. Perhaps they struck a deal in the morning with one of the farmhands—if the weather was bad, he'd take mercy on the youngsters and hitch up the team. They'd all pile into the back of the sleigh, and there'd be a stop at each farmhouse on the way home, children dropping into the snow at front porches like clumps of slush falling off pine boughs.

At times, these endless winters may have felt much like Charles Dickens' winter of despair. And as in all Dickens tales, there is a spring of hope. In the countryside on the west end of Syracuse, spring was a glorious time. Robins returned to nest in towering maple trees where buds popped out all at once in June. Winter would be forgotten, and the children at Terry Road School could see there was much to look forward to—summer was upon them, a season of light and hope and all that was good in the world.

It was 1902 when Marion and her sisters learned firsthand about loss, about grief and loneliness. Their mother, Mary Anna, died one night while the girls and Willis stood watch, helpless to do anything to comfort or save her, not even with the help of the doctor. They had watched their mother's health deteriorate since her second or third serious bout of pneumonia. She grew pale, losing more and more weight until even the smallest of her heavy cotton frocks hung on her body like wet sheets on a clothesline. During the final two weeks, Mary Anna did not get out of bed, and her family stayed at her bedside day and night, desperate to hold on to her.

After that, all three Parsons girls stayed home from school until their father told them it was time to go back, to show the rest of the world how strong they were, to set a good example for other children. Life would go on. And it did.

Despite the hardships—despite the anger and resentment Marion and her sisters felt when their father married the housekeeper, Allain—life on the farm was wonderful. The days were filled with simple satisfactions like the sound of a woodpecker in a hollow maple, breakfasts of hot oatmeal, and pitchers full of fresh milk. Farmhands came in from the barn for a meal and were considered part of the family. There were miles and miles of pastures, woodlands, and rolling hills.

After finishing eighth grade at Terry Road School, Marion attended Solvay High School on the other side of the turnpike, over a hill. The year before she graduated, the year before the United States was officially at war in Europe, her father purchased another large acreage of orchards, pastures, and a rambling farmhouse where a farm manager would live. Willis bought the farm and all its contents in July 1913 from a Mr. E. H. Wheaton. Located to the west of the current property that would come to be known as the Lower Farm, its frontage abutted the turnpike near the town of Camillus. Willis would call this the Upper Farm. Though Allain objected to this "extravagance," as she called it, it was there that Willis would grow some of the finest apples in the state of New York. Allain eventually had to concede it had been a good decision.

Still, there was bad blood between her and the girls. Allain had grown up on a plantation in Ceylon and then in Nyasaland in Africa. She had had her fill of betting on crops, staking a family's fortune on the fickle marketplace. She left Africa on a steamer ship as a young woman and never returned. Listening to Allain's stories of tigers, snakes, and the largest rats on the planet, Marion developed a curiosity for the other side of the world, and she had to admit that her relationship with Allain wasn't all bad.

Mary Anna and her brother, Viniah Clowes

Marion and her friends took pleasure in Sunday afternoon strolls through the Upper Farm, wandering its gently sloping pastures, rows and rows of prolific apple trees. For Papa, though, this new operation was far enough away from the Lower Farm to make it a time-consuming journey in a horse and buggy.

Later that year, Willis sped up to the house in his first automobile—a touring car from H. A. Moyer Automobile Company. Willis loved that old roadster, shiny and new when he brought it home.

Marion and the girls had all run out into the barnyard, yelling and screaming with a mixture of shock, joy, and fear.

"Willis, where in heaven's name did ya get that contraption?" Allain was the first to speak.

"I bought it directly from the plant." Willis rubbed a speck of dust off the fender with the sleeve of his jacket. "From Mr. Moyer, who has made all my buggies and wagons for years, so you can count on this vehicle. Not only that, the Moyers have a fine reputation for building first-rate carriages, and they sell them all over the world."

With this, he could travel between the two farms much more easily, although daily trips were still out of the question. Unfortunately, the car was made so well—no corners cut to produce

Papa could be seen puttering down the turnpike on Sunday afternoons. One such September afternoon in 1915, he loaded his grandson, John, and several friends and young cousins into his Moyer. They puttered off down Cherry Road in celebration of John's first birthday. Marion and Grace wanted to go, but the car was filled with children. They took pictures with the family's new box camera instead. The Cole house, having just gone up not long before, can be seen in the background.

the finest of automobiles—the company fell out of the business of car manufacturing in 1915. Willis wanted to keep up with the times, though. After the Moyer, he took to driving Franklins. He loved his automobiles; they gave him the mobility to manage his farms and visit other farmers.

☙

When Marion was far away in Omak, her father wrote to her of fair-goers camping in his orchard: two young couples from Interlaken came to the Fair, and camped at the lower end of the orchard. This was the sixth time they had been here for the Fair and same camp.

Above, Fishing party in Nyasaland, Africa; Below, Nyasaland, Africa,

Allain Imlah Parsons'
brother-in-law, Henry Brown

Martha, Grace, John, unknown woman,
circa 1915

Her father had no doubt seen an opportunity to make a little extra cash by turning parts of his farm into a campground during fair time. Marion grinned when she read Papa's words. Later that evening during dinner with her frontier friends, she repeated the story and they all chuckled at Marion's description of the old man, at his attempts to make a living off his land, at her stories of life back on the farm. It had been fun to make light and laugh with friends.

In the decade that followed Mary Anna Parsons' death, the world in which her girls lived changed drastically. For the first time in history, a war affected countries on both sides of the world, a terrible war, the Great War. Cousin Jim Parsons, who only a few years earlier had studied medicine at Syracuse University—living an idyllic life in a fraternity house with friends and classmates, visiting his cousin Grace on weekends at Alfred University, then marrying the prettiest girl on campus—would find himself stationed as a medic in a foxhole in France. Cousin Charles F. shared a letter from his brother with Marion and her sisters one night at dinner. It had arrived the day before. Dr. Jim had written from the front lines in Europe:

> *20 March, 1918*
> My Dear Brother—
> Nothing since March 9 I fear, from me. That is not commendable but I hope for forgiveness … If there were nothing else learned in this war of [this hellish war], men learn how to do with anything they have. After reading an article discouraging too free play of sentiment in sending things over to friends I would advise that very little in the way of non-essentials be sent me—not because I am unappreciative I am sure but because a shell or a rifle or other tool of destruction or necessary equipment for men in the ranks, would more quickly finish the Hun.
> As I see more I cannot but hate him more—as righteous a hate as hatred of evil of any sort. One day I saw a man of my

battalion whose life probably had been saved by the deflection of a bullet, by a whistle in his pocket, so that it just grazed his abdomen. Otherwise it would have gone through his chest. I was still marveling at it when another lad was brought in with both hands and one leg blown off by a shell, the other leg being badly wounded. I sent him on & know he lived to reach a hospital, may be alive today. No, a man so badly wounded doesn't suffer much pain, he is so nearly unconscious … that at such times is for the damnation of the bloody ruler who started such a war when he, more than all others, knew how horrible he could make it. The God he trusts in is only the God of War, that is certain. Plainly, the duty of civilized nations is to use the only argument that appeals to him, viz. resort to equally horrible measures. Anything else would be an abject yielding to the devil.

I have written letters with shrapnel falling on the roof over my head. Have seen a high explosive shell enter the roof of a hut fifty feet away and pass through the far end of the hut in which were four men, explode outside and not wound a man. One of the men had been in the same hut 24 hr earlier when a shell casing came through the roof—harmlessly & 12 hours before that in the midst of a barrage of gas and high explosive shells. I had seen that barrage about a mile from the foxhole I occupied, playing on a duckboard track. The night before that two gas shells had struck & partly destroyed—gas shells do little harm through explosive force. In such places we keep two heavy blankets over the entry & in the above instance we got very little gas in the pill box, but had to use our respirators for a time. Just the day before the place from which I had moved in the early morning was heavily gassed. With it all, the escapes are far more wonderful than the casualties.

Maybe it's unkind to give so vivid a picture—if it is a vivid one—but Americans are at war & should know what it is as Sherman thought he did though he had then but a very meager idea. The fact that it is so makes, I believe, all who enter it willing to do their utmost to remove it from the world—possible only through the overthrow of the Huns. I must say I have very little fear in it all. I can't explain that, further than that I'm here (to my complete satisfaction) and that I couldn't get away if I would, so there's no alternative but to take things as they come.

After all we are a very fair part of the time quite removed from all the annoyance of the front line. And the country in much of the territory I am in is very pretty. Not that I've seen anything the equal of American country nor American rural prosperity, but still very pretty. It is interesting to meet the peasants & they enjoy it too. I recall one little French girl whose father, in the war since 5 days after its onset in 1914, was coming on leave from Italy. She was about 8 and was very overjoyed. She told how her father had once been in a cave for 5 days with no manger, no "boire," while the Germans were passing. The youngster talked fair English, I, worse French. But, I seldom find anyone I cannot communicate with, after a fashion....

As the Tommies say, I'm "sweating on leave." Was told today that I might be granted leave before April 1. I plan to spend my time in Glasgow and Edinburgh, perhaps a bit elsewhere in Scotland ... Will probably go there for a day. I have asked if possible to have the last 2 or 3 days in Paris where I might see a few acquaintances—Davis, an old S.U. oarsman ... and probably some others I would locate there through him or otherwise ...

It is not impossible I will next write you from Britain.
Much love to you all,
JJP

It was a scary time. Young Marion saw the fear in her elders' faces. One day she asked her stepmother, who had been born in Scotland and had lived all over the world, what she knew about the war.

"Well, it's without precedent, Marion," Allain replied, stopping as she hurried toward the clothesline. Wiping her hands on her apron, she sat next to Marion on the back porch. "Ne'er have so many na-

Lieut. J. J. Parsons

Reported Seriously Wounded in France.

Lieut. James Jerome Parsons of this city, mentioned on General Pershing's casualty list as severely wounded in action in Flanders on April 12th, is widely known. He is now in an English Red Cross hospital.

Lieutenant Parsons is chief medical officer of the King's Own Scottish Borderers. His wife, who resides at No. 102 Summit avenue, has received word from him by cable that he is doing finely and will recover.

He sailed from this country September 8th as a member of the American Medical Reserve corps.

April 29, 1918 Syr. Herald

Cousin "Jim" Jerome Parsons

tions taken up arms at one time, ne'er has the battle been so vast, so gruesome. It's the Great War, for sure, and this world will be changed forever. Take my word."

Marion lay awake that night as her father's snores filled the towering farmhouse. She missed her sister Grace who had finally married Claude Cole and was expecting a baby any time. Papa had given them a lot over by the cherry orchard and bought them a Sears house kit—a house that came pre-built in pieces—for a wedding present. It seemed as though Grace had been gone forever.

Papa said they would all be making bandages at the grange for the holidays. There would be no presents—anything extra would go to the troops. Besides, he wanted them all to be reminded of the importance of helping others, of pitching in when their country needed help. Marion could see that, yes, he was right to think that.

☙

As the country shook with unrest, Marion and her

cousins ended their tenure at the one-room schoolhouse and then graduated from the high school on the other side of the hill, where they didn't know, weren't related to, their classmates. Many changes had taken place since Cornet Joseph Parsons had landed on the rocks at the edge of the New World colonies three hundred years earlier. From a fledgling settlement belonging to a confluence of Indian tribes and some English and Dutch settlers, a new wave of immigrants had turned the countryside into a nation that was quickly becoming what the newspapers called a "world power."

July 4, 1916: Martha Parsons, Grace Parsons Cole, Marion Parsons, John Parsons Cole

When Marion's generation came of age in the small agricultural community on the western boundary of Syracuse, their modestly prosperous parents did what they could to help their children go to college. Boys went to college if they could, or they inherited their father's farms. Girls went to normal schools and universities too—studied business or medicine, science or art. Willis insisted that all three of his daughters go to college. He had instilled in them a love of learning and the high standards of self-discipline and respect for others that he had learned at his father's knee.

Terry Road School, Circa 1916

Terry Road School, Circa 1925

Chapter Six
Terry Road School, End of an Era

What we call the beginning is often the end.
And to make an end is to make a beginning.
The end is where we start from.

—T. S. Elliot

By midwinter 1926, the board of trustees decided Terry Road School would close for good. After nearly seventy-five years, the old building had simply worn out. It had been exactly one year while Marion was still in the West during the blizzard of 1925 when the little school was shut down for weeks.

The afternoon of the storm, January 29, 1925, several children were stranded at the school with the teacher. It had snowed all morning, relentless wet snowflakes the size of large gold coins. The school was buried. No cars or streetcars ran for at least a week. The Terry Road School students and teacher were finally rescued by sleigh. For days, the world as they knew it shut down. No one went to school or work, but hardly anyone complained. It was their way of life. But the community grieved when one elderly farmer died trying to shovel a tunnel from his back porch to the road. He never made it.

֍

Now that the school was closing for good one year later, Marion asked Mother and Papa for permission to hold classes in their parlor until other arrangements could be made, or until the new school was finished. Marion and Allain pulled the settee, the chairs, and Willis's rocker to the edges of the room. The farmhands brought benches from the school and lined them up in the center. It was warmer there than it had been in the drafty little school building, but it was also crowded, and the Parsons' home was now overrun.

Marion moved from her room upstairs to a vacant room at the home of Uncle Charles and Aunt Allie Parsons, whose property hosted the old Terry School building. Marion loved their company and was glad to be out of sight of her stepmother and father. She loved Papa, but he could be overbearing at times, looking over her shoulder whenever letters came. She had said no when a young man at church invited her to a holiday social. It would have been too much trouble to explain the occasion to Papa. When he objected to her leaving home, she promised him she would move back in when

> **That night we went to bed with the snow falling down in big [flakes]; it snowed all night and on Friday morning the snow was three feet deep. We were literally buried in snow; the landscape was one vast mantle of dazzling white, everything buried deep. It took me several hours to make paths to the sidewalk and when they were made they looked like deep, narrow canyons. I didn't go to work that day—I couldn't. Nobody did; it took all day to dig ourselves out of the snow. All day long there were no streetcars and no automobiles. We didn't get any newspaper that day nor any milk delivered, nor any mail. On Saturday things began to move again—a few streetcars and sleighs. The streets were piled high with embankments of snow like big dugouts.**
>
> **The snow came down silently stealing through the warm night and buried us deep while we slumbered blissfully under the warmth of the snow mantle! In other days we would have considered this quite natural and proper; but now people look upon snow as an enemy to be fought. So-call modern (pseudo-) civilization and snow don't hitch together very well. Only children appreciate snow as they always did.—**
>
> **George N. Terziev, January 1925**

The youngest at the Parsons' parlor were called The Tots, circa 1926

spring came and the older children's class would be moved out to the barn. Papa could be a tyrant, but Marion somehow understood his goodness where others might not. Perhaps that was the reason she could put up with certain things. The man had worked so hard, had lost so much, and what he did he did for his family.

Winter turned into spring, and by April, several of the older boys and girls started meeting in the barn to begin a new program Marion had learned about during summer study at Boston College. It was a series of classes in woodworking design and domestic arts—a system of teaching based on an old Swedish curriculum called Stroid. They built dollhouses to apply what they were learning in math.

This arrangement at the Parsons farm would have to be temporary, and if they weren't successful in their attempts to build a new school, all the children of the area might have to be absorbed into surrounding schools. These families had gone to school together for almost a century. Now their children might be sent to school in other neighborhoods, or worse, all the way in downtown Syracuse. Marion and her father as well as Judge Farnham, Mr. Terziev, Mr. Coulter, and the other trustees would not let this happen. The community had to remain intact. They were a close-knit family—most were related by blood somewhere along the line, sometimes two or three times along the line. All the neighbors attended the meetings at the grange hall, crowding in until there was no seating and hardly any room to stand. No one escaped Judge Farnham's office without a gentle nudge about the school.

Marion's dreams of returning to her life and friends out West began to feel more and more out of reach. She put her hopes and dreams for a family of her own aside. A letter she received went unanswered,

Parsons family picnic (Willis far left, standing)

a long distance phone call missed. There was hardly enough time in the day to tend to teaching and planning a new school, let alone personal matters.

Whenever Marion's father—a towering man with a distinctive white beard who always wore a suit—came into the barn, the boys considered him from the corners of their eyes. They were careful not to catch his attention. Willis Parsons wasn't someone to cross; he was Miss Parsons' father, and this was his barn.

Marion tried to shield her students from Papa, but one boy learned the hard way, setting an example for the rest to mind their ways around Mr. Parsons. Young Phillip was not a boy to get in trouble, but one spring morning he arrived early for school at the Parsons farm. His father was driving their Model T to the Barge Canal office and had dropped him off out on the turnpike. It was their very first car, and Phillip never passed up a chance to ride in the shiny new Ford. After his father pulled away, he wandered around the back of the barn, not wanting to disturb the Parsons in the house, and tried the door. It was locked, probably too early for the farmhands, or maybe they were down in the potato field. Plowing had already begun.

The boy kicked around in the dirt along the fence line, over by the newly planted orchard. He was going to be like Willis Parsons; when he was old enough, he'd buy some property, maybe that piece he'd seen not long ago on the other side of the Jerome pasture, on the other side of the hill. He checked the door again, and it was still locked, so he wandered over by a circle of boulders where someone had recently burned a pile of logs. A mound of charcoal still smoldered in the fire pit. Phillip picked up a piece from the edge and scratched it on a fencepost lying nearby. It made a sharp black line. He drew another line on the side of the barn. It was crisp and smooth, and he liked the curve of the arc. He decided to write his name along that line. He was just finishing when Willis Parsons strode around the corner of the barn. Mr. Parsons, who

Above: Willis examines his prize apples;
Below: Willis and grandson, John Parsons Cole

was usually friendly and encouraging, wasted no time in grabbing Phillip by the scruff of his collar.

"Fools' names can always be found on public places, young man. I want you to go home, change your clothes, and return prepared to work. The first thing you will do is clean this building until there is no hint of this crime. Do you understand?" Willis's face had turned blood red, his sparkling blue eyes clouded with rage.

Other children had begun arriving and stood back, frozen by the corner of the barn.

Sunday picnic–Marion far left, Willis far right, circa 1916

Willis hadn't been the same since young John's death on Christmas Eve in 1920. He rarely smiled anymore; he only went riding in his auto when he needed to go to the Upper Farm, visit another orchard, or attend a meeting at the church or the grange. For a while, he stopped going to church altogether. Maybe God's grace was a myth after all. He kept this thought to himself. The pastor had told Willis he would find the grace within himself when he was ready—and that his daughter Grace needed him to give her strength as she grieved her son. He was tired. He loved his daughters, but he was tired.

After the twins were born, Willis came around again, doting on his grandson, David, and his granddaughter, Helen. His greatest pleasure became taking them riding in the car, just the way he had once taken young John and his playmates. They took picnics out to the creek or the lake. Sometimes the entire extended family gathered for Sunday picnics.

Allain had hoped the trip to Panama would cheer Willis, and it did, but only for a while. She was also certain that Marion's return would rekindle his fire and drive, but he seemed more agitated than enthused most of the time. The pressure of the new school and the bad weather was on him. He was a farmer at heart. Change was hard for someone like him.

It was a Monday morning in early May, 1926—the first signs of spring popping through the remains of old snow and slush around the perimeter of the Parsons farm. Marion's students had been looking forward to summer, to spending their days playing in haylofts, swimming in the creek, trapping muskrats down in the swamp. She had them write essays about what they would do during the summer months. They wrote about the county fair and the state fair; they wrote about Mr. Jerome's farm. One of the Mitchell boys wrote how he and his brother like to go up to the big barn and pretend to be working, pitch a little hay, and gaze at the cows. If Mr. Jerome wasn't too busy, he'd let them ride on the wide back of the enormous white horse.

The Jerome dairy wagon, filled with ice to keep the fresh milk chilled, would come up the rutted dirt roads in the mornings. Children ran out to grab slivers of ice, and sometimes an ice-throwing battle would ensue.

On the second day of May, it rained hard during the night—loud claps of thunder, brilliant flashes of lightning illuminating the sky above Westvale while people slept. But now the rain had stopped, and the temperature was cool enough that you could see your breath in the thin air, the way it is sometimes after a good rain has settled the dust.

It had been a particularly cold spring. In April, the temperature plummeted to eighteen degrees. Willis worried about his orchards, some already in bloom. Marion and the children watched him quietly from the corner of the barn where they worked on their projects. He came in and out carrying lanterns, loading charred black globes into the back of the wagon. If the temperature were to drop again, he could lose all his fruit. This would be the end of him, the ruin of his orchards.

On this morning, a growing crowd of children waited at the back door of the Parsons' farmhouse. Overhead, gray thunder clouds swam angrily across the morning sky. The door was usually open as farmhands passed in and out for scrambled eggs and coffee, but today not a soul was in sight. A tenant farmer came out the door on the side of the barn, turned and locked it, then strode across the potato field without a glance at the children huddled on the back stoop.

Finally the housekeeper opened the windowless door just wide enough to peer out. "Go home. There will be no school today," she said, and the door closed, the sound of its slamming an exclamation mark.

Willis, Helen, Grace, David, Allain, Marion, 1925, shortly after Marion's return

The children wandered back up the turnpike. Some wondered if they oughtn't go over to Terry Road School, but no bell had rung there, so they gathered in front of the service station on the north side of the road. Some of the boys played in the mud where the storm had soaked the dirt. Van Jerome said he'd go find his dad, and he took off toward the pasture out behind Francis and Sara Parsons' place.

Two girls huddled by the edge of the road, clutching their small pile of books. Belle Jerome—Nana Belle—opened her front door and headed across the lawn. She stood with the children, and together they watched one of Willis Parsons' farmhands walking up the road. He took long, even strides and kept his gaze on Belle, who fingered the hem of her apron and kept an eye on the man as he approached.

Willis Parsons was dead. He had died of heart failure early that morning.

༄

When Marion and Martha—both living back at the farmhouse with Papa and Mother—came downstairs that morning the house was dark. Allain stood by the window, staring through a small crack in the curtains at their own mother's flower garden. Tiny spears of iris buds poked through the ground, as they did every spring. A few yellow splotches of buttercups jutted out from the dreary and soggy piles of leaves left untended from last fall. Papa would be upset to see this neglect, but it made no difference now.

Someone from the barn had gone to get Grace at her house around the corner on Cherry Road. She and Claude and the twins would be up with the new baby. Grace had survived the death of a child; she and Claude had learned to endure the worst life had to offer. They would all get through this somehow.

The day of Willis's funeral, people came from all over the state—members of the fruit growers' associations and the grange where Willis once served as president; parishioners from the Congregational Church where he, and before him his father, had sat on the board; cousins, brothers, and their wives; Willis's sister, Mary Amelia Parsons Jerome, whose husband, James Schuyler Jerome, was himself near death.

Throngs of neighbors gathered in the large parlor in the Parsons farmhouse, where just days earlier, children had giggled behind cupped hands when the stately gentleman strode through the room. On most days a hub of activity, the three-story farmhouse was as still as death itself on this day. All the rooms on the main floor were filled with family and neighbors. Shutters flapped in the spring breeze but made no sound. From the outside, the big white house towered in a quiet reserve on its perch above the corner of the Genesee Turnpike and the Parsons' farm road. Willis's prized Franklin automobile, polished, sat empty alongside the road, waiting to take him for one last ride up Myrtle Hill, to the cemetery where his parents, sister, cousins, aunts, and uncle were already buried.

The Parsons girls gathered around the kitchen stove, asking questions, wondering aloud, trying to get at the bottom of the mystery. Had their father known he was sick? Is that why he worked so hard to divide up the land and create the community he had begun to envision only a few years ago? In each deed of sale, Willis Parsons included stipulations to ensure his efforts would result in a quiet, upscale neighborhood free from the vagaries of drink and idleness.

His terms of sale included restrictions that would never hold up in a court of law. But that didn't stop Willis from demanding that there be no consuming of alcoholic beverages and that garages—for no more than two cars—be built for each home. Every house constructed on his estate should be of a certain caliber.

The first to buy into the neighborhood were fellows Willis looked up to, knew he could trust—his good friends Terziev and Farnham. In his vision, a red-brick schoolhouse would be at the center—and now his wish to entrust his daughter with the matter of the school would come to fruition. Now it was Marion's job to build a school everyone would be proud to claim, especially her father. They would call it Cherry Road School in remembrance of the cherry orchard that would make way for the school. The new community built upon the Estate of Willis Parsons that had been built upon the Salt Springs Reservation, had been designated Westvale; its boundaries were in-

The Parsons and Jeromes bring in the hay on a Sunday afternoon

side the town of Geddes.

Up on Myrtle Hill, the Parsons family plot overlooked the long outline of Onondaga Lake at the western edge of Syracuse. After the mourners had tramped down the winding road alongside the cemetery, climbed into cars and buggies left at the bottom of the steep hill, they headed back onto the turnpike. A soft spring breeze wrapped around the Parsons girls as they stood alone at the top of the hill. They huddled near the family monument, a tall granite stone marking the place where those who had already passed had been laid to rest. Someone had planted lilies at the front of his headstone, perhaps Papa's friend Farnham. Marion traced the engraved names of the dead with her fingers: her mother, Mary Anna; her grandparents, Edwin and Julia Parsons; her nephew, young John Parsons; Aunt Sarah; Aunt Emma; Amanda, her father's younger sister, and others who had died too young.

Back at the house, the Parsons sisters stood back, surveying the crowd they had known as family their whole lives. They realized what many of us do sooner or later, that the older generation had become too old and too feeble to carry on. It would be up to the younger ones—the three of them plus Ned and Harry, Julia, Charles F., Jim, Laura and Bessie; even Herbert and Guy, and Esther and Bertha who had moved away—to carry on the dreams of Willis Parsons and the others.

Marion put her arm around Grace. "I hope we keep the family together as it has always been."

Grace nodded.

Martha added, almost under her breath, "We're responsible now."

Cousin Esther smiled at the sisters from across the room, as in agreement. She lifted her hand in a half wave, half salute.

Ever since the Great War ended ten years earlier, the world had been changing faster and faster. The war had almost torn them all apart. Cousin Jim had come back from the front, where he'd worked as a medic, a changed man. Once fun and carefree, after the war, Dr. Jim sat quietly in the corner at family parties. He moved his young family to a small community in the southern tier of the state and set up a medical practice. Then they left for California with hardly a word of warning. Willis's older brother, Mahlon, had long ago transplanted his family to Michigan. Though the Parsons girls had once idolized this uncle, now they rarely saw him or heard from him. They all knew that one day soon, the quiet idyllic farmland would be left to the past, though no one spoke of it, especially on a day such as this.

After the Great War, the economy boomed. Though the upswing that followed seemed secure—people invested heavily in the stock market—in many rural areas where families depended on farming to support their livelihoods, people began to struggle. Bad weather had ruined more than one year of crops, and as time wore on the nation began to feel the recession. There had been a time when Marion's father could earn a fine living from the farm, but now they would have to sell more lots for houses if they were to keep both farms running.

Willis Armstrong Parsons, 1857-1926

It's dangerous to be closed off from the world, Marion had thought as she looked out over the city from the top of Myrtle Hill, while they had still been up at the cemetery. It's treacherous to be too comfortable if others are suffering. Aunt Allie once told Marion that she inherited her cautious sentiments from her father.

Marion understood that in order to help usher her students into the disposition of the twentieth century, the school would have to grow and change with the times. It would be up to her to ensure this happened. Her mind was constantly working these days, and now even more so. Marion felt a sense of urgency and panic with her father gone.

She wasn't sure yet what Mother had in mind for the farm. Marion would stay at the house as long as Allain needed her. They had never gotten on, really. Neither she nor her sisters had approved of her father marrying the housekeeper, and so soon after Mama's passing. They distrusted the woman who could be crabby, spoke with a thick Scottish brogue, and had once lived in the servants' quarters in the attic. Nevertheless, Marion would be kind and caring and would do the best she could to hide her feelings.

After the funeral, Marion and Allain adjusted to the tedious emptiness in the house, the terminal quiet in the barn. The Parsons sisters saw to it that the chores Willis would have wanted accomplished were done. Each struggled for perfection in her own way. Martha, the youngest, was probably most like her father—organized, tidy, with a strict management style.

James Schuyler Jerome died four days after Willis

Grace, the eldest, was the family artist and sometimes a little disoriented, especially since her son's death. Her sisters fussed over her, straightening her hat or her shirt collar, reminding her of one thing or another. Grace had been the only sister to marry, and both Martha and Marion shared in the joys and the tragedies of Grace's family. Marion, the middle sister, loved children and thrilled in exploring the world and all it offered; she cherished a red cardinal perched on her back stoop as deeply as she reveled in a flowing red cape at the opera. She coveted a nice hat and a suit made just for her by her seamstress. Mostly she loved the idea that one day she would have her own family with whom she could share these small joys.

For now, though, she would share in her sister's jewels. Baby Peter, only three months old, felt like her own as she rocked him in their father's Queen Anne rocking chair, the one with the musical creak. He was a special baby, so sensitive, but Grace seemed preoccupied with the twins and her lingering grief for John. Marion had seen Grace hang back by the young boy's grave at Papa's funeral, and her heart broke again as she watched her sister in the cemetery.

One night after the children had been tucked into bed at their grandparents' farmhouse—how Willis had relished having the grandchildren overnight—the sisters and Allain gathered around the fireplace, talking softly for the first time about the future. They agreed that the school would be built in the cherry orchard where Willis had wanted it. Each had heard him say at one time or another, in one way or another, that he was certain the cherry orchard was the perfect location, that a school built right there in the heart of their budding neighborhood could serve children from one end of the Parsons estate to the other, and beyond. The location was central enough and large enough to accommodate every family in the growing community. Youngsters could easily walk to school and home again for lunch. Willis had thought of everything. Grace and Claude, the executor of Willis's estate, had set the wheels in motion to sell more lots, where more houses would be built and filled with young families.

Marion carried in an armful of small logs and stoked the fire while everyone sat in silence. She turned to her sisters and Allain, wiping the charcoal from her fingers. "Papa didn't trust the big boom, even if he did invest in a few stocks."

She paused, waited, but no one spoke. She looked directly at her stepmother. "He believed that land and learning were the only sure things. That's why he wanted to turn his land, our land, into a place where children could get an education without having to leave home, leave family behind. We need to respect that." She quickly chided herself for this affront to Allain. The woman was trying. She and her sisters had not always been fair with her.

Nevertheless, Allain had not shown much enthusiasm about the school, and though she never came right out and voiced a complaint about being left out of the Lower Farm in the will, Marion had sensed her displeasure. She was surprised when her stepmother said, "Your father and his cronies were right when they declared there was 'nothing surer—the rich get richer and the poor get poorer.'"

The four women chuckled softly. This was the first time they had gathered together peacefully in a long time, and it felt good; it felt right.

Marion commented to Grace later when they stood beneath the waxing moon on the back porch, "There's no time for childish foolishness if there is to be a place for the children in the fall."

Marion recalled her father catching up with her one morning on her way to the barn. "There's no time to be lost," he had said. "We have to get started; we have to get that hole dug."

Grace stepped off the porch and trudged toward the field in the moonlight, heading to the shortcut back to her house on Cherry Road. "We have to build that school, for Papa!" Marion called after her.

Chapter Seven

The Brass Bell

*How can we live without our lives? How will
we know it's us without our past?*

—John Steinbeck

A FEW DAYS AFTER their father's funeral, Marion and Grace were approached by George Terziev about the school. He and Willis had been close, their love of nature and education their bond. The Terziev house had been the second to go up on what became Cherry Road. He bought two acres of wheat field from Willis in 1920 and farmed the land with flowers and vegetables until he built his house in 1925. His beautiful garden abutted Grace and Claude's backyard.

The two families had a pleasant relationship, and Grace had warned young David to stay out of Mr. Terziev's garden more than once, but one day he ran home with a fistful of daylilies. She grabbed her son by the collar and marched him over to the neighbor's back door, where the shy boy with the dark curls apologized to the giant man with the thick shock of mustache. David offered to return the blooms. With a hint of an accent, George Terziev told David to give the flowers to his mother for her painting studio.

Terziev had learned the value of school in Bulgaria as a boy, when at the age of thirteen he walked forty miles to school, learning English from American missionaries. He grasped the transformative power of education and, after struggling to get to this country, he eventu-

Willis Parsons' cherry orchard where school was built

ally earned a master's degree in chemistry from Harvard University.

Now that Willis had died and Marion was tasked with seeing the school through to completion, Terziev had come to offer her the use of his chicken coop as a temporary schoolhouse. "It hasn't been used for chickens in quite some time—hardly at all." He bowed to Marion and Grace in his kindly European style.

He was a shy sort, his nose always in a book, even as he walked in the mornings to his job at Solvay Process. The man never owned a car, and he seemed at ease only with his flowers—rows and rows of colorful hollyhocks, borders of bright orange and yellow tiger lilies, roses, and hedges of iris. Marion admired his springtime garden that always promised an explosion of color and a sweet scent that wafted all the way to Lydia Hicks' house on the corner of Cherry Road and the Genesee Turnpike. Terziev was even known to sprinkle seeds as he walked and read, and he soaked in the fresh air and nature all around him so much that he was later given the Johnny Appleseed Award by the Men's Garden Club of America.

"Why don't the two of you follow me there right now?"

The little structure was situated at the corner of his garden, directly across from where the school would be built. It was surrounded by fruit trees, hollyhocks, and a narrow stone wall. The three made their way up the path and, pushing aside a clump of spider webs, Terziev shoved open the wooden door. Marion and Grace followed him into the dark, musty room.

"I'm not using the building, you can see, and well, with a little fixing up, it could serve the purpose for now. What do you say?"

George Terziev had teamed with Papa, Judge Farnham, and Sidney Coulter, another neighbor and attorney. Together they had dreamed up the vision of the school in the cherry orchard, though Farnham was the first official Trustee. Now this generosity from Mr. Terziev.

Marion's throat tightened, but she cleared it once and turned to the man with the big mustache. "Mr. Terziev, I won't let you down. Papa would be so grateful."

The imposing man took her hand in his, and she felt the warmth of him, allowing her to relax for the first time in a long time.

Later that day she pleaded with Leona and Marie, two women working in her father's cherry orchard, to help her clean out the hen

George Terziev and his children, July 19, 1925

The Terziev house 109 Cherry Road, chicken coop out back

house. It would serve just fine as a makeshift school while the new brick school was under construction, but she needed help to transform it into a usable classroom.

Later, when Marion's students would nestle onto the floor with blankets for their afternoon rest time, she would gaze out the windows of the old chicken coop to watch the new school going up. She cringed every time she saw a tree fall—soon the landscape would no longer be recognizable as the cherry orchard. She felt the weight of duty.

Grace and Claude, along with the twins—David and Helen—and baby Peter, were a constant presence while Marion and the others cleaned up the chicken coop and put together the temporary school. David or Helen would arrive with a plate of sandwiches and cookies sent by their mother late in the morning, before the heat and humidity set in. Sometimes Grace would push the baby carriage down the bumpy path, the twins trailing behind. Twins would be in the first grade this fall, along with several other children in the family and from the neighborhood—little Van Jerome, Cousin Ned's son; Leland Mitchell and his sister, Mildred, and older brother, Lloyd; the Terziev children, John, Marc, and Frances; and the young Farnham

Helen and David Cole, the twins, in Mr. Terziev's garden, July 1923

boy. Marion thought it hardly seemed possible that these children had grown up so fast while she'd been gone.

Claude was away much of the time looking for work since he had lost his job at Solvay Process. If he didn't find something soon, he would have to take the position he'd been offered in Niagara Falls. Marion couldn't bear the thought of losing her sister. And though she said nothing, Marion could see this new stress in Grace's eyes, in the way she walked across the room.

In no time, a path between Grace and Claude Cole's house and the chicken coop took hold, a narrow trail of worn grass at first and then nothing but dirt. The little outbuilding was buried beneath a well-kept garden of vines, leafy trees, and berry bushes overflowing from Mr. Terziev's garden. They pulled vines away from the windows to let the light in; they pulled weeds away from the path. They painted trim around the windows and the door. Baby Peter on her hip, Grace was always there when Marion needed a hand or an artistic touch for the new classroom. She fashioned colorful pictures for the walls. She decorated benches with painted flowers and filigree.

She had taught art and music out in one of the tiny Finger Lakes villages for two years after she graduated from Alfred University with a degree in fine arts. She'd ridden the trolley there and back every day. After her son John was born, she stayed home; after he died, she couldn't go out. Marion was happy to see her sister smiling and painting again.

◈

Throughout the sweltering summer months, Marion and her helpers worked to clean up the chicken coop, determined to be ready in time for the start of school in September. They rolled up their sleeves and, when the heat and the humidity became unbearable, ladled water from a big metal bucket the neighbors kept filled outside the door. Everyone pitched in, working together to turn the dream of a new school into a reality.

Never one to wear pants—raised in nineteenth-century long skirts, modest and sensible—Marion labored in a cotton dress covered by a kitchen apron, its deep pockets filled with supplies and the soft embroidered handkerchiefs she used to clean her spectacles. When they were alone, Leona, Marie, and Marion worked harder and faster—they swept out layers of dust, straw, and feathers; they scrubbed windows; they scoured walls. The little building was filled with an endless hoard of dirt and grime.

The floors were scuffed planks of rough-hewn maple. After the room was fumigated with a dust pump, the neighborhood hauled wooden desks and long wooden benches over from the old school. When that job was done, the women covered the walls with Grace's artwork and distinctive lettering. One day the three women stood at the front of the transformed room, taking a rest.

"I don't know how to thank you," Marion said. "I'm certain you didn't imagine doing this kind of work when you signed on to work in the orchard."

The women shook their heads and laughed. Marion had grown fond of Leona and Marie, had learned about their families, about Leona's husband's bad leg, about Marie's daughter's bout with diphtheria. She saw tears in the corners of Leona's eyes when she hugged her, but said nothing. She remembered her as a girl, when they were both young, coming in the late spring with her father to pick cherries. She was embarrassed she hadn't remembered Leona's name—that when they were children, they hadn't invited the fruit pickers' children to join in their play in the orchards. Now, she and her sisters worked alongside them. She would go to St. Joseph's to see Marie's daughter later in the day. Perhaps Helen had an extra doll they could share with the girl.

"Imagine our beautiful classroom filled with children," Marion said. The three women folded their arms and surveyed the room. "Well, back to work, we'll never finish the job standing around." Marion had a way of sounding like she was inviting you to a picnic when she was ordering you back to work.

For the next few days, this became their ritual at the end of the day, to stand in front of the room and conjure up the image of children sitting on the benches, working at their desks. At a certain time of day on these late summer afternoons, bright shafts of light streamed through the small windows, a thin haze of dust reflected in the sunlight.

After the women had fulfilled their promise to help, Marion mailed each a handsome check, not wanting to embarrass them or let on to the trustees about what she had paid them from her own money.

Since arriving back home, Marion scarcely had time to miss her friends out West. She barely noticed that she hadn't received a letter from Tom in a long time, hardly gave it a second thought… hardly ever.

The trustees' meeting overflowed with neighbors, family, and friends who had come to hear news about the school. When would it be built? Had they raised the money? Was Marion Parsons going to be the superintendent? Marion sat off to the side. She should have dressed up, should have worn a hat, but she had no idea anyone but the trustees would attend. She sat listening to snippets of conversations and began to imagine forthcoming objections. Who was she, after all, to take the helm of the school? She would have to face them and tell them about her past teaching experiences in New Jersey and out west, about the classes she had taken at Boston and Harvard and would continue to take. She looked around the room for her sisters, but they were not there. Marion wiped her forehead with her handkerchief, quietly asking her father for strength. She hoped he could hear, that someone could hear.

It was only late August, but leaves on the giant maples outside the grange had already started to turn color. It had been unseasonably cold. Meanwhile, parents were nervous about the impending school days. More people streamed through the back door—Mr. Babcock, Mrs. Andrews, a man she didn't recognize. Then Judge Farnham called the meeting to order.

"You've probably wondered why I asked you all to come out this afternoon. I apologize, as I know many of you are busy getting ready for harvest." He smiled over at Allie Parsons, who had been Allie Terry before marrying Uncle Charles. She was sitting in the front row with Aunt Mary Jerome. Then the judge looked straight at Marion. "Miss Parsons, Marion, I'd like to ask you to come to the front of the room, here, next to me."

Marion's legs felt like rubber beneath her skirt. It was too late. She should have worn her suit. Her knees had been bothering her lately, and her hearing was going. It had been a long, hard year. She took careful measured steps toward the man who had been her father's friend for as long as she could remember. As Marion approached, Judge Farnham reached under the desk and pulled something out. It made a loud clanging noise. Marion stopped and placed her hand on the desk to steady herself. Judge Farnham held out the brass bell, the one Miss Allen had rung all those years ago, the one Marion had always longed to touch, to ring. He placed it on the desk between them.

The judge adjusted his glasses and began riffling through the contents of a thick folder. *Has he forgotten I'm standing there?* Marion wondered. "Close to sixty thousand dollars has been raised thanks to the generosity of our friends, all of you. There will be a school. For now, it's a matter of architects, contractors, and construction decisions. Open meetings will continue to be held on a regular basis." The room filled with applause, and he turned again to Marion. "Miss Parsons?"

She cleared her throat and touched the bell with the tips of her fingers. "I will do my best to make all of you proud, Judge Farnham, Mr. Terziev, Mr. Coulter." She looked at the others in the room and added, "And my father." She smiled at her sisters, Martha and Grace, who stood together by the door. "You will hear this bell every morning school is in session. The ringing of this bell, our bell, will remind us all of the possibilities for our children and their future. This year, as last, we will be confined to temporary quarters, but we'll make the best of it, as we always have." She would be their Miss Parsons.

George N. Terziev in his lab at Solvay Process, 1910

Marion held up her hand to silence the clapping. "I'd like to share my recollections about this bell." The room fell silent again. "Back in the nineties when we were girls and boys at the Terry School"—she glanced at Allie, whose father had donated the old building—"our Miss Allen rang this bell every day. We lived our lives by the bell.

"Sometimes we would wander off, follow the sheep over the hill looking for wildflowers; the boys may have been looking for trouble. Miss Allen would stand on the back stoop and ring this bell for all she was worth, and she was a small woman herself."

Marion paused, lost in memories mixed with the legends she had heard. No one moved or interrupted the silence that hung in the room. Marion surveyed the crowd, looking for Allain, but she had not come. After a while she said, "The girls would be screaming, the boys laughing, perhaps we couldn't hear her calling. Even in the dead of winter, she'd stand in the open doorway. I can see her frozen breath forming a halo around her yellow hair. She rang this bell until we were all safely inside. She rang it to signal the start and the finish of the day." Marion held the heavy bell up in front of her.

She looked at Aunt Allie, who returned her gaze with a smile. Marion could see the tears in her eyes. "For me, the sound of the bell stood for what was important. I wanted to learn about the world. She wanted us to learn about responsibility and integrity. This bell and my days at Terry School shaped my life in ways I didn't understand at the time."

Chapter Eight

The New School

Who bends not his ear to any bell which upon any occasion rings?
But who can remove it from that bell which is passing a piece of himself
out of this world?

—John Donne's Devotions

SOMETIME DURING THE SECOND week of September 1926 the National Broadcasting Company launched the golden age of radio, an event that would change the world forever. For the first time, Americans in every corner of the country were connected by airwaves; they could listen to the same news on the same day, could gather round and hear the president of the United States, or Arthur Godfrey, or Will Rogers. We had become a nation not only in geography but also through a new electronic media that would shape our changing culture, politics, and eventually, our education system.

On the same day, the first day for Cherry Road School, Marion stood on the front step of the old henhouse to announce the start of class. Her heart raced as she raised the brass bell high into the air for the first time. She let it fall to her side and then lifted it high above her head again, brass clanging against brass, again and again, a signal to herself and to the neighborhood that this was the opening day of Cherry Road School—each resounding knell an exclamation of her resolve.

Her heart felt heavy as she thought of her father not surviving to see his dream come true—even if it was coming to pass in a chicken coop. She wanted to cry at the sight of the now nearly tree-less orchard that Papa had worked so hard to make productive. She wanted to cry because he was not there. But she also wanted to sing to the treetops to celebrate the new neighborhood, the new school in the making, so many of Papa's dreams now a reality.

The little makeshift schoolhouse was not much tighter and not much roomier than the one-room school they had left behind. Sometimes in the afternoons Marion let the children gather around the window and watch the cherry orchard come down, watch the new school rise out of the old grove. They'd gaze in awe as trees crashed and dust flew. Huge sweaty horses dug their hooves into the mud as they strained to haul fallen logs to the side of the road. To the children, it was exciting. They saw their world change before their eyes. Soon they would have a real schoolhouse with plenty of room to learn and a furnace to keep them warm.

Halloween on Cherry Road in 1926
David Cole, left; Peter Cole, sitting; Helen Cole, right

Warm weather held. Big trucks thundered in and out of the construction site. Before long, hardly a tree was left except one small grove of pine and cedar along the far end of the old cherry orchard. Across the road at the chicken coop, peering from the window, Marion was distracted by fleeting memories of her childhood—a small girl climbing on gnarly branches, her friends calling to her. These orchards had been a wonderful place to play hide and seek. Then her thoughts drifted to the friends she left behind in Omak and California. Why hadn't she heard from Tom? Her chums and colleagues had not mentioned him once in their letters, and she was too embarrassed to ask after him. After all, if he'd wanted to talk to her, he would have written more than the one letter. It had been awhile since her father intercepted the mail—not that he would hide a letter from her. Would he?

At the end of the day, after the children had gone home or out to play—some in search of one last pickup baseball game before winter set in—Marion would stand at the front of the humble classroom summoning images of her parents. Her father had had such enthusiasm about education, the power of ideas, and the need to nurture the genius he believed inherent in all children. She could picture her mama in her long, high-collared dress. It had been during one of her afternoon tea parties that young Marion overheard Mama tell Mrs. Babcock that girls could accomplish anything, same as boys. She remembered the woman's disapproving look and wondered if she should have been embarrassed for her mother. Both her parents held firm ideals about social responsibility—about lending a hand when a hand was needed, about women's rights and responsibilities. Papa especially believed that women should be educated. Grandmother Julia, her father's mother, had graduated from Cazenovia College in 1839, a most unusual circumstance for those times. Not everyone in the community shared Papa's ideals, though. Marion was aware of this but believed in her father's wisdom.

Marion's favorite holiday was Halloween. She thought of it as a sort of harvest festival, a celebration of crops and other achievements. She loved everything about it—costumes, parties, apple bobbing, candy apples, bonfires, trick-or-treating, and the celebratory sensations it evoked. She looked forward to dressing up her nephews and niece and some of the younger cousins. She enjoyed helping with the handcrafted costumes and masks. Everyone pitched in.

One day close to Halloween, she was out on the porch. She could smell ripe pumpkins rotting in the nearby fields where spent milkweed plants loosened their pods and let go fluffy wings carrying seeds across the meadows. Her own childhood came to her like a prairie flood. She saw piles of horse chestnuts spilled on the ground, bulging brown casings trailing toward pastures to the south where dried grasses and cornstalks tumbled like fallen soldiers. It was these smells in the air at this time of year that transported her to another time in the same place. It was in these very fields and orchards that they had frolicked as children and strolled sedately as young women in their long skirts.

Tomorrow the neighborhood children would gather in front of their little schoolhouse at the end of the day. Parents had been instructed through notes sent home to return to the school at three o'clock sharp. Boys and girls, young and older, would change into their costumes. No one was too old to participate. With the help of the mothers, Marion would lead a parade up Cherry Road and down the farm lanes, over to Terry Road. It was a celebration everyone wanted to attend, and the children had looked forward to it since the first day of school. Neighbors stood on their porches and lawns cheering for the children wearing homemade masks, old sheets, their fathers' jackets, their mothers' old dresses.

After the festivities were over, Marion lingered on the back porch at the house where she had grown up, where she still lived with her stepmother. Dogs barked in the distance. She suffered from nostalgia at this time of year and shivered later on when the wind wheezed through the windows in her bedroom on the second floor of the east side of the house. She lit the kerosene lantern on her dressing table and watched the shadows dance on the walls of her childhood room.

There were nights when she felt out of sync with the rest of the world, like she was falling apart in slow motion. She took out a piece of her best stationery. After she wrote Dear Tom, though, she could think of nothing to say that would mean anything to him. She put the paper and ink pen away. It was time, it seemed, for her to make permanent plans to stay, move out of her parents' home, and build a house on the lot her father had left to her near the new school.

Chilly autumn days turned to icy winter days, as they do in Central New York. Firewood had been piled beneath a cover outside the door by generous neighbors. When winter came on with a vengeance, cousins and friends came by to see if Marion and Allain were OK, if their fires were burning, if the Parsons women were in need of anything. Of course, if they had been, they wouldn't have said.

At school, the older boys, and sometimes Marion, fed the pot-bellied stove throughout the day. As winter wore on and twilight bore down in the afternoons, gales of bitter wind wrapped around the tiny wooden building. Marion watched the children working on their arithmetic numbers one afternoon, the swish of sleet pelting against the windows. She was grateful to be home, nasty weather and all. She busied herself washing the day's lessons off the slate board at the front of the room, and the snow kept on for the rest of the day and all night long.

It was May of 1927. Almost a year had passed, and Marion and her students had survived winter in the henhouse. With Claude gone to Niagara Falls, leaving Grace and the children alone in the big house up the road, sometimes for weeks at a time, Marion had taken up the habit of going over after school and helping out. Baby Peter had had a bad cold all winter, and little Helen took to bed in the afternoons with sick headaches. And David had gotten into trouble more than once lately. Marion tried to spend more time going over the new grammar books with him in the mornings before school. Helen missed her father, and Grace kept to herself, aloof with her endless grief. More often than not, Marion took one or more of the children home to sleep at her house to give poor Grace a break, to be certain someone would be there to comfort Helen in the night.

It had been an especially hard winter, so Marion was surprised at the sound of machinery when she was leaving Grace's house at dusk one evening in early May. David in tow, Marion followed the noise until they discovered an enormous hole had been dug toward the front of the flattened orchard. This would be the basement of Cherry Road School, where one day soon, workmen would install a giant coal-eating furnace—next school year there would be no more woodstoves, no more outhouses. A crowd of people had gathered around the hole. Mildred Coulter walked through the mob with a plate of cookies, baby Bobby on her hip, little Betty following close behind.

In the days that followed, Marion watched from the windows of the temporary schoolhouse as cinder blocks were laid one by one; then the beautiful red bricks that would come to represent Cherry Road School were carefully wrought and set with mortar around a distinctive oval-shaped front door.

By late May, school was let out for the summer. Construction workers kept busy from daybreak until nightfall all summer long. They worked in the baking sun, and they worked in the rain. They kept on working when the architect showed up one day with a change of plans. Whenever there was a stall of one sort or another, they found something to do, another way to keep going. Not a minute went to waste in the building of Cherry Road School, not until a single-level building with three rooms and an office was complete. The new brick building sparkled compared with the old one-room clapboard school it had replaced. It was a fine piece of work.

Neighbors came from far away that summer to watch the construction, and then to celebrate its completion. There was always a crowd, sometimes small, sometimes large, lingering near the site where once there had been a cherry orchard. Now the red-brick building stood sturdily among piles of dirt, tree branches, and old fence posts.

Chapter Nine

A Red Brick Schoolhouse

The philosophy of the schoolroom in one generation is the philosophy of government in the next.

—Abraham Lincoln

By September 6, 1927, the day had finally arrived. Children streamed into the brand-new brick building, some running and some walking cautiously down the wide, lustrous hallway. Slick, polished wood floors echoed their footsteps. A crowd of older boys ran shoulder to shoulder along the main corridor, stumbling into one another, laughing, pushing.

Marion appeared at the door outside her office to meet the swarm of boys. Leland, Van, Edward, David, John, and Lloyd skidded to a stop. Taking David by the ear, she asked, "Is this the way we'll behave in our brand-new school?" She had decided it was important to show the children there would be no favoritism for her nephews, niece, or cousins.

David's face burned. They all hung their heads, and clearly no one wished to speak, to answer this question to which they all knew the answer. They loved Miss Parsons and wanted only to please her, to be her favorite.

Marion released her nephew's ear and placed her hand on his shoulder. She was wearing a crisp suit with a flower in her lapel. Her red hair was coifed in soft waves around her face. She needed to say no more.

The New Cherry Road School

Unlike the chicken coop, the new schoolhouse had an office where Marion could retreat, where she would be able to meet with teachers and students one at a time. She had thoughtfully designed the arrangement of the office. If a student was summoned, he must first enter an outer office where a secretary would serve as gatekeeper to the inner sanctum of authority. Sometimes when Marion arrived in the morning, there'd already be a young boy waiting to tell her why he had been sent to her, his head hung, his face long. Over the years, these rooms would come to symbolize a place where fear, anxiety, and trepidation played out in scenes of reprimand, reproach, and calculated approval. They embodied power. They were a place some dreaded, some anticipated, and some imagined longingly.

From the new office windows, Marion could see out into the ever-changing Cherry Road neighborhood. She saw Mr. Coulter mowing his lawn, new houses growing under construction. Cherry Road was being extended. She sat behind her formidable wooden desk and glimpsed the outer office, sometimes watching the comings and goings of teachers and students, listening to parents talking to the secretary. Her brass bell sat on the front corner of her desk. A large bookcase with gleaming glass doors held books on education theories and advancements and more books on phonics, art, and culture. In there, Marion kept some of her favorite fiction: Jane Austen, the Brontë sisters, William Blake, and others she intended to read soon. She had read one or two of the Austen books over and over. On the wall next to her desk hung a framed William Blake quotation in her sister's sprawling script:

> *Father, O Father! what do we here*
> *In this land of unbelief and fear?*
> *The Land of Dreams is better far,*
> *Above the light of the morning star.*

☙

Syracuse Herald
June 3 and October 7, 1929

Modern Trend Closes Era of 'Schoolhouse'
By Roy C. Fairman

The little old red schoolhouse is no more.

The last vestige of the 'schoolhouse' of a generation ago, some of which had lingered in Onondaga County and other parts of Central New York, was removed during the summer vacation this year.

Thousands of rural pupils express surprise and delight at the improved conditions under which they are now attending school.

Residents of rural areas ... can recall their own school days in weather-beaten buildings, heated by wood-burning box stoves.

Uncomfortable seats such as their fathers and grandfathers had studied in were still in use. Oil cloth or painted wooden blackboards were the rule rather than the exception.

If the interior of the classic old time rural school building was unattractive, the exterior was doubly so ... Bare rocks, scrub bushes and trees constituted, more often than not, the environments of the old red schoolhouse in towns and villages around the country.

But a new era has come for the country school. The 'little red schoolhouse' has become a thing of the past. The school trustee paints it a beautiful white or some other attractive color.

Not for many years has there been such a general improvement of buildings and equipment as during the summer just past. Practically every rural schoolhouse in Central New York has been painted or shingled or improved in some way ... and is directly traceable to the new school legislation enacted by the last legislature.

This legislation aimed to help poorer districts improve their equipment without having the cost become a heavy tax burden. As an incentive to making the schoolhouses and their surroundings more attractive, the State allows to each rural district which spends as much as $1,000, a similar amount. This aid makes it cheaper for the districts to improve their plans than to refrain from such improvement. Country schools are getting much needed equipment ... playground apparatus ... library books ... and ... where small windows have been the medium by which light entered rural buildings ... glass now covers nearly one side of almost every schoolhouse ... This is arranged in such a way that the desks may be set so that the light comes over the left shoulder of the studying pupil.

Modern desks, adjustable to the various sizes of the pupils, have been installed. Slate blackboards have replaced the old wooden or oil cloth ones. Steel or straight wooden flagpoles have taken the places of bent old poles from which the American colors have been suspended in so many cases.

School grounds, too, have been improved. In many cases, flower gardens have been developed and the grass is kept trimmed ... Heating plants have been improved. In some schools ... where more than two teachers are employed, furnaces have been installed.

Pupils in the Cherry road section of the town of Geddes are in a new brick building which has three teachers. This replaces the old building erected on Terry Road more than 100 years ago.

Neighborhood women and their children arrived in cars with covered-dish casseroles teetering on the backseats. It was Cafeteria Day. Some women came on foot, pushing plates of food in giant baby carriages and strollers. They carried their babies while toddlers and schoolchildren followed behind.

The Mitchells were the first to arrive, and of course they were on foot. Mrs. Mitchell had made Spanish rice and homemade rolls. Lloyd carried a large box for his mother, who had a small child in her hands. Marion admired Mildred Mitchell. Her family had so little, and yet they had so much. They had all been living in their garage while John Mitchell worked on the house in his spare time, when he wasn't working at the Social Services Office over in Solvay. He worked side-

The Coulters, Mildred and children

Claude and Grace Cole and Family, circa 1930

by-side with his children, hammering nails, carrying boards, climbing ladders. No matter how hot or how cold, no one complained. They had been taught to work hard. The children did chores, cleaned the house and helped with the cooking; they walked to school in snow up to their waists, back for lunch, and back again.

The Mitchells reminded Marion of times gone by when her cousins would gather on a spring day to bring in the hay, or later in the summer to help with the picking. Now that Papa and Uncle Jim Jerome were gone—he had died only four days after her father's death—the family didn't get together as often. She was grateful for the occasional Sunday dinners at the farmhouse.

Marion stood by the front door until all the mothers had arrived, greeting each woman as though she had come for tea, as though she were the most honored guest. Then she rang the brass bell, oversaw the raising of the flag, and read the morning announcements. She reminded students that today was Cafeteria Day, that those who had not brought pennies with them for lunch would walk home as usual.

It made Marion's heart ache that there were families who couldn't afford three extra pennies for a school lunch. More than once she slipped a few coins into a child's pocket so he or she could stand in line with the others. The idea of the monthly Cafeteria Day was to raise money for the eighth-grade trip, so she couldn't very well excuse anyone from having to pay, and she never wanted to embarrass a child.

By the time Marion arrived at the gym, mothers were already setting up tables, putting out the food they would ladle up later. The gym smelled of baked beans, macaroni and cheese, chicken casserole, and fresh baked bread. The mothers had outdone themselves as usual.

She walked up and down the lines of tables covered with linen cloths, stopping to greet women she had not seen earlier out front, asking after their families, talking quietly to her neighbors and friends. These were fine women, and she admired each one. There was only one thing she didn't share with them: they had children, families, and she did not. They talked among themselves about their husbands, their sons, their daughters. When they went home, they took their children with them. Marion was thankful for Grace's children. They were as close to her as if they were her own. Helen and her friend Betty Templar would spend the night with Marion on Friday, and she had given them permission to plan a party for their friends.

She walked out through the gym door and onto the new lawn, inhaling a sweet current of air from the Terziev garden. She strolled around the building, checking the windows, admiring the bricks, looking for anything out of order. She liked knowing everything was tidy. As she walked, she surveyed the grounds, the stand of pines, the baseball diamond. She strode across the field where the boys played ball in the afternoons, mostly unsupervised. Beyond the field, two young neighbor women were playing on the new tennis court. She waved, and they waved back. She stopped to admire the new playground. As she neared the far corner of the building, she glanced past the corner lot at the spot where the chicken coop had once stood. After it was no longer needed for the school, George and Kate Terziev had torn it down to make way for a house for Kate's mother, Mrs. Hawkinson.

Rounding the front corner, rubbing the palm of her hand on the bricks, she strode past the side doors where she usually entered the building, if only to set an example for the children. It was she who had created the rule that the front door would be reserved for com-

Cherry Road School teachers, 1938

pany; side doors were for girls and boys, girls on the left and boys on the right. As she turned one more corner to the front side of the school, a gust of a breeze picked up the flag, flapping it back and forth, canvas and metal on metal. She stopped and fingered the rope where the boys had tied it off earlier in the morning; satisfied, she headed for the front door.

Once she entered the building, she noticed a young boy sitting alone in the row of chairs outside her office, head hung low. She took a deep breath and asked him to come into her office, where she would learn what he had done.

Chapter Ten
The Mothers' Club

One good mother is worth a hundred schoolmasters.
—George Herbert

SURROUNDED BUT NEVER completely engulfed by the city of Syracuse, the new community called Westvale sat atop a piece of earth that just four hundred years earlier had been a wilderness stewarded by the Iroquois Nation—the Onondaga Indians. Their footprint had been so light that when the French stopped to settle, set up camp and open a trading post, they paid little mind to those who lived in their longhouses beside the beautiful lake just over the hill, growing corn and enjoying the beauty of rolling hills, meadows, and swamps. Eventually the fur traders were encouraged to move on, and they did so quickly rather than risk a potentially deadly raid.

It would be another hundred years before James Geddes and others came along and discovered the salt marshes, signed treaties, and established the Salt Springs Reservation upon which Willis Parsons' tract was built, upon which Westvale and its new school was growing. Before it was Westvale, small family farms lined the Genesee Turnpike, and the children who lived on these farms attended small, one-room schools up and down the turnpike. Cherry Road School would be a new kind of school for a changing world. Marion led by including others, giving everyone in the community a sense of ownership in the school.

Peter Cole (this author's father) and his older brother, David sit on a bench in Marion's new front yard facing the south side of the school, circa 1932

One of the first acts Marion performed as principal of the new school was instituting the Mothers' Club. You might say that she instinctively knew the power of parent and community participation. You could also say that the Mothers' Club ran Cherry Road School right alongside Marion and the trustees. The first president was Allie Parsons. Marion had grown up alongside Allie's two boys, Herbert and Guy, and it had been their grandfather, Guy Terry, who donated the original Terry Road School. Appointing Aunt Allie as president may have been the first and last gesture of Marion's that could have been construed as nepotism. Perhaps she caught wind of some criticism, as her relatives played a very minor role in the school from that time

David, Peter, Helen Cole, Cherry Road School in background, circa 1932

forward.

The mothers didn't need much organizing—they organized themselves. They held monthly meetings. They discussed the business of the school, made recommendations and hosted guest speakers who might, in some way, raise the awareness of Mothers' Club members and keep them informed of the goings-on in the education field, the community, and society at large. One such speaker was the chair of the state panel on child entertainment; another, the principal of a neighboring junior high school whose speech was "The Influence of the Home on the Lives of our Young People." They raised money for special events and school supplies. Perhaps most importantly, they helped make the annual eighth-grade trip possible.

The Mothers' Club found ways to enrich their children's lives without breaking the bank. In those days, families gathered around their radios at night listening to Will Rogers turning a yarn chocked with homespun philosophy and cowboy humor. They all leaned in close as Walter Winchell dished out the scoop on big shots and celebrities of the day. Life centered around home, school, and church, and the mothers were the organizers of it all.

> It was a wonderful place to grow up. We had teachers who opened the door to the world. We were encouraged to do our best and try hard. Everyone looked out for each other. We learned to be kind to people.
> —Mary Kate Parrott Quick, class of 1949

Within the Mothers' Club, there was a committee in place for every occasion and every task. When guest speakers came, the Arrangements Committee invited trustees and their wives, Miss Parsons, and members of the faculty. For the Annual Supper, the Entertainment Committee coordinated music and dancing, the Decorations Committee livened up the gymnasium with crepe paper and flowers, the Refreshments Committee organized covered dishes, and the Publicity Committee made sure an announcement was placed in all the local newspapers. Every mother participated short of a deathbed excuse.

Parents and neighbors flocked to card parties, and the proceeds went to support school activities or charities like the United War

Cherry Road School Mother's Club, officers, September 29, 1940, prepare a series of lectures on child study. The upcoming lecture will be "Growing Up."

Council of Mothers' Clubs Elects

MRS. ROBERT BALLARD of the Cherry Road Mothers' club was elected president of the Council of Mothers' clubs at the annual spring luncheon meeting yesterday at the Mizpah. Officers for the coming year, shown above, left to right, are Mrs. Herbert Wright of Thomas Meachem Mothers' club, treasurer; Mrs. Ballard; Mrs. George Pappas of Brighton Mothers' club, vice-president, and Mrs. Gerald J. Finney, Jr., of sentatives. Mrs. Harry Jewett was luncheon chairman. Retiring officers are Mrs. Lloyd Richardson, Jr., president; Mrs. Joseph Novack, vice-president; Mrs. John Callahan, treasurer, and Mrs. Melvin Denny, secretary.

Individual groups have pledged to adopt sponsorship of victory gardens as summer projects. Various clubs have already arranged to take over vacant lots for planting, members being assigned

Cherry Road School, early 1930s after the addition of the gymnasium

Cherry Road School mothers, Marion Parsons, left

Cherry Road teachers, June 19, 1936

Seventh and eighth grade girls, Cherry Road School, 1934; Marcella Merrill, Virginia Murphy, Emma Sager, Helen Cole, Dawn Mellen Jeanette Haight, Mildred Mitchell

Fund or the Red Cross. If there was an occasion, there would be an afternoon tea party to commemorate it. The Mothers' Club hosted Open House for Parents, and they sponsored Children's Book Week. There was an annual mother/daughter banquet organized by the Girl Scouts and supported by the Mothers' Club. No one sat home. There was always something to do, and there was always a scheme afoot to raise money for more activities.

Syracuse Herald
December 8, 1938

Cherry Road School Mothers' Club to Have Christmas Dance, Card Party Dec. 10

On Saturday night, the Mothers' Club of Cherry Road School will have a Christmas dance and card party. Christmas decorations will be used and buffet refreshments will be served. Dancing will begin at 8 o'clock in the school auditorium.

These committees are in charge: Decorations Committee, Tickets Committee, Refreshments Committee, Publications Committee, Reception Committee, and the Features Committee.

In addition to the fun and socializing, the Mothers' Club and eventually the Parent-Teacher Association were always on hand when it was time to dedicate a new wing of the school, a new playground, or a new classroom.

Everyone agreed that Miss Parsons was a great leader. From the start, she set the stage and the tone for the school. One student from the forties, Marilyn Lewis Marcy, who now oversees student teachers for the State University of New York at Oneonta, sees Cherry Road School as Marion might have:

It was her whole world. She observed what we today call good teaching practices. She knew every one of her students

Marion Parsons (right) and Cherry Road School Students, 1932

and cared about each one. Every child was treated the same and yet was allowed to stand out in their own way.

There were no pull-out programs, but somehow it was always arranged that a mentor or tutor would be on hand, without sticking out, to help a child with reading or math. We had teachers who introduced us to the love of literature by reading to us every morning. I was hooked when she read us The Secret Garden. We had what today they call hands-on projects and worked with our peers in groups, learning how to interact with others in what Miss Parsons would have called free time, time to talk about what we were learning.

And we were always preparing for our eighth-grade trip in one way or another, learning about our state, about money, about collaborating. The Mothers' Club was a huge force for good at Cherry Road School, and let me tell you, none of this would have happened without Miss Parsons. She prepared us for the world, and we thought we were having fun. We elected officers for our eighth-grade class; we were taught how to look out for others. It was her world, and she created a model school.

We had a basketball team and a band. Everyone knew everyone, and we had what I would call a core education.

Sometimes Marion, sometimes teachers, or sometimes community people or close-by neighbors, bought books for the library. Dr. Seuss was a popular emerging children's writer, using rhyming words to engage children in reading. The year his first book, *And to Think That I Saw It on Mulberry Street*, was published, several copies were ordered for the library.

Syracuse Herald
January 13, 1932

Cherry Road P.T.A. Will Have Dedicatory Exercises Friday

The Parent-Teacher Association of the Cherry Road School, District No. 1, of the town of Geddes will dedicate the new school addition Friday night at 8 o'clock in the new auditorium/gym. John Farnham, a trustee of the school, will preside. Prof. James A. Shea, principal of the Lincoln Junior High School, will speak, Warren Rothwell will play violin solos, accompanied by Mrs. Albert Raaflaub. Among the guests of honor will be P.M. Hefler, district superintendent.

Money from Cafeteria Day would go to the eighth-grade trip fund. If a trip was coming up, and they were going to take the train to New York City, Marion could hardly wait. The children and their mothers worked tirelessly for months to raise enough money to offset the cost for each student.

Times were tough, and Marion often wasn't sure that one student or another would have enough from their families to go on the trip. What should she do? After all, part of the reason for the program was to teach them how to raise money, wasn't it? She wanted the students to have these experiences, and no children should be left out just because their family couldn't afford it. So she would do whatever she could to make certain everyone went along. Maybe she would hold another card party over at the farmhouse, maybe she'd slip in some of her own money.

One morning, drifting through the halls of Cherry Road School, Marion stopped in the library. She had encouraged the teachers to bring their students there as often as possible. This particular morning the paneled room was filled to capacity. She loved this room—shelves filled with books, walls lined with wooden benches and cabinets made by Cousin Herbert; cabinets stuffed with toys and decorated with paintings of bears, thanks to Grace, who had done her work quietly and thanklessly.

Marion noticed a faint smell of pine as she sat at one of the wooden tables next to Karen, a young girl paging through one of the new Dr. Seuss readers. Karen sat up in her chair, and Marion put her arm around her shoulders. She was proud of Karen for working hard

Fall, 1934, Cherry Road School students. Back row: David Cole, Jeanette Haight, Mildred Mitchell, Mike Lemp; Front row: Ralph Bristrol, Marcella Merrill, Helen Cole, Dawn Mellen, Virginia Murphy, Brad Sherry

to overcome a reading disability. Only Marion and Mrs. Robinson, Karen's teacher, were aware of how hard she struggled.

Wanting to talk to the girl outside of the filled library, Marion asked Karen to follow her to the office. Once there, she smiled and launched into her proposal. "Karen, as you know from this morning's announcements, Children's Book Week is coming up in two weeks."

The girl nodded, but kept her eyes on the floor.

"I'd like you to help me organize a display of books, a selection of books that we used in our health education and in our school banking programs. Would you like that?"

Unknown boy, Frances Terziev, Penny (cousin from Bulgaria), David Cole, 1935

The girl looked Marion in the eye, and her mouth trembled when she smiled.

"That's wonderful, Karen. Meet me back in the library tomorrow right after lunch. I'll talk to Miss Robinson."

Marion remembered her own experience of being singled out, the sensation of being told, "You are special." Miss Allen had asked her to help the younger children with their reading, and that's when Marion decided she wanted to be a teacher. Because of Miss Allen's encouragement, she realized she might have something to share.

Marion hugged Karen and sent her back to the library, shutting the door after her.

When a young woman knocked on the front office door awhile later, Marion motioned her inside. She had almost forgotten the interview for the fifth-grade teaching position. A tall, attractive woman with tightly curled blond hair arranged above her ears entered the room.

Marion offered her hand. "Marion Parsons. Won't you have a seat?"

Boys in Mrs. Amedro's eighth-grade class, 1938; Front row: Jimmy Rowe, Dan Salisbury, John Sherry, Bill Hourigan, Bill Brady Second row: Quentin Wells, Richard "Joe" Owen, Brad Vineal, Jimmy "Red" Sherlock, Bob McArdell; Third row: Maynard Young, Jack Hackbarth, John Pyle

The woman, Miss Healy, clutched the front of her coat as if someone was about to steal it, so Marion decided to sit next to her at the front of the desk, next to the bell. She pulled up two chairs.

"At one time we held all of our classes in two classrooms," she started.

"I see."

"With a recent addition to the building, we are finally ready to add yet another teaching position. We are growing slowly but surely."

Children came in and out of the outer office to buy lined paper and pencils. They noticed Miss Parsons sitting close to a woman they had never seen before and wondered about it, but they knew better than to stare. They glanced quickly and then scurried back out into the hall.

"Should we decide you are the right person, you will have the fifth- and sixth-grade classes, Miss Healy." She beamed at the young woman, who loosened her coat and returned the smile this time.

"Tea?" Marion lifted a tea cozy off the teapot she had prepared earlier. Thankful the tea was still warm, she poured the dark brew into a delicately flowered cup, placing a sugar cube in the saucer without asking one way or the other. I must arrange a set-up for lemon and milk in the future, she thought. Surely they can find a way to put a refrigerator in the kitchen.

"You will be working closely with Miss Cummerford, who has the younger children. I have worked with her myself, and she is a first-rate teacher. She's been with us from the beginning, when we had eleven children in a chicken coop. The following year we started here in the new building with fifty students, three rooms, and an office. A few years ago we added another classroom, purchased more property, and then added more classrooms and a gymnasium."

The two women sat in silence and understanding—Miss Healy would join the small team at Cherry Road School.

"We are a happy place. We can't afford much in the line of extras. Even so, everyone here respects and admires the other. We can't afford to have it any other way."

Chapter Eleven
Our Miss Parsons

Only nostalgia makes us think that the places we've left are still there. We must practice memory—rehearse it over and over again.

—Natasha Trethewey

Even after they were grown, the students remembered dark afternoons when there were no lights at the school but Christmas candles in the windows. They remembered how Miss Parsons would make these days special occasions.

When nighttime fell, they'd climb into Ned Jerome's sleigh by the side of the school. They could see little puffy clouds of breath around the big white horse's nostrils in the freezing night air. Miss Parsons would stand in the doorway reminding them to keep the blankets wrapped tightly around them—she'd be waiting with hot cocoa when they returned. Some say they can still hear the bells jingling on that horse's tack and Miss Parsons' cheer as they pulled away into the night. They sang carols in the moonlight that reflected off the snow; they laughed and pinched one another. When they got back to the school, some threw snowballs, but no one wanted to make Miss Parsons mad, so they cut it short.

They remember these olden days like this:

On the way to school in the mornings, we'd throw plenty of snowballs. We thought nothing of walking to Cherry Road School in the snow. It would be up to our waist, but we didn't mind because we loved our teachers, and we wouldn't miss school for anything.

In the summertime we'd build a dam on Geddes Creek so we could swim. When wintertime came, it would flood the field and freeze over where Wegman's Supermarket stands now. There'd be a big skating rink. We'd build bonfires and skate in the dark, nothing for light but a giant bonfire. When the wind came up, sparks would fly and settle on the snowbanks. We remember the Jeromes coming down the road in their bobsled. Boy, could that thing fly.

Some of us remember the chicken coop school. It was overgrown when we first got there. It had a potbellied stove, and there was a blackboard up front. We were always kidding around; we were full of it. We'd have a joke when Miss Parsons was writing on the blackboard and whisper, "Is that chalk or chicken poop?!" We loved her.

We remember in the old days, Cherry Road was pretty barren, only a couple of houses back then. After the school went up in the orchard, more houses started being built around the school—the Coulters, the Vineals, the Moons, and then Miss Parsons' house, the Sherlocks, and the Salisburys.

We remember Halloween parties—Miss Parsons parading us kids around the roads in our costumes. We'd wave as we went by the houses, and people waved back. We used to start Halloweening about

Miss Costello, Miss Kendell, Miss Parsons

two weeks before Halloween—getting our costumes ready, making candy apples, making goblins. Later on, after the neighborhood built up, one family counted four hundred kids at their door one year.

We remember recess and lunch hour. We didn't spend a second sitting around. We were out there playing ball. We beat the hell out of each other—just plain fun—no adult supervision. How could we have gone out there and organized ourselves and played ball and done what we did without any coaches, without anybody? But that's the kind of school it was—and certainly Miss Parsons was watching over us.

> An awful lot of common sense—that's how she educated. She didn't have any hard-set rules. Back then, when you were principal, you called the shots. To my knowledge, she always called them right. —George Kinder, class of 1943

We remember the flagpole and the thrill of being asked to raise the flag in the morning, to be asked to come to the office and give the morning announcements. Miss Parsons would come into the classroom and ask one of us to follow her. Sometimes we didn't know why and we'd follow behind her trying to keep up, worried, and then relieved when she'd say, "Please give the announcements."

One time Leland Mitchell cut his arm bad when he and Dave Cole got to raise the flag. They were excited and raced back inside. Dave got there first and let the door go behind him, and Leland put his arm through the plate glass on the swinging door. Both his hands were bleeding like the devil, so Dave took Leland to Miss Parsons' office for first aid. She poured salt all over both hands to stop the bleeding, and it worked.

We remember the neighborhood being safe. Parents were involved and watched over us. You could go anywhere, day or night, with never a thought of danger—and everybody was watching. Judge Farnham knew every one of us by name. Mrs. Sherlock knew when we were going by her house. All us kids had paper routes, or we were out there shoveling snow, mowing lawns—some of us got allowance, some of us didn't—a dollar was huge.

We were poor. We didn't know it, but it didn't matter because it wasn't what your dad did or how much you had in your family. We measured each other against each other, for who each person was. We all got along great. The school was the hub, and we radiated out of there. We spent our weekends there—we'd go early in the morning and play basketball games that lasted all day—scores of up to 9,000. We snuck in through the windows. Mr. Lamphere, the janitor, would come down there and decide it was time to chase us out. He'd say, "I'm going to call Miss Parsons." Miss Parsons let us do a lot on our own. It was like a family, and she was like the mother. You can't help but look back and say we had a good time.

We published our first all-school newspaper, The Cherry Leaf, in December 1932. On the front page of the first edition, we posted a list called "Ten Commandments for School Children." Someone found this in another school newspaper from the other side of the world written by Czechoslovakian students in a town where their

Cherry Road School, class of 1940: First row: Margaret Patterson, Elsie Tait, Joanne Farnham, Julie Rowe, Polly Schwartz, Janet Hicks, Helen Cooper; Second row: Donald White, Jack Trowbridge, Richard Tetrault, John Gould, Eddie Vineal, Barney Windhausen, Dickie Ryan
Third row: Vernon (unknown), Dennis Owen, Jim Ryan, Bill Haight, Bob Garrett, Loren Raulston, Peter Cole

grandfather was born. We believed in what it said, and it sounded a lot like what we were learning from Miss Parsons, Miss Robinson, Miss Cummerford, Miss Healy, Miss Miller, Miss Muench, and all the rest:

1. Love your schoolmates; they will be your companions for life and work.
2. Love instruction, the food of the spirit. Be thankful to your teachers as to your own parents.
3. Consecrate every day by one good useful deed and kindness.
4. Honor all honest people …
5. Suppress all hatred and beware of insulting your neighbor, be not revengeful but protect your own rights and those of others.
6. Observe carefully and reflect well in order to get at truth. Deceive not yourself or others and beware of lying, for lies destroy the heart, the soul, and the character … Radiate love and peace.

> It was a wonderful school. We have eighth-grade reunions once a year. We have a great time still.
> —Bob Salisbury, class of 1949

7. Consider that animals also have the right to your sympathy and do not harm them or tease them.
8. Think that all good is the result of work; he who employs without working is stealing bread from the mouth of the worker.
9. Call no man a patriot who hates or has contempt for other nations, or he who wishes and approves wars. War is the remains of barbarism.
10. Love your country and your nation, but be co-workers in the high task that shall make all men live together like brothers to peace and happiness.

We remember Miss Cummerford and Miss Healy. We had two or three classes in one room. Miss Cummerford was there in the chicken coop with Miss Parsons. We loved those teachers. Miss Healy dated Mr. Amedro and we loved when he came to the door when she was teaching because we knew they were dating. We had a lot of good teachers, and we had to do a lot of reading. We don't remember complaining about any we didn't like.

Marion Parsons in her backyard

We remember that Miss Parsons was a terrific principal—she handled problems easily without getting upset. Someone started a Girl Scout troop, and she let us meet at her house. She taught us how to act if we went to a tea. We always joked about it. If you put lemon in it, don't put milk. You put sugar and lemon in a cup of tea or just plain milk. Some people were forgetting and didn't know the difference. She was so good to everybody. We all just loved her. She was loved.

She was firm, but she was fair. She didn't stand for monkey business, but she would go out of her way to help us have fun. We can remember parties at Miss Parsons' house when we were older. We always knew she was around, but she kept invisible. Those parties were wonderful. She was a very special person.

When they built the gym—that came along later when the roads were built—we'd have one of the boys on a Friday night, he'd unlatch the window in the gym. We boys were all crazy for basketball, and we'd meet there on a Saturday morning. We'd boost someone up in the window and then he'd go open the window for all of us so

Miss Marion Parsons, principal, tells Edward Donnelly about bell she used in old one-room school where she was a pupil and later teacher.

February 28, 1941

we could get in and play basketball.

We had a janitor who came and checked the boiler every Saturday morning when we were there, and we knew we had to do something to let us know when he was coming in the building. Mr. Lamphere came in the back of the building, and there were stairs down into the basement, and then across the basement up toward the gym, there was another set of stairs. Well, our Bob, who was often thinking when the rest of us weren't, says, "We'll put up an alarm system and then we'll know when he's coming." So he ran a string with cans on it up in the gymnasium at the top of the stairs, across the basement, and up the stairs to the door where Mr. Lamphere came in. When he pulled open the door, those cans came runnin' down the stairs and we scattered. That worked one time, but we couldn't do it again because he'd be wise to us.

We got legitimate after that. Miss Parsons was one to listen to you. She must have trusted us enough after hearing the gym was being invaded. She said, "Well why don't you boys come over and get the key at my house?" From then on, she OK'd us to come over and get the key on Saturday morning, and we played all day long.

> During the war, we had one janitor, Mr. Lamphere. His daughter taught there. They were still on coal—this is before they went to oil. Mr. Lamphere was pretty elderly, and they had to come back nights and stoke the boilers. I can remember Miss Parsons would get us boys to help—no pay. You did it because she asked you to, that's all.
> —Bill Eriksson, class of 1943

The boys from Cherry Road were outstanding basketball players. When we went on to high school, many of us made varsity. Leland Mitchell became captain of the Solvay High School team. It was primarily the training we had from Cherry Road. We played all day long on Saturday, and then Saturday night we'd go downtown and play in the church league—that's how much we loved the game.

We loved baseball too. Those were the days of Joe DiMaggio, Babe Ruth, and Lou Gehrig. The White Sox and the New York Yankees ruled the game. Opening day of baseball in Syracuse was nothing short of a reverent occasion.

A couple of us boys learned about honesty one afternoon on the opening day of baseball season for the Syracuse Chiefs. Everybody went to opening day—we skipped school, we did anything we could. Two of us boys were worried we'd be sitting in Miss Parsons' office till we were old if we just skipped, so we went down and asked her if we could be excused to go to the ballgame. She was kind of taken aback. Then she said, "Yes, I guess so." So we went to the ballgame—we were excused, but the rest of the boys who skipped school all had to come down and sit in Miss Parsons' office.

Unknown, Miss Parsons, Miss Costello, Miss Robinson, Miss Hannigan, Miss Bedwell, Mrs. Miller

Miss Parsons and our teachers showed us ideas and people we would not have known about otherwise. She gave us freedom and opportunities to unlearn our prejudices by engaging us with people and places we might otherwise be afraid of. When we had to go over the hill to Solvay for high school, some of us were anxious. We had heard things. We didn't know those guys. But we'd learned to interact with new things. We played ball with the other kids. We became good friends. Later on, during the war, we all had each other's backs.

The teachers who taught under Marion, those who are still alive, remember her with love and respect. They recall that everyone respected her, that she was personal with everyone, that she made you feel like she was a friend. If one of them got married, she'd have a shower. They said she was terrific, let them do plays and trips with the kids, let them have cookouts, and every spring they'd have a special daylong outing on the farm.

Marion Parsons

The few teachers who are left recall Miss Parsons like this:

We loved her because she cared as much about us as she did about the students, and that made us better teachers.

Sometimes we'd have as many as fifty students in our class—we had all different levels in one classroom in the beginning.

"We would never think of calling her Marion—she was always Miss Parsons," Tibby Dumanian-Muench, now in her nineties, remembers. "There was a great deal of respect. She let you try innovative things and never held you back—as long as she knew what was going on and thought it was OK." Tibby tells the story of having more than forty kids in one classroom but never having to send anyone to the office. "You never felt like she was on you. She was friendly, warm, and wonderful. It wasn't formal, but she had a way. She was a terrific person, and she is in the memory of so many people."

Chapter Twelve

The Great Depression

The past wears an armor that thickens.
—Kim Stafford

NOT A SOUL IN THE BUILDING—students, teachers, and even the janitor had gone for the day. Blessed stillness washed over Marion like a warm breeze in early spring. She unbuttoned her suit jacket and leaned back, letting the spine of her chair support her tired bones while she finished reading the letter from Amy Kinney. She had grabbed it off the vestibule table that morning and saved it in her pocketbook all day. Now she reveled in the news of her Omak friends in the solitude of her office, where less than an hour ago three boys had been lined up for a dressing down. They had been talking in class, so she'd made them stand in the corner and talk—to no one in particular, just talk. Perhaps she had been too tough, but times were tough, and they had to learn to behave. Well, they were gone now, and hopefully they had been impressed by the severity of her reprimand.

Marion skimmed Amy's stories once again, eager for news about Tom, Mrs. Eary, and Amy's mother. She wondered how they'd held up since the stock market crash. Amy never mentioned their financial situation, but Marion was sure they must be struggling like everyone else, like the people she read and heard about—starvation in the streets, despair everywhere. For the most part, Marion and the others in Westvale were lucky compared with the thousands who stood in line for bowls of soup.

She thought for a moment about Mr. Lamphere down in the basement and decided he might be down there after all. They had finally let the coal furnace run cold for the season, but it would have been like him to be down there sweeping up coal dust, organizing tools, fixing a broken chair. He was known to come around to each classroom at the beginning of the school year to measure students' legs from their knees to the insole of their feet, matching these measurements to the chair that would be theirs for the school year. The man was a stickler for maintaining a perfect fit for each child—the top of the legs must rest firmly on the seat of the chair; feet must touch the ground in the flat position. Marion had seen him fiddling with one chair over and over to make sure no child would spend the

The old coal furnace, basement, Cherry Road School

year in a chair that did not fit properly. For one small girl, he finally brought two red bricks to the classroom and arranged them under her feet so they would be flush with the floor.

Having read Amy's letter twice, Marion folded it exactly as it had been and replaced the linen sheets in the envelope she had pried open with her special letter opener. The long silver utensil had been her father's, and she turned its mother of pearl handle over in the palm of her hand, ran her finger over the swirling P—almost indistinguishable now. Marion's eyes rested on the brass bell. She couldn't help but think about Papa. He would be aghast at the results of all the speculation. Grace and Claude had sold yet another parcel. When would it end? She wiped her face with a soft hankie that had belonged to her mother. She folded the embroidered cloth into fourths, like a petal, and tucked it between the buttons of her blouse next to her hearing aid. Then she stowed the letter and the opener in the top drawer of her desk.

Amy had written again to beg Marion to come back out west for the summer—the third letter of its kind in six months. How could she leave Westvale now? She missed all her friends in Omak and her cousins in California, of course, but a journey across the country would be out of the question. She would stay here at Cherry Road until the school budget was stabilized, until plans for the school addition were finalized and voted on by the community. How could she leave the Mothers' Club now? How could she leave her sister, her niece and nephews? The twins had been through so much lately—seventh grade is a difficult time for most children. And what about her new house? It was almost finished. She felt guilty about spending money on it when others had lost their jobs and their shirts. But in the end, it made sense. She had to get away from her

> I came [to Cherry Road School] in the eighth grade from Split Rock, and it was a remarkable difference. Split Rock was an impoverished community, and the parents did not work—they were unable to find work. My dad and a few others worked all the way through the Depression. When we got to Westvale and I started at Cherry Road School, everybody's father worked, and Mom was always home. For my brother and me, it was a remarkable change. At Split Rock, a lot of the kids did not have shoes. Mom used to make an extra sandwich to share at lunchtime.
>
> My brother and I looked at the Cherry Road School kids as rich kids, but what we found was that Miss Parsons set the tone. There was a demand that we reach our highest potential. She had a way of coming in the classroom at just the right time to deal with us miscreants. She would always be shaking her finger at me. I never had a beautiful report card like that since.
> —Joe "Rich" Owen, class of 1938

stepmother, be on her own finally, be near the school. The workers had promised to cut corners wherever possible, and they did. The new house was small, its ceilings low. Marion had already fallen in love with the little house on the edge of what was left of the orchard. Would the visit out West have to wait? She'd decide later.

When Judge Farnham had stopped by the week before, he talked about his confidence in the school's finances. His demeanor somehow made him seem taller than he was. You couldn't help but trust him when you looked into those eyes. Marion and Judge Farnham had frequent conversations about the budget, or lack of it. The new gym and auditorium had cost more than expected, but with help from the community, they would be OK. The judge repeated this several times, and what choice did Marion have but to believe what he said? And President Hoover had said that lack of confidence is foolish, but then, hadn't he lost in a landslide to FDR?

Cherry Road School was lucky for the support of its neighbors, to be sure, but it wasn't enough to keep the school stocked with the books and supplies needed for the kind of curriculum Marion wanted for her students. She read in the *Herald American* that illiteracy in the United States was as high as 6 percent. This would not happen in her school; not while she drew breath. Money was scarce; she could not expect parents to cover the cost of pencils and the nice lined paper you could get nowadays. For some of the families, it was hard enough to find the cash to buy clothes for school, a sled, a bike, sometimes food for the table. High school kids over in Solvay and down in the city were quitting school to find work—to put food on the table.

> I'm glad I was able to live during that time. You knew everybody, and parents didn't mind their kids going out after supper and playing kick-the-can. The signal to go home was when the streetlights came on. —Betty Templar Jerome, class of 1935

Marion and the trustees knew it was possible they'd have to cut teachers' salaries soon. Well, she would take the first cut. She would keep an eye on Cherry Road families. Times were tough for every-

Rooms for rent at 3012 W. Genesee Turnpike

one, and every penny counted. She wouldn't trouble the judge with her concerns just yet.

As for the library, if Marion decided the Dick and Jane books were worthwhile, she would pay for them out of her own pocket. She had made promises to herself. Like John Dewey, she believed in hands-on exploration, that it was the best way to learn the pursuance of a self-fulfilled life. And she appreciated how lucky she was, as a woman, to be afforded this much authority. There were many places in the country where classroom teachers were supervised only by men, local businessmen who knew nothing about teaching, she thought, nothing about what makes an effective classroom. Well, she would find ways to make things work.

Marion heard footsteps in the hall, and she rose from her chair. Grabbing her coat, she headed toward the door. Forget about the letter and the money worries. These are tribulations that pale next to troubles in other places. She stood inside the door and watched Mr. Coulter examining his new front lawn. He liked to joke that he'd built his house just in time for the Depression. The sky was already pink with fading sunlight. She waited until he was out of sight.

For heaven's sake, what about all those Midwestern farmers who've lost everything? Her mind settled on images of bread lines and soup kitchens. Things here weren't so bad. Just the other night, the whole community showed up for a celebration of the new gym—a wonderful and well-organized event, thanks to the Mothers' Club. Without her having to lift a finger, they had arranged an orchestra, a women's double trio, and three violin solos. It had been lovely.

Marion would write to Amy, tell her about her responsibilities. Amy would understand. She wasn't sure about Tom. She hadn't heard from him in a long time. Just as well. She had a life to live here. Cherry Road needed her. They all counted on her.

≈

The day the stock market crashed, everyone was seized with panic. It was contagious. Banks closed their doors, and what became known as Black Tuesday marked the beginning of the Great Depression. That was on October 29, 1929. Over the years to come, things got worse for everyone. No American went unscathed. People lost what they had, went without, did whatever they could to survive.

> Family farms were once a way of life throughout rural America, proverbial red farmhouses dotting landscapes in communities across the Midwest ... In 1930, farmers made up more than 20 percent of the American labor force. There were 6.3 million farms throughout the United States. Agricultural exports consist[ed] of one-third of the total American exports. But the Depression and the infamous Dust Bowl left farm families in bankruptcy. Sons of the fathers wandered the countryside in search of hope ...
> By the 1940s, as a result of war rationing and price controls, more and more farmers were throwing in the towel, migrating to large cities in search of jobs in an emerging industrial economy that dealt the final death knell for the American farm family.[1]

It was a perilous time for public education. Parents were called on to outfit their children with supplies and textbooks, but with money in short supply, most were hardly able to provide the ba-

Cherry Road School, 1944

sics of clothing and food, much less school materials. School boards struggled to find ways to make the dollar stretch—they shortened the school year, combined classes, cut teachers' salaries, and in some cases charged tuition even at public schools in order to keep their doors open. It was not unusual for older children to simply leave school to find ways to help the family survive.

All across the country, these were terrible times. Between 1929 and 1932, unemployment rose as high as 25 percent, and the average household income in the United States fell 40 percent. Life expectancy for men was fifty-eight—for women, a little over sixty-one. Annual incomes were lower than today's monthly incomes, though milk was about 14 cents a quart, and bread, nine cents a loaf. From one end of the country to the other, people suffered and wondered what had happened to the spectacular rise of the stock market in the mid-1920s. For some, life was a nightmare of handouts, government relief, and shantytowns called Hoovervilles.

In the new community called Westvale, like elsewhere in the

country, people did what they had to do—whatever they could do—to survive, to outlive the Great Depression. They took in boarders, sold fruit and vegetables from roadside stands, sold corsets door-to-door. Often they went without. Instead of buying new shoes, they resoled the old ones when they wore through, sometimes with nothing but cardboard. Mothers darned socks, sewed their children's school clothes and reused old buttons on new clothes. Nothing was thrown away, nothing wasted. They lived by the motto, "A stitch in time saves nine." Every family did what they could to put food on the table. Many of the fathers held two jobs, walking from one to the next to save on gasoline. But unlike many places in the country, no one in Marion's community went hungry or slept without a roof overhead.

> I remember my mother coming one evening and talking to me up in my bedroom and saying my father needed to get into my bank account—I had a little bank account—because things were so tough. And what am I going to do? I can't get it anyway. So he took it out and paid me back one day. —Jim McClennen, class of 1949

❧

The stocks Marion's father left her were all but worthless; banks were failing every day. Last week, Judge Farnham had concluded his presentation to the Mothers' Club with a pronouncement that more than 13 million Americans had lost their jobs since 1929. They would cling to what they had here in Westvale. Hadn't each year gotten better for them since the new school was built? Marion expected more new students in the fall. She wasn't sure they could support many more students, but she would never turn a family or a child away from Cherry Road School. They would probably have to consider adding on to the school building again soon.

❧

Marion's shoes crunched on the gravel and dirt that was her new front yard at 303 Cherry Road—her new address. Cherry Road now extended past the schoolyard, past her driveway, and down into what was left of the wheat fields and cornfields. She still hadn't gotten

Miss Parsons and Miss Robinson on front steps of school

used to coming here after school or to waking up in her new room with the pegged wooden floors and pretty wallpaper. The tiny front upstairs windows in her bedroom were covered with wooden filigree patterns that let morning sunlight stream through and pool into a pattern of gold on the floor.

She had worked closely with the architect to cut corners on the design and construction of her little house. She wanted it to reflect her family's New England heritage, like an old down-east dwelling with flower boxes and a welcoming front door. Even with all the gloomy talk of tight money and difficulties she was sure to face, the house had come together, and the result was similar to what she might have imagined.

Even though Papa had given her the property, a schoolteacher's salary was meager, and she felt lucky. Her luck had started when

303 Cherry Road, Marion's house was the first built past the school, but the neighborhood grew fast

she met a young architect with a reputation for colonial style work who convinced her that materials, labor, and construction costs were at an all-time low. So her house took form, and by saving every inch of floor space and keeping her ceiling height low, the plan he put together made every inch count. She cherished her old-fashioned fireplace, the small-paned windows where sun streamed in, casting shadows across pine floors and walls. She could look out at the familiar tree-covered hills, the same ones that had always surrounded the farm; she could gaze at the south end of the school and watch new houses going up across the street. Today the workers were laying a stepping-stone pathway from the road to her front porch.

To outsiders, the people of Westvale might have looked rich in comparison to Dust Bowl survivors and soup kitchen denizens of the day. But, like many towns and villages, the natives and newcomers of this small farm community on the edge of Syracuse struggled to make ends meet, and they all shared what they had with one another. They stuck together, and the school would not go by the wayside. In fact, it was the heart of the community.

Around the country, as many as a thousand people a week lost their homes or their jobs or both. Mostly, jobs were nonexistent. Around Cherry Road School, people hung on as best they could, to the school, to their way of life, to one another. They were, some recall, an extended family, with Marion the matriarch. Even if times were tough, those who look back wouldn't trade their memories for anything else.

Thirty-some years after the fire destroyed Willis Parsons' barn, the rebuilt barn was demolished again, this time to make way for houses on the old farm road. The potato field, the plow, and the team of horses were all gone. The area would now be a street for car traffic where children rode bikes and mothers pushed carriages. During the heat of the Great Depression, more and more parcels of land, once part of Willis's prized farm, were sold off, and new landowners opened up the dirt road to make a street. They named it Parsons Drive.

More streets and roads went in and were soon lined with houses. The community Willis had dreamed of took shape, and they called it Westvale. Marion's plans to return out West—her dreams for a family of her own—seemed more and more remote. This was where she belonged, she knew. This would be her life. Opportunities had

Marion's living room, right after the house was built

I was one of five brothers and sisters. I started at the brick school. I remember trudging the seven blocks to school and home for lunch and back again, back and forth. I remember sports being encouraged. You go to Cherry Road School on a Saturday and play basketball—the gym was open, the baseball fields were available—whatever you want. There was no concern. If I got a 75 on a test, I got a star.

I remember the first time I got on the back of that horse up behind the Jerome barn. It was as wide as this table, and I couldn't stay up there and fell off. It was an exciting place. One of my favorite activities was to go around the neighborhood with four stainless steel milk cans. I'd go down to the Turpening's farm and get the milk cans filled up and come back and deliver those to the families. Then the next few days, it would be another person's turn to get the milk cans and come down and get the raw milk.

We were raised on raw milk. The Turpening farm was down about where the shopping center is now. You could go to that area where the shopping center is; it was all open. It was Geddes Brook, a great place to go down and fish for little trout. There was a big bend in Geddes Brook—it came from Fairmount right from across Genesee Street, right about where Tully's is now—a beautiful little bend in the brook where we used to go skinny-dipping right in the middle of the farm field, which is now under the pavement of Wegman's parking lot. There was Terry Woods where you could build a tree house. Really happy memories.

Westvale ran from West Genesee Street to Clover Road. All the area around that was farm country. Then there was the transition when it went from a wonderful farming community to a new type of development. There was the Grange Hall up the road from where I lived on Terry Road. The Grange Hall was a center of activity, and I remember going to a lot of suppers at the different farms. You could go out and have a covered dish supper. It was a great community to grow up in and live in.

—Jack Mitchell, class of 1948

passed her by, but there would be others.

Farm communities disappeared throughout the country. Westvale was no exception. Family farms were sold off to pay bills, feed children, and keep a roof overhead. It wasn't unusual for extended families to live together in one house; some of the big farmhouses were divided into two-family homes, half rented out to tenants.

In places like the Midwest, large productive farms turned into small dirt farms where people were barely able to scratch out enough vegetables to make a meal. Mostly they ate dust, and they waited for the weather and the market to change. Others simply gave up, loaded their cars and trucks, and drove off in search of another way to make a living, in search of a meal.

> Our families were very frugal—you only got things if you really needed them. I wanted a record player in my own room more than anything else in the world at one point. But I never got it because I didn't need it. That's the way it was.—Martha Ballard Lacy, class of 1949

Marion's cousins, Ned and Harry Jerome, managed to hang on to their small dairy farm. As Jerome Dairy had grown over the years, Ned had given up the wagon and, with the help of his son, Van, his daughter, Connie, and his friend Clayton, delivered fresh milk from the back of a Packard automobile. This would change again during World War II when gasoline was rationed, and the Jeromes went back to delivering out of the old milk wagon pulled by the big white horse.

These were tough times all right, but many who were there look back at a simpler time when life seemed less complicated than it is today. Without denying the struggle—counting pennies, going without, worrying—they still remember those as the good old days. Perhaps they were.

They lived simple lives in complicated times. Same as everywhere, they did what they could to entertain themselves with what they had. There were no televisions; some had radios. Families had only one car; some had none.

S. B. Coulter
Attorney at Law
516 Loew Building
Syracuse, New York
June 29, 1939

My Dear Miss Parsons:

Bob's leaving Cherry Road School is very much in the nature of his going away from home. He has never attended any other school and his attitude and reaction to his association and work over there is remarkable in its affectionate and serious meaning to him. It isn't the usual thing for a boy his age to feel toward his school as Bob does about Cherry Road School.

Mrs. Coulter and I cannot let the opportunity go by without our expressing to you the lasting appreciation we feel for your efficient, kindly, and gracious care of Bob during the past eight years. I want you to know that we are very happy over the fact that you came into his life at the time when you did and we consider ourselves very lucky in these troublesome times to have so important a phase of his development in your hands.

We hope that you will have a very happy and restful summer and return back to Cherry Road School this Fall and many more Falls to come, continuing your very excellent administration of our school affairs.

With our best personal greeting I beg to remain,
Very faithfully yours,
Sidney Coulter

Chapter Thirteen
The Discipline

A hero is someone who has given his or her life to something bigger than oneself.
—Joseph Campbell

IT WAS SO QUIET in the new gym that night that if a pin had dropped on the floor, it would have echoed from one end of the room to the other. Marion stood in front of the boys, all the boys. The girls had been sent home.

By the close of that October day in 1933, every teacher had been alerted to bring their entire class to the gym instead of releasing them from school. The boys from each class filed into the gym, and no one spoke as they brushed past Miss Parsons where she stood at the door, lips pursed. A few glanced at her and smiled; most kept their eyes straight ahead or to the floor. When the last child had been seated in the auditorium, Marion walked out into the middle of the gym and looked up at the crowd. No one made a sound.

The sun was already starting to set behind the Coulters' house across the street. The feeling of growing darkness filled the gym, even though the lights were glowing.

Finally Marion said, "We have a problem." She paused, and the silence that hung over the room was louder than her words. "Someone has been so foolish as to urinate all over the wall in the boys' lavatory." A wave of surprise flashed through the crowd.

"Hush." Her one word stilled the crowd. "I expect the guilty party to come forward." Marion looked from face to stricken face.

Cherry Road School teachers, 1940. Top row: Miss Hannigan, Miss Steinbeck; Middle row: Miss McCluskey, Mrs. Walti, Miss Muench, Miss Wallace; First row: Miss Robinson, Miss Miller, Mrs. Haskins, Mrs. Swartz

"There will be no punishment other than to clean the mess. But until someone comes forward and admits to what has been done, no one will leave the building."

Heads began to turn. There was a low murmuring among the crowd of boys, ranging in age from five to thirteen years old. One of the younger boys sitting toward the front covered a giggle with both hands.

"This is not a joke, George." She looked at the boy, and his face turned red. "Do you know who did this?"

The boy shook his head.

"What about our parents?" someone asked.

"Your mothers have been called," she said.

Boys fidgeted and looked from side to side, a few turned in their seats, but no one spoke; no one doubted Miss Parsons would not back down or that their parents would wait as long as it took the principal to discover the culprit. They also knew that the longer this took, the angrier their parents would be when, and if, they were set free.

The stillness and the anticipation lingered like a bad odor in a closed room. One, and then two hours passed. Boys were allowed to go to the bathroom or get a drink of water, one at a time. One boy who had diabetes was taken to the front door and let go in his mother's care.

Marion thought about the nights her father came into the bedroom she shared with her sister, Martha, wanting to know the answer to this mystery or that mystery. They both knew there was no sense holding back because he would maintain his ground until satisfied he had gotten the truth. She would do the same. Some of the boys looked angry. The Lundy boy appeared scared, but she knew he wasn't the culprit because he had been in her office all afternoon.

A boy sitting alone up in the top row of the bleachers slumped down in his chair and put his head in his hands. His shoulders heaved up and down. Tired, Marion climbed the stairs slowly and sat in the empty seat next to him. When she asked if he knew who had dirtied

Eighth-grade graduating class, Miss Costello in middle, early 1940s

the bathroom, he put his head in her lap and began to sob. "It's OK," she said. "Go down to my office and wait for me."

"Did he do it, Miss Parsons?" They all wanted to know when she told them they could go home, that their parents were waiting for them out front, that Mr. Lamphere would walk them to their cars two at a time.

"Just be glad it wasn't you." She patted one of the smaller boys on his shoulder. "Sometimes we make mistakes and we have to own up to them. Have I made myself clear?" She spoke to everyone. No one had moved yet. The boys were still too frightened to speak, but they all nodded their heads, eager to agree and eager to get out the door.

The guilty boy stayed to clean the bathroom, and the janitor helped while Marion talked softly with the parents in her office. After she inspected and approved his work, that would be the end of it—the incident would never be mentioned again.

She stood at the window in her office and watched the family pull away in their old Model A, rusted out all along the bottom. She thought about her empty house and what she would have for dinner now that it was so late. Maybe she would just have some of that frozen custard left over from Sunday dinner with Grace and the family. *It is lovely having a freezer,* she thought as she pulled on her coat, turning off the last light and closing the office door.

Chapter Fourteen

The Circus

*Life isn't about waiting for the storm to pass,
it's about learning to dance in the rain.*

—Vivian Greene

"Normally I would stay at the farmhouse with Mother while the workers are at my house, but you know she's left, moved to Buffalo." Marion struggled to hold the cumbersome phone receiver to her hearing aid, the way the doctor had coached her these past few years. "We have tenants in there now. Two families—" She paused. "What did you say?"

"I said come up here and spend the night with us, dear." The static overtook his words momentarily. "We'd love to have you; we always do, Marion. Grandma Harkness is here—Ruth and Janet have come up from Delhi ... We'll make an evening of it."

Marion watched the cloud cover roll across the tops of the trees in front of the school. She yelled into the voice piece. "Thank you, Uncle Charles. I'll be there as soon as I stop by the house. I'm worried about this wind, and it's already started to rain."

"Yes, it's going to be good one. I predicted it this morning."

"Oh dear ... I better check, make sure the workers closed up the garage. Tell Janet I look forward to seeing her."

She could barely hear Uncle Charles, but it sounded like he was talking to Cousin Guy. He said, "Grandma and Janet just came in the back door ... armfuls of peonies ... we're trying to save ... the garden

… hustle … get on over here as fast as you can."

Marion put the phone back into the cradle just as Judge Farnham came through the door. Ducking his head, he was across the room in two long strides. Holding his fedora with one hand, he extended the other to Marion. "What's this I hear about a circus?" He didn't let go of her hand.

"Oh my!" Had she forgotten to tell the trustees? He had startled her, and her heart was pounding.

Farnham pulled up a chair. Marion hesitated and then sat down behind her desk. She wished she could tell him in plain language how much she appreciated all he did to help her with the school. Without the judge, there would be no school. She also wished she could tell him she was in a hurry, but as always, she would have to let him take his time. Wind and rain began to bang against the closed window. She'd have to go straight to Charles and Allie's.

"This sounds like a lot of fun, Marion."

"Well, it was all the children's idea. They dreamed it up, planned it, for the parents."

"Marion, that's a splendid idea, and a darn good use of the gym, I might add."

"A few mothers have helped organize. Two of the students called the Herald-Journal and talked to the reporter themselves, can you imagine? I let them come in here and use my phone"

The lights went out.

"We better skedaddle before this storm gets any worse." The judge uncrossed his legs and leaned forward but didn't make a move to get out of the chair.

A tree limb slammed against the window. Three flashes of lighting cut the sky.

Mercifully, the judge rose, grabbed Marion's coat, and held it while she slid one arm in and then the other. "This kind of rain gets to the dogs," he said. "I used to have a pair of hounds that would run off at the first hint of lightning or thunder—wonderful dogs, just scared of a storm. One night they ran off and didn't show up for a week. We found them over by the fairgrounds."

Marion laughed. "I'm off to Uncle Charles and Aunt Allie's to spend the night. I have workmen at the house."

She let the judge pull the heavy front door shut, wrapping the front of her raincoat tighter around her middle against each blast of wind, thick with debris from the front lawn.

Head down, Judge Farnham gripped his hat, pulled the catch on the door with his free hand. It was really raining now. "Let me give you a ride!"

"I have my car!" Marion shouted into the wind.

They ran down the sidewalk toward the street, turned away from each other, and scurried in opposite directions. She turned and watched him for a second and then made a dash for her car.

The Chevy started on the first try. She held the choke out and let the car warm up while she tried to rub the fog from the inside of the windshield.

The car jerked, and she backed out onto the street where rivers of rain poured down onto Cherry Road, filling ruts, forming raging rivulets. More unbearable claps of thunder chased explosions of lightning. Marion's foot shook on the clutch, but she managed to get the car out of reverse and into first gear as another car inched past. It was pouring so hard, she couldn't see who it was. She broke into a song she made up on the spot about buckets of rain. This was something she did sometimes to calm her nerves, made up songs and sang out loud when no one was around.

She'd be lucky to make it to Charles and Allie's, but she told them she was coming and they'd be worried if she didn't show up. The phones were likely out by now. She thought about the cherry orchard at the Upper Farm. What about the plans to go down there on Sunday to pick early cherries? The weather had been so hot, they would be ready to pick. That's what the farm manager had said the other day. This rain could be the end of the cherries.

Her car crept along Cherry Road, and Marion clung to the steering wheel. She hadn't been able to see out the window driving past Grace and Claude's house, but she thought she saw Mr. Terziev in his garden. Still in first gear when she reached the intersection at the turnpike, she could barely see the road. The wipers made loud flapping sounds but weren't doing a bit of good against torrents of rain. Was that a river running down the turnpike? The inside of the car was completely fogged up, and someone pounded on the window over on the passenger's side. She couldn't see a thing, and then the door flung open. A familiar-looking man stooped over the seat. He was saying something about a tree. She recognized him as one of the McArdles' hired hands. "Get in before you drown!" she yelled.

The man's dark hair was plastered flat to his scalp, rainwater running down the side of his face, his words drowned out by windshield wipers, pounding rain, and thunder. "I said we need to get to higher ground!" He leaned closer; his breath smelled of something sinful.

"I'm on my way to Allie and Charles Parsons' place just up the road." Her vocal cords trembled, and her foot would not stop shaking on the brake pedal, but no matter, she was grateful to have this stranger for company in the middle of the storm.

"My name is Frederick, ma'am. I'm on my way to talk to Mr. Jerome for Mr. McArdle ... grass seed he's been developing? Mighty nice of you."

Still only blocks from home, Marion decided to drive on.

Before the intrusion, she had been waiting, stalling, too frightened to pull out onto the road. Now she gunned the car, and it drifted to the other side of the turnpike. She eased the steering wheel around until they were moving along the road in a westerly direction.

"Careful, ma'am. Try an' get just enough traction for the car to keep goin' steady."

Something crashed onto the roof of the car.

"Just a tree branch. Keep goin'."

Marion whispered a quick thank-you to the heavens for this passenger from out of the blue, out of the storm—her father would have disapproved of having someone in her car with spirits on his breath, but there was so much argument these days about repealing the prohibition law and she was in no position to be picky about who helped her navigate the storm. She clung to the steering wheel and wiped at the window with her white cotton glove. No time for moral judgments in the midst of a tempest.

Frederick used the back of his sleeve to clear the windshield. "Be careful of that there horse and wagon over in the other lane." She could see no wagon or horse—hadn't seen one on this road for years—but she would take the man at his word. She had no choice, even if he had tipped a bottle.

Marion kept her eyes fixed on the road—or where she imagined the road to be—and her foot on the accelerator though her leg trembled up and down uncontrollably. She was driving upstream and couldn't stop the car now if she wanted to. A wake formed behind them—she could see this in the side mirror.

"You're doin' fine, Miss Parsons. Keep 'er steady."

Uncle Charles' driveway would be coming up soon. She would have to turn across the road again, and there was no way to see what might be coming. She rolled down the window, signaled a left turn with her arm, praying no one was behind her or coming the other way. With her foot on the accelerator, hands shaking on the steering wheel, she gave the moment all she had in order to maneuver through the creek bed forming at the bottom of the driveway. Tires spun and rainwater pelted in through the window, soaking her sleeve and the side of her face. There was no time to roll it up again, no time for second chances. She would either make it up the driveway, or they would be in the ditch.

The car lurched, stopped, hissed. Marion rolled up the window, and they sat in silence while a barrage of rainwater bombarded the hood of the car. A row of birch trees along the driveway swayed almost to the ground.

Suddenly, someone was banging on her window.

"What in heaven's name?"

It was Helen. "Nantie Marion, come into the house!"

Marion turned to Frederick, but he had already disappeared into the downpour.

Helen, who had grown into a tall young woman, was trying to

hold on to a gigantic black umbrella, trying to keep it upright, but it bolted back and forth and then blew inside out and flew out of her hand. She leaned into the car and took hold of Marion's arm.

Marion clung to her niece. Rain pelted against her face as they struggled arm in arm toward the back stoop. Her hair whipped across one side of her face, and a blast of wind almost knocked both of them over. Helen reached for the railing. Marion hung on to Helen's jacket, but still she slipped on the first step, grabbed the porch railing and cast her gaze around wildly. In one glance she saw devastation in every direction—tree limbs covered the ground and an old screen door was plastered against the fence. A pine tree lay sideways on the ground over by the garden, or what was left of the garden. What must be a hurricane had created a haze of backsplash that covered the front of the property all the way down to the road.

Grace stood in the open doorway, one hand gripping the other. She looked tired. Then again, she often did.

Inside, Grandma Harkness stood at the wood cookstove on the other side of the large kitchen, stirring her giant cast iron pot. Never one to get keyed up, she waved at Marion without even turning around.

Everyone started talking at once.

"Is that Mother's silver?" Marion pointed to the wooden box on the kitchen table.

Helen started to cry. "Uncle Charles called and told us to get up here right away. Cousin Ruth was at the house and grabbed a few of our clothes and the silverware, and here we are!"

Marion put her arms around her niece. "Let's get out of these wet clothes. It will be all right, dear, just a little storm—a hurricane more than likely." Then, "Where is Uncle Charles?"

"He's out back, probably in the barn," Grace said. "You know him, 'Save what you can.'" Grace had slumped into one of the kitchen chairs. "The water was so swift, it destroyed everything," Helen said, wiping her face and wringing her drenched dark curls. "You should have seen it. I can't believe you made it here! How did you? Oh Nantie, the beautiful new lawns on Cherry Road are all ruined."

Grace handed Marion a dry towel, and she wrapped it around Helen's shoulders. Helen cried, choking out words between her sobs. "I checked the cellar before we left, Nantie, and it was knee deep. Mr. Terziev was out in his garden, trying to do something. Bless his heart … his beautiful garden."

Grandma Harkness came up behind them with a woolen blanket for Marion.

By the time the phone service came back on, it was dark and everyone had dried out. Grace was pulling a pan of brown bread out of the oven when the phone rang. They had kept the fire going, hoping to keep the house warm all night and to dry out the wet clothes.

Claude had been trying to reach them for hours. Without a car, he was stuck at the house, but he had news. Judge Farnham had come over after dinner, after the storm died down. One of the department stores down on Salina Street had nine feet of water, and the loss was extensive, devastating—rugs, furniture, clothing. They were already estimating crop losses on the west side in the range of $200,000.

"Peggy Mable's doll house floated away with all the dolls in it." Grace told the story to all the anxious relatives while hanging up the phone. Her hand rested on the receiver, trembling. "We were luckier, just a little water in the cellar, and Mr. Terziev's garden is totally wrecked." She paused with the realization of it all. "He's been working on that garden for fourteen years."

The rain had stopped. In the darkness following the storm, it was hot and muggy. They would be up for hours—too hot to sleep and too worried to rest. Marion could hardly bear to think what might have happened to the school. Where would the money for repairs come from? She couldn't think straight right now, but now she knew for sure she would put her summer travel plans aside.

The school took only minor damage during the big hurricane, and in the days that followed, there was always a crowd of people—

neighbors, students, friends, and family—helping Mr. Lamphere drag tree limbs, branches, and debris and heft it on top of the big pile. Others came by to haul wood home to burn in their stoves and fireplaces.

Now they would get ready for the first-ever Cherry Road School Circus.

Syracuse Herald-Journal
June 1, 1934
Cherry Road
Pupils Offer
Circus Acts

—

500 Parents See Parade
and Other Features
of Big Top

—

School Grows Fast
14 in 8th Grade Scheduled
to be Graduated on
June 23

by Roy E. Fairman

Pupils of Cherry Road School, which has grown from an enrollment of 11 to 163 in 12 years, staged a circus before more than 500 parents and friends in the school building last night.

The circus, conceived by the pupils themselves, and planned and developed by them, included all the acts common to shows under the "big top."

Trained animals, acrobats, tight rope artists, boxers, dancers, magic acts, clowns, cowboys, cowgirls, Indians, music, all intended to bring back to the adult audience memories of the sawdust ring.

The performers, gaudy in paint, powder and tinsel, staged a real circus parade as a preliminary to the big show, headed by a band, many of whose instruments the pupils made themselves.

In addition to the circus, an ice cream sale and exhibit of school work in the classrooms of the school were features of the program.

When Miss Parsons, principal, took the teaching job in District 1, Town of Geddes, the school had 11 pupils in a one-room building on Terry Road.

Today, the school has six teachers and 163 pupils in an attractive brick building on Cherry Road. Nineteen of these pupils are non-residents.

Four years ago, when the first unit of the present building was completed, Miss Parsons had one assistant and the school had an enrollment of 50 pupils.

Two rooms were completed in subsequent years and last year an addition with two classrooms and a combination auditorium and gymnasium seating 320 persons was completed.

The school has the enviable reputation of never having a potential graduate fail in the final Regents tests. Fourteen pupils in the eighth grade are slated to be graduated on June 23. The greater number of them will enter Solvay High School in September.

The Regents examinations, part of the New York State Education Department's requirements, were the oldest educational testing service in the United States, predating the College Board, the Educational Testing Service, and the American College Testing Program. Marion knew it was rare and commendable for a school to achieve a 100 percent pass rate, and she took quiet pleasure in this.

Chapter Fifteen
Cherry Road School

Don't cry because it's over. Smile because it happened.
—Dr. Seuss

THE YOUNG BOY STANDING in the doorway looked as though he was about to cry. Perhaps he had been crying. Marion was in a hurry to get the financial report done for the April trustees' meeting, but she closed the ledger book and folded her hands on the desk. "Come in, William."

She could see the mud on his shoes. He hesitated, looked down at his feet and back at her. She felt like crying for the agony of the boy.

"Please, come in and sit right there in that chair." She hadn't meant to sound gruff, but the boy scurried to the chair, twisting the cap around in his hands.

"What is it, William? Is there something I can do for you?"

Marion knew the name of every child in the school. She knew how they were doing in class—who needed help with reading, who paid attention, and who did not. She knew each family, how many children each housed, and which fathers were out of work. She wrote personal notes on every report card, reminding students and their parents that she was paying attention.

The boy said nothing, just looked at the floor.

Marion was about to ask him again when a gust of cold wind rustled the morning newspaper she'd left open on her work table. The chill on the back of her neck made her jump from her chair and run toward the window, where another blast of air blew across her face. The smell of burning leaves and a faint hint of overripe fruit filled the room, and the window slammed shut, harder than she had intended.

The boy did not flinch but watched her closely. She turned, grabbed the back of her chair and reached across the desk. "William," Marion lifted the brass bell. "Have you ever seen the bell up close?" Since that very first day of school, Marion had made a point of standing out front by the flag pole every morning and ringing the bell. When students came into the office, they would eye the bell, but she never allowed anyone to touch it. After all, if she permitted one, she'd have to let everyone hold it.

"Come here, William. I'd like you to see the bell up close."

William lifted himself off the chair, inched his way over to the desk. Marion felt the courage wash over the boy, and she offered him the bell. "You may hold the bell, but you may not ring it because, you will notice, I've removed the ringer, as I do every day." He didn't look up while she told him the story about the day she had been late for school. She could hear the bell all the way from the Terry Road School, but she knew she wouldn't make it in time for the start of class. She'd had to make a decision right then whether to tell the truth. Would she tell her teacher that she had overslept or make up a story to show herself in a better light?

"What did you do, ma'am?" The boy looked Miss Parsons in the eye.

"I told the truth, Will. Now how about you tell me what's bothering you this morning?" She took the bell, put it back in its spot on the desk and placed her hand on the boy's shoulder.

"Well, ma'am," he turned his hat around in his hands, pulling at the visor.

Marion waited. She could see through the window to the outer office—a row of young boys filled the chairs lining the wall. A small group of girls poked their head through the door from the outer hallway and giggled at the boys. She hardly ever saw any girls in her office.

The boy spoke, "It's that trip you asked us to sign up for? Well, my dad, he only works a few days a week, and we don't have no money to go on no trip—that's what he told me last night. We haven't got any money to go on a trip."

Marion's throat clenched. She wanted to hug the boy. "Well, William, I'd like to ask you a favor. Perhaps you can help me out." Marion had a habit of clearing her throat at certain times. "You see, I have storm windows that need changing at my house, and I need someone to do it for me. I wasn't sure who might do that until just now."

The boy stepped back, his face opening in a wide grin.

"You know," she said, clearing her throat again, "I know of two other women in the neighborhood who do not have anyone to do work. Would you be willing to help us out?"

"Yes, ma'am!"

"Then run along and I'll expect to see you at my house on Saturday morning. No basketball this Saturday, and no more talk to anyone about not going on the trip."

"Yes, ma'am."

"One more thing, Will."

"Yes, Miss Parsons?"

"Someone, I'm assuming it was several someones, put a very large wagon full of pumpkins up on the roof on Halloween night. It took the janitor and several men to get that down. Thankfully no one was hurt or killed. Do you know who did that, William?"

The boy shook his head, looking again at Miss Parsons.

"I believe you, William. I believe you don't know. And I'm not going to ask you to tell me if you happen to find out. But if you do, take a good long look at those boys and know that they are headed for trouble in this life if they don't straighten up and consider the consequences of what they do."

She heard William running in the hall as the next boy stepped across the threshold. She would never get any paperwork done today, but it didn't matter. A glint of warm sunlight radiated through the windows; children's voices exploded outside her door, wafted into her office.

Cherry Road School had survived the Great Depression, and Marion had kept the promise she had made to herself over a decade ago to show the world to her students. When it had been time for eighth graders to graduate, the Mothers' Club organized fundraisers for a trip to New York City, sometimes other cities around the northeast. They hosted dances, card parties, bake offs, and crafts bazaars. Everyone enjoyed these events, and they were profitable too. By the time spring rolled around, the eighth graders always had earned almost enough money to fund the adventure of a lifetime—the kind Marion had spent years dreaming about and planning for. One year, to make up for the rest of the money needed, the Mothers' Club took up a silver offering at an emergency meeting, netting an additional twenty-five dollars for the trip. Marion contributed twenty dollars at the last minute so everyone could go. The kids promised to pay her back by serving more lunches after they returned, and they did.

> That school has had so many additions; it seems like every summer something was being done.
> —Helen Wright, school secretary

Those who were there remember one year, the day they left on the train for New York City. Even Miss Parsons and their two chaperones were excited. They pressed their noses to the dusty train windows. As their coach pulled away from the station, nobody said a word—they just watched out the windows as Syracuse faded away. Some of them were leaving for the first time in their lives. They were on their way to New York City. They had planned the trip carefully and thoroughly, spent hours researching what they wanted to do when they got there. They went to the library and looked in books, they talked to neighbors who had been to the city, and they asked Miss Parsons to tell them about the times she had been there.

On the first day, they ate at an automat, rode a double-decker bus and walked through Rockefeller Center, the planetarium, and Grand

Central Station. They rode on the subway, they visited St. Patrick's Cathedral, and they even had tickets to a musical comedy called The White Horse Inn. Some of the girls shopped in a fancy department store on Broadway.

On the second day, they went to the Bronx Zoo, and a girl got lost. Miss Parsons told all the other children to stay with Miss Robinson. She and Miss Muench went to find a policeman. Two girls cried while Miss Parsons was gone, so they sang songs and talked about the penguins, how they walked and how they could swim under the water. When Miss Parsons and Miss Muench still hadn't returned, Miss Robinson said not to worry. Though some children had to go to the bathroom, Miss Parsons had said no one was to move, so they stayed put on the benches. When they saw the grown-ups heading their way, they all cheered. It had been less than thirty minutes, but they still recall their fear. By the time they got back to the Hotel Bristol, everyone was ready for bed.

Piling off the train in Syracuse on Friday night, the students were

CHERRY ROAD SCHOOL CHEER LEADERS—Dressed in their green skirts and white sweat shirts with green letters, CR, the cheer leaders of Cherry Road school lined up as follows after a busy basketball season, from left to right: Joan Guth, Mary Lou Jerome, Rosemary Ryan, Roberta Kendall, Joan Kleintop, Bernice Crolick, Virginia (Ginger) BeVard, Maureen Ashe, Joan Donnelly and Martha Ballard.

The Post Standard, November 4, 1949

all talking at once, running toward their parents waiting on the platform to tell them all about the trip. Says one student who was there, who remembers the day as vivid as last night's dream, "It was exciting and noisy, thrilling, colorful, and busy, and we were glad to be back home. The only thing on our list we were unable to do was ride on the Fifth Avenue bus."

From then on, the neighborhood grew as fast as Mr. Terziev's flower garden in early spring—there were more houses and more babies, especially after the war. A common sight along Parsons Drive was women pushing large, clunky baby carriages, strollers made of metal and wood. Toddlers and young children often traipsed behind, hanging on to their mothers' skirts or cotton housedresses. Some rode tricycles or bicycles. From the first year the school was in operation, for about three or four years, more classrooms were added each year. Students all remember that when the gym was built in 1931, it changed everything. The gym became the center of their lives—it was all about basketball, dancing, choir, and covered dish get-togethers. From then on, the school and the neighborhood grew every year.

No matter how many changes happened over the years, how many additions to the original school, the gym was the students' favorite place. They played basketball, had band practice, used it as an auditorium for evening events—plays, movies, and concerts. When it was an auditorium, they had to carry chairs up and out from a door that led to the locker room under the bleachers—double-folding chairs that were heavy. The students all helped to set them up and remove them afterward. There were big dances in the gym—they'd decorate during lunchtime.

The gym was the place they'd try out for chorus—walk up from the basement with flashlights covered in cellophane, a strange ritual that many remember but don't remember why the flashlights or the cellophane. One former student who had wanted to be in that choir more than anything remembers: "They'd call us out one at a time. Some of us made it, and some of us did not."

Several students remember standing in line at the door of the gym at the beginning of the school year to get inoculations, polio shots. Some remember the smell of rubbing alcohol just before the prick of the needle. Some had to sit down with their head between their knees, some passed out, a few had to go home.

Wooden rails ran along one side of the wall, and they were used in gym class for exercise. During lunchtime, the stage curtain was pulled across and the stage was used for boxing. The students were allowed to do the boxing all by themselves, and they worked things out by themselves too. Some Friday nights they watched movies like *Drums Along the Mohawk*.

The Mothers' Club sponsored football dances and dances for the eighth graders. On Friday nights, they held round and square dances and danced the jitterbug to 78 rpm records in the gym. Sometimes their dances were semiformal with orchestral music, and every student was encouraged to take lessons at the Arthur Murray Dance Studio in formal ballroom dancing—the four-step waltz, the tango, the cha-cha, and the fox trot. Some kids rode the bus downtown after school. In the 1940s students pulled out the record player during lunchtime and jitterbugged to Hank Williams Jr. Some did the swing dance to big band music like Tommy Dorsey and Gene Krupa. The girls wore saddle shoes and hoop skirts that flared out when they twirled around. They wore their hair long so it would spin too. Everyone had a great time, and the evening dances brought in money for the class trip.

Students remember it this way:

We could hear echoes in the gym locker room as we changed into

School Additions
1927: Cherry Road School opens to 50 students (three rooms)
1928: Another classroom
1930–31: Two classrooms plus a gym/auditorium
1941: Four classrooms and girls' lavatory
1946: Three classrooms and boys' lavatory
1949: Six classrooms and cafeteria
1953: Six classrooms and a new one-acre playground

Cherry Road School band, 1955

those blue gym suits. We played basketball, and girls could only go half court, so the guard passed to the forwards on the other half and they made the baskets. Girls were cheerleaders for the boys' teams. We wore green circular skirts and white long-sleeved turtleneck shirts, and white and brown saddle shoes.

We had music classes in a small room off to the left of the stage in the gym where the chorus performed at eighth-grade graduations, and we had a band too. The eighth-grade dances were so special when we jitterbugged to records. Up in the back of the gym, there were about eight rows of seats with backs and fold-up seats, and we were comfortable up there watching whatever was happening on the floor. This was really the finest school in Onondaga County.

There was a small lunchroom toward the back side of the school, in the basement. We can still smell the overripe bananas down there. Everyone had one. A makeshift kitchen toward the front had a stove and an oven. One of the teachers showed us how to put old records in the oven to soften them up and then bend them into bowls as presents for our mothers.

When the additions were being built, we went right on with school. We managed somehow, like we always did. We met for classes in the gym, in the basement, anyplace they could find room or a quiet place. Because we were so proud of our school, no one complained about the inconvenience or the noise.

One year we went to school in the coal bin in the basement. They had already switched from coal to oil, and the old coal bin was bigger than some classrooms so they just whitewashed the walls and put two curtains across and made four classrooms out of it. You couldn't do that today—no windows, no air circulation.

> While we were going down there, I was talking quite a lot in the class. The teacher, she says, "Bill, you're going up to see Miss Parsons." She says, "I want you to get some adhesive tape. And if she asks you what it's for, tell her it's to tape your mouth shut." I got up there, and sure enough she asked what it was for. And she taped my mouth shut and said, "Now if that tape doesn't work, you can spend some time with me after school." How can I remember that and not know where I put my glasses?
>
> Back then, you knew everybody—if someone mentioned a name of somebody who lived there, you knew them. Anybody, even if they didn't have children. We had a kid in our class who had a lot of problems—he'd lost his mother and had some deformities from being in the crib too long. He lost his kidney when he was young. Anyway, the kids were picking on him one day because he wore shorts. We went home for lunch and told our mothers about it, and they said, "After you finish eating lunch, go put on a pair of shorts and go back to school. If any of those kids make fun, kick the snot out of them." It was different then—there was no bullying, and if there was, we corrected it ourselves.
>
> There was another situation—a girl who had real physical problems and would wet her pants in school. But nobody made fun of her. We all helped take care of her. It was because Marion Parsons said, "This is what we'll do," and we did it.
>
> School was the focus of everything. We had buddies at school. We'd walk up there in the summertime. After school, it was still the focal point. And at Christmastime, we usually had some kind of play for Christmas along with Christmas carols. Whole families would be there. —Bill Eriksson, class of 1943

Chapter Sixteen
A Time to Remember

Some days in late August at home are like this, the air thin and eager like this, with something in it sad and nostalgic and familiar ...

—William Faulkner

So many, now way past retirement, remember in the summertime going up and having pick-up baseball games. It wasn't anything organized, they recall, they just got a bunch of guys together. They get together now and reminisce about the parties they had at various houses.

They were rambunctious and sometimes little hellions. They were what you'd call 'good kids' who knew how to have a good time, who understood the importance of respecting their elders. *They remember it like this:*

The parties were well supervised. One of the things we used to play was Wink. The girls would sit in chairs in a circle, and the guys would stand behind them. One chair would be empty, and that guy would wink at a girl and she'd run over to his chair, but the guy who'd be standing behind her chair would grab her.

There was a quarter-mile race track behind Lundy's that was for midget cars with real engines. It wasn't very big, so those things would rip around there—it was great. We loved it. You could hear them all over Westvale, but our mothers hated that. They got together, and they had that thing gone. Very quickly.

Boy Scouts. We'd meet at the church on Bronson Road. Around

nine o'clock they'd let us out, and it'd be kind of dark. We'd go out in the fields and start little fires. Well, we were Boy Scouts—we had to do this, right? Some of the fires would get out of hand, and we'd all streak out of there as the fire engines came.

You'd wake up in the morning on a Saturday. What do you want to do? Well you played ball—you could go to Cherry Road and play basketball. We loved to go over to the Jerome farm. We went mainly to play. Sometimes we thought we were working. We helped a little bit with the haying or putting the corn in the silo. Some fields were still plowed with a single horse and plow. We would ride with the hired hand on the way to the field. We remember riding in a buckboard wagon with a single plow in the wagon. When we got to the field, the heavy plow had to be removed from the buckboard, the horse and plow hitched up. One of the hired hands would plow all day, one furrow at a time. In order to plow those long fields straight, the field hand would sight a tree or bush between the ears of the horse and aim for that point.

> I thought someday I might be paid for doing all that work. I could become one of the hired hands, but that never happened. As I look back, I have received my pay many times over in memories.
> —Jack Mitchell, class of 1948

After we watched a little plowing, we would get bored and walk back to the farm for the next adventure. When the corn was ready to be cut, it would be loaded onto wagons, taken back to the farm, chopped by a machine, and then blown up into the silo. We were never allowed near the chopper because it was a dangerous, hungry monster. We were allowed to go up into the silo and help move the silage around while it poured down from above, though. We can still feel the wet corn chips hitting our faces and going down inside our shirts. It was also a great place to wrestle—a self-contained rink with a soft floor of chopped-up corn.

Mr. Jerome would lead one of the work horses out of the barn and let us ride him if we stayed close to the barn. It's hard to believe in this day and age that he would leave us to have such a good time, but he did. No worries about liability or lawsuits. And there were other chores to help with, feeding the cows silage from a wheelbarrow, giving them hay, sweeping floors.

Going to Cherry Road School opened our world. We walked the mile home for a warm lunch. We never wanted to miss a day, even when everyone else had the mumps and we could have gotten away with it.

At Cherry Road School, sports, scouts, the arts, and playing in the orchards and barns kept us busy. We don't remember ever being bored. We remember excitement playing in cow barns, abandoned tunnels, swamps, meadows, orchards, and frog ponds. At school, there was the never-ending planning for the annual eighth-grade trip. Our parents didn't have to force us to go outside to play; it was all they could do to get us back inside by dark, to keep us out of troubles such as skunks and bee stings.

We walked everywhere and didn't think a thing of it—rain, snow, or sleet. Nobody was concerned about where you had to walk. We remember walking on big piles of snow along Genesee Street to get to Parsons Drive, to Meadow Road, with the cars whizzing by—nobody ever thought, Oh, that's dangerous for these kids.

We had our scout meeting at the school—all the mothers were leaders. You got a card saying you were a member. It was important for girls.

McArdell's Gas Station, a hang-out place

Chapter Seventeen
The Class Trip

We could never have loved the earth so well if we had had no childhood in it.
—George Elliot

THE EIGHTH-GRADE TRIP was the highlight of the school year. For some, it was the highlight of their life. They rode on the train down the Hudson Valley. It was fascinating to ride along the Hudson River. Mrs. Amedro had them reading about early American history, so they learned about Henry Hudson and the early Dutch, and then they knew why all those towns had Dutch names. Across the river they saw the Catskills from Rip Van Winkle. They saw tugboats, river boats, and big barges dredging the river.

When they got to New York, they stayed at the Hotel Bristol. Miss Parsons took them to see the Rockettes at Radio City Music Hall. She took them to the automat where they put nickels into a slot to open a small window for meat, veggies, or pie.

> My big fear was my father finding out if I had misbehaved—if I had to go to the office. I was much more afraid of what would happen when I got home than I was of being sent to the office.
> —Bob Coulter, class of 1940

๛

On one class trip to Detroit in 1949, the long-awaited day arrived and they all got on the bus—eager, energetic eighth graders and three chaperones—and off they went to

1938, Marion Parsons and students who have just returned from New York City

Buffalo. Though this was not the first class not to go to New York, it was a big class compared with the others, and the way the story goes, there were some pranksters on board.

Here is how some of them remember the Detroit trip today:

We think we had the best trip ever. When we got to Buffalo, we boarded a Great Lakes Steamer, a giant side-wheeler built in 1812. It cost $25.68 each to go on the trip. The inside was brass and mahogany, and it made the ship look so elegant. We spent two nights crossing Lake Ontario. In Detroit we visited the Edison Institute, Greenfield Village, and the Ford auto plant. We had lunch at a famous place called the Little Brown Jug. As tired as we were, we got back on the boat that night and did not sleep.

The cabins were on the outside, and the whole middle was filled with opportunities. It was great fun watching water balloons plummeting to the lower decks. Something came over us. We were rambunctious eighth graders, and our twelve-year-old excitement came uncorked, boiling up in more energy than manners. We kept the chaperones up all night.

We made memories to last a lifetime. But because of our rowdiness and the challenges we gave those three chaperones, there were great restrictions placed on future eighth-grade trips.

We were part of a large family. We knew that our parents, our teachers, Miss Parsons, and even the neighbor on the corner were watching out for us. We felt that what we were doing was relevant to our lives because everyone cared so much about what we were doing. We were proud of our school. If we were asked to raise the flag, give the morning announcements, sing in the choir, or be a Patrol Boy, we felt honored.

At Cherry Road School, the entire community agreed on the goals and the rules and supported each other. We knew what our boundaries were and dared not venture too far beyond. We followed rules of mutual respect, courtesy, punctuality, and honesty, and they were strictly enforced. We were never treated unfairly, but we knew if we broke the laws of the school, there would be hell to pay when we got home.

Neighbors always pitched in. One time they all got together and donated trees and all sorts of plants for a school flowerbed that became a great source of pride for everyone. When a large clock was inlaid above the front doorway, they hung lanterns on either side. We remember standing there,

> I was class president at the time and oversaw the raising of the money for the trip. I remember standing in the middle of two classrooms that were separated at times by a folding wall, conducting class meetings.
> —Martha Ballard Lacy, class of 1949

> We were studying the Wild West one time, and I rode my horse to school. My husband owned a horse stable, and we'd have cookouts and all sorts of fun. Westvale was like a little community. Times have changed. Back then, the adults were all on the same side—it wasn't the parents against the teachers.
> —Tibby Muench Dumanian, teacher

looking at those new lights—the four steps leading into the school reached out and pulled us in even though we knew we were supposed to use the side doors.

Our parents and the neighbors loved the school grounds. They came over when school was out to play sports. We had festivals and pageants on the school grounds. Sometimes we gathered around the flagpole.

Our school grew in size as the neighborhood grew, and the neighborhood grew because the city of Syracuse grew. Westvale was thought of as a nice place to live and a great place to send children to school.

Teachers have equally fond memories, the few who are left.

They loved their jobs. They felt like a family. At that time, not only did they teach academics, but they might also have taught gym, music, or art. They remember that they were always in training. They did plays with the kids and took them on trips. Miss Parsons would let them try new things.

At that time, the area was all countryside—hardly any houses. Mrs. Muench-Dumanian recalls her days at Cherry Road School as times when, "…parents were active and involved and interested in what was going on. We were like a big family. All the teachers got along together."

Fred Fuller, Jean Miller, Marion Parsons, John Garafalo
Chaperones: 1950 trip to New York City

The class of 1950 did not go to Detroit and get on the boat—that was for sure. But we did go on the train to New York City. Some of us had never been on the train or to New York City, so it was a big deal. But before we went, we had to earn the money. So the mothers put on this play about an old-time country school. There were all girls in the play and there was supposed to be one boy, but we couldn't get any boys to do this, so one of our mothers took the part of the boy. There was a big crowd, and we made the money.

Our parents got a notice that was sent home with us about the trip:

Children report to the classroom at 10:00. Leave for New York Central at 10:30. Train leaves at 11:18, train #40, and arrives back in Syracuse on April 4 at 9:05 p.m. Each child must have their own lunch for Monday. Each child will need 85 cents for lunch at the airport and a dollar for a box lunch on the return trip. There will be little opportunity to spend money, so we suggest bringing only a small amount.

It was a big thing to have an autograph book then, and we passed them around on the train. While we were in New York, we ate at Schrafft's. We went to the Empire State Building, Grant's Tomb, and to a Rockettes show. We stayed in a hotel.

Marilyn Lewis Marcy—class of 1950

Chapter Eighteen
Our Miss Parsons

Ring the bells that still can ring.
Forget your perfect offering.
There is a crack in everything.
That's how the light gets in.

—Leonard Cohen

IT WAS A FRIDAY AFTERNOON in December, 1941. After the last child and the last teacher and finally the janitor had left Cherry Road School, Marion walked down the hallway toward the door, her steps echoing inside the empty brick building. After locking the large double front doors, she headed home and went straight to her kitchen. She baked two batches of molasses cookies, and when they had cooled she boxed half of them for the Salisburys, her next door neighbors, wrapping them neatly in waxed paper and arranging the bundle of sugary slices inside a Christmas box from the attic; she would leave them on their back porch later on.

Saturday morning passed in silence but for the crackling of the first fire of the season in Marion's fireplace. Peter and David came by in the afternoon and raked the last of the leaves from the poplars and maples. The trees were all bare now and the wind had shifted, blowing in from the east, a large gale teeming with tiny flakes of snow and rain. She watched out the window while her nephews scurried around the yard, bundling leaves into baskets away from the wind. Peter was now in his first year of high school, Dave at Springfield

College in Massachusetts.

She shivered and wrapped her arms around herself against a chill that had slowly been filling the dining room since the morning fire had died out. Cherry Road was empty of cars and people, and all she could hear was the clock on the mantle and the dripping of water into the rain barrel at the back corner of the house. The clock had belonged to her grandfather Edwin, its pendulum measuring the passing of time, back and forth. The water from the roof dripped steady droplets, louder and louder as the rain picked up, loud enough for her nearly deaf ears to hear.

Bare trees against gray sky gave the impression of a painting behind glass. A lone car passed by, and Marion imagined the lapping and splashing sounds its tires would make on the rutted street, now filling steadily with ice-cold rain.

Marion's hearth

She stood by the window until the sun set behind her Cousin John's house across the street. Clouds had drifted off, and stars sparkled in the clear moonlit sky. Marion thought longingly about nights like this on the farm when she was a girl. She and Grace would sit on the front porch looking for the Milky Way, waiting for the big round harvest moon to appear from behind the hill, its fullness yielding deep shadows crossways over the pasture on the far side of the turnpike. Stars quivered in the mist, and bare tree branches looked like witches on broomsticks.

When the clock chimed ten times, Marion pulled down the window sash, picked up her needlepoint, and made her way up the dark stairs, coaxing her tired body up each step, slowly and carefully, hanging on to the railing with one hand and her tapestry with the other. Her bedroom door creaked when she pushed it open.

Today her students from over a half-century ago remember Marion with the bell in the morning—she'd come out on the sidewalk and ring the bell. One of them would be chosen to raise the flag. One of those students who went into the Navy remembers waking up in the morning at boot camp. He remembers the other fellows saying, "What an awful night! That lousy flagpole banged and clanged all night long."

And Bob Coulter would say, "I slept like a baby. That put me right to sleep."

They'd say, "What do you mean?"

"Well, I grew up with the school flagpole right across the street from my bedroom on Cherry Road—so when I heard that, it was heaven. When I was a kid, that's what put me to sleep. When the wind blew and it would crack up against the pole, that sound put me to sleep."

> One day Miss Parsons called me into her office and gave me a year's membership to the YMCA. I can tell you I made good use of that membership.
> —Jack Mitchell, class of 1948

They remember feeling like they were all alike back then. Some of them may have had a lot more than others, but no one ever paid any attention. The kids who had more learned by example to help those in need.

They remember Miss Parsons most of all:

We remember her coming down the hall when we were only about six or seven years old, and we'd stand taller and walk better when she went by. When Miss Parsons came down the hall or into your classroom, she commanded respect. There was something about her—we loved her from the first day. It may have been the sparkle in her eyes; it may have been her unusual demeanor—a mix of friendliness and yet a command for respect. To this day we still refer to her as Miss Parsons. We would go to her little house, and she'd serve us tea and

Cherry Road School basketball team, Fred Fuller, middle. 1950

molasses cookies.

We remember how she'd ring the bell at recess and greet kids as they arrived for class. She knew everybody's name. We remember how she'd add her own notes to every single report card and sign her name.

Everybody respected her so much that if she called up your house and said there was a problem, the parents took it as a problem. If she or somebody from the school called, there was no questioning by the parents—you'd get it. And back then, you got spanked.

> One night a bunch of kids broke out all the windows in Banister's greenhouse—four hundred dollars' worth. Our mothers heard about it and took us all the way up to Cherry Road School to pay our share even though we weren't in on it.
>
> Miss Parsons seemed to have a way—just out of respect for her, you would do what was right. And she could do things back then that no principal would dare do today. If a kid got sick, for example, Miss Parsons would ask one of the other kids to ride them home on their bicycle. We weren't supposed to ride two on a bike, and we probably missed two classes, but it was good sense. She was willing to break her

own rules and even the rules of society for our benefit.

We asked her one day if she'd drive us over to Solvay to buy squirt guns, and she did. She might have taken them away from us on Monday, but she drove us over there.

—George Kinder, class of 1943

We knew she was watching, even when there were almost seven hundred of us. She was open to change and kept abreast of emerging technologies and methodologies—new trends in education.

We remember learning not only the basics, but also about people and the value of each individual. While many friendships have come and gone after seventy years, some of our Cherry Road friendships still prevail. That's one of the things a small community imparts on the soul! In today's world, we marvel at the simplicity from which we came, and that somehow imparts a responsibility that we rise to—in memory of friendships—good friends and caring teachers, who in spite of our shortcomings gave us a roadmap for life. When we think of Miss Parsons, we are reminded of how much respect we held for her—we were in awe.

> She devoted a lifetime to it, that's what she did. And it was the Lord's doing she didn't have kids of her own so she could do that. God bless her.
> —Bill Eriksson, class of 1943

A few of us stopped in one day, not long after we'd left Cherry Road School, to say hello, and she was so gracious. We were so young and curious. It brings a smile to remember gentle kindness and a bit of humor in her eye; we remember those eyes and her gracious warmth.

Miss Parsons was a wonderful lady. She may have disciplined us, but she also made sure we learned, and that led us all the way through school.

We started in kindergarten and went all the way to eighth grade in one building. Our classes changed a little as some people moved in and out, but many of us remained with the same people all that time—so we made some friends. But one thing that we remember the most is that Miss Parsons would write on every one of our report

> They were doing miles—how long is a mile? I did it in inches. The teachers said it is correct, but it's not anything anyone would know but you and me. But I was stubborn and wouldn't change it to feet, so I had to go down and see Miss Parsons. And she said, "Bill, I know you're right, but we measure a mile in feet." She said, "If you put that on your paper again, I'll hear about it."
>
> So I went back to class, and I wrote it right out in inches again. So I had to go to Miss Parsons' office, and she said, "Bill, you may not like this. There's a sidewalk out front. I'm going to give you a ruler and a piece of chalk and you're going to measure a mile with a ruler. Then you'll see why you don't want to write inches on your paper again."
>
> So I had to work on that every night for an hour. She would come out and see how I was doing. I can't remember how long it took me, but when I was done, she gave me a pat on the back and said, "Maybe it's not so good to stick with something if everyone else is doing it one way and you're doing something odd but you know they're right. Maybe you will remember this." She asked me, "Have you learned a lesson from this?"
>
> And I said, "Yes, I did. Thank you very much."
>
> —Bill Ballard, class of 1955

cards. She knew everyone and was so proud of what went on in the school.

We scored high on state standardized tests and won spelling bees. Some of us toughed it out—some of us who might otherwise have fallen through the cracks went on to be highly successful in life. She was probably one of the reasons several of us kept going to school, or we would have dropped out.

Some of us get emotional because we see things the way they used to be, but everything has changed. Those of us who have moved away would move back tomorrow if we thought we could get away with it. We know that nothing is the same, but the memories are.

A few remaining teachers remember that Miss Parsons exuded passion for her job and for them. She was their leader with a clear vision of right versus wrong. She was kindhearted, they recall; she respected others' ideas; she was approachable. She knew how she wanted the school to run, but she let others help steer the boat, and she made it look easy. As teachers, they look back longingly.

As teachers, they knew she would back them up. "She appreciated the individual qualities each of us brought to the job," said Tibby Muench Dumanian, who taught off and on at Cherry Road for over twenty years "When I got the job, I felt right away that she would back me up with anything. I remember that when they put the upstairs story on, our class was in the gym and we were in the school while they were building all around. No one complained."

Miss Parsons led by example and never asked anything of her staff if she wouldn't do herself. She was out front every morning ringing the brass bell, letting the community know school was about to begin, letting her staff and her students know their principal was on board. She let the Mothers' Club and the Faculty Club and the Parent Teacher Association participate alongside her and the board of trustees. It was a team, and she was in charge, and everyone appreciated that. Every family and every student felt they were equal in the eyes of the school.

Marion poses at her hearth at her home at 303 Cherry Road

Chapter Nineteen
World War II

I cannot remember what I saw in the mirror as a child.

—Anais Nin

It was the heart of winter, 1942. Marion came to school early to make sure the furnace had run without problems throughout the night and to read the morning newspaper. She waited for her hands to warm before removing her coat with the big fur collar and hanging it on her special wooden hanger.

She wore one of her favorite gabardine suits and a rayon blouse that almost matched the color of the suit. Cousin Belle had put a tuck at the waist, making the bottom of the jacket flare for a slimming effect, something she certainly needed. She checked to see if all the buttons were fastened, her hearing aid tucked securely out of sight. She had also asked Belle—one of the best seamstresses in the city and who happened to be married to Cousin Harry—for pleats in the back. The entire effect was pleasing. Belle kept Marion's hems in line with the fashion of the day, and Marion appreciated the extra details she added to her suits and dresses—belts, double stitching, covered buttons, and kick pleats. It was bad taste to go without a modified corset. The loose, drop-waist dresses, fashions of her younger days, were no good for her—they just made her feel shorter and, well, plumper than she really was. At least the new tailored look was easier for her to wear.

Earlier that morning she had looked herself over twice in the full-length mirror and then added a string of pearls and matching pearl drop earrings. But a final glance in the mirror confirmed what she had been thinking: school marm. Maybe it was the sensible brown lace-up shoes. But that's who she was, after all.

She settled in with the paper but couldn't get past the front page's stories of war. The world had become a scary place. Battles were being fought all over Europe—Holland, Belgium, France—as armies were destroyed, countless people declared dead. Here in the United States, they had been lucky, but now the war was getting closer. With Pearl Harbor bombed, war was officially declared on Japan, in addition to Germany.

David and Peter—and all of her schoolboys, the ones she had scolded, loved, cried for, and laughed with all these years—had gone from Cherry Road School, some still at high school on the other side of the hill, over where the strangers lived, the ones who came to pick the fruit. Now they would all be going to war together. She felt them all close by, somehow. She could feel them playing ball; she could hear it bouncing on the gym floor, their shouts drifting from the playground. Was that Joe Owen? That kid was a born leader. She would have to put her boys out of her mind for the day. The children at school now were her charges, and they needed her more than ever. Wartime was scary for young people; they didn't understand things like blackout curtains and air-raid drills. How could they?

A letter had arrived yesterday from Amy—she sent news that Mrs. Eary, the janitor's wife at the Omak school, was sick, had been in the hospital. She was the lovely woman who had once urged her to follow her dreams. Have I followed my dreams? Marion wondered. She hoped to one day have the chance to ask Mrs. Eary what she thought, but Omak seemed so far away and unreachable now. She appreciated Amy's regular correspondence, and she felt a pang of regret when she read that Tom had joined the army, shipped out two weeks ago. Wasn't he too old for the service? Why had he never married? Amy was clearly concerned that no one had heard from him since he left. Well, surely Amy would let her know if anything happened. They had all been such close friends back then.

Her fingers had thawed, tingling, aching. She wasn't as hearty as she once was. It was going to be another endless winter, and the children were already restless. She would organize an assembly in the auditorium, talk to Penny about playing her harp for the other children. It must be difficult for the young girl from Bulgaria; Marion could only imagine. She had come all this way to live with her relatives, the Terzievs, who had sponsored her escape from Europe; the girl was so shy, and she had been sickly too and had missed too many days of school. Because her first language was not English and because of her extended absences, she needed personal help with her spelling and grammar. Yesterday, Miss Robinson brought one of Penny's papers for Marion to see. She had spelled neighbor as nabor and had lined up a row of commas at the bottom of her paper with a note saying she didn't know where to put them. Marion smiled again at the thought of this ingenuity. When the group from Ann Robinson's class came down for spelling and grammar help later that day, she sent Penny back to the classroom, telling her this conversation was not for her. What Penny needed was to feel at home. Playing her harp, sharing that amazing instrument with the rest of the students, just might pull her out of her shell.

Gazing out the window at the snow-filled street, Marion's mind wandered to a day when she was a young woman, when the last big war was starting. It must have been 1914. She and her friend Florence were planning to take the trolley out to Marcellus to watch Dan Patch race at the Chaney Amidon Racetrack—a great social event and something she had to beg her father to allow. He did not approve of horse racing and all that went with it. But he had finally capitulated, and Marion and Florence were getting ready—packing picnic hampers and picking out their clothes—when a cry from Allain sent everyone racing to the parlor. The Austrian Archduke Franz Ferdinand and his wife, Sophia, had been assassinated.

Her father had whisked the paper away from Allain and forbidden Marion and Florence from going to the race. After that, she remembered clearly, the world changed.

And today, once again, she was reading the newspapers, listen-

Martha Parsons, Peter Cole, Marion Parsons

ing to the radio, and watching on the sidelines while mere children enlisted in the service—where was the country headed this time? She trembled with that same frightening uncertainty. She knew her brother-in-law Claude held no confidence in FDR, but she did.

Marion pressed her forehead against the icy windowpane. Even with the furnace running day and night, it was cold in the building this time of year. Big wet flakes of snow pelted against the window.

She jumped when someone knocked on the door. Betty Jerome entered the office quietly and began lining up a row of papers on Marion's desk. Betty Templar had married Van Jerome several years ago, and Marion hired her former student to work in the office while her husband was overseas. It was hard to believe that young Betty, Helen's dearest friend, was all grown up. Wasn't it just yesterday the two young girls had spent weekends at her house, nights by the fireplace eating popcorn? And the parties—she missed the parties, and all of Helen and David's friends.

The two women chuckled at Marion's apparent alarm. "It's going to be a big day today, Miss Parsons."

"Oh, I know. Betty, the yarn for the afghans is on the table. I brought several colors and more wool sweaters than we had planned, but after the church drive, my car was filled with used sweaters. Since the boys will be knitting too, I brought twice as many of the number-nine needles."

Marion pulled skeins of brightly colored yarn from a Dey Brothers shopping bag. Then she placed the bag of yarn and needles on top of wrinkled paper bags filled with donated sweaters. The children would take them apart and re-knit the wool yarn into afghan squares.

Betty tidied Marion's desk one more time. "Oh, and the Mothers' Club will need the gym by four o'clock to start preparing for the card party."

Marion cleared her throat, straining to listen, trying to catch an echo of what Betty had said. Then she heard it. She would have to get her hearing aid checked. She had an urge to reach out and hug Betty, but she held back. "Let's have Mr. Lamphere dust mop the gym."

"By the way, there's been three more skiing accidents up on the hill at the end of Walberta Road," Betty said, crossing her arms in front of her, grinning.

"Pshaw. What can their parents be thinking? I would suppose all of our families should know better. Just as well we let the boys play inside on Saturdays before someone gets killed. I'll have Jack come over to my house Saturday morning and pick up the key, let those rascals into the gym before someone gets hurt." They laughed out loud.

Frances Terziev, Navy Wave, 1945

During the war years, they all joined in and helped out. They bought bonds at the school, students brought in a few coins to buy stamps to put in their bond books, and the money went to the war effort. Burlap bags were handed out, and over the weekends they filled them with milkweed pods from the fields, brought them back to school, and stacked them up against the wall in the gym. Milkweed pod bags were stacked up to the ceiling. "Someone came and got them," recalls Jack Mitchell, "we heard they were used for life jackets or parachutes. We collected tinfoil and rolled it into blocks."

Many of their brothers were in the service.

David Cole, John Farnham, Marc Terziev

Former students who were at Cherry Road School during the war remember it like this:

Miss Parsons taught us to be proud of our country. When we grew up, some of us went into the Marines together, some of us in the Air Force, or Navy, or Army. We all served during the war. Some of us served in the Pacific. One of us was Air Corps and shot down. He survived, but he had lifelong health problems and issues from the German prison camp treatment. Several of us were pilots, officers. Some of us were so young, we enlisted before we were eighteen.

Those of us who could, joined the service—all our buddies were doing it. Our parents had to sign a permission form. We went down to a recruiting office on Salina Street. When we left, some of us rode on a train to Buffalo. Some of us went to Seneca Lake, or Tennessee, Florida, or California—different stations all over the country for training. Then we shipped out.

During the war, those of us who were still in school learned to

Marine Lieutenant J. Richard Owen takes a helmet bath during a break in fighting the Korean War, 1950. In later combat he was twice wounded and awarded the Silver Star Medal for gallantry in action against the Chinese Communist Army

be satisfied with simple things—movies, games, books, gathering together with friends and family. Miss Parsons and the Mothers' Club organized events for us and our parents. Sometimes we had to do with less, sometimes nothing at all. One year there was no eighth-grade trip. We had a big party, like a dinner dance, over at someone's house instead. Then we went to Green Lake for a picnic.

One kid couldn't go because he had a muskrat trap line set at the end of Meadow Road where it was all swamp. That morning there was a skunk in one of his traps and he thought, Well, I'll just get him out of there. Nobody wanted him at the picnic after that.

Sometimes we were scared, and Miss Parsons would tell us to be brave. Our families gathered around enormous, static-filled radios and listened while the president talked about banks in crisis, about the war, national defense, and inflation. He talked about battles being fought overseas. For many of us who had brothers over there, this was our lifeline. We clung to our radios, hoping to hear any piece of news. At school, Miss Parsons taught us to take the air-raid drills seriously. We may or may not remember the science or math we learned back then, but the air-raid drills are imprinted in all our memories.

During these drills, we all had to go out into the hall and sit down with our backs against the wall. We covered our heads and necks with our hands. "Don't talk," we were told, "and wait for the all clear."

If we were at home and there was an air raid, all the lights had to be turned off and the shades pulled. A volunteer block warden patrolled the street and knocked on your door if he saw any light from outside. Some of our fathers volunteered to go into the city and sit on top of a building to listen for the sound of approaching enemy aircraft. They were trained to listen to certain engine types so they could distinguish friendly planes from the enemy's. Some of our fathers worked extra jobs over at Solvay Process or at Crucible Steel on the night shift in addition to their regular jobs in order to help with the war effort. The steel they were making was used for military weapons.

Some of us were little during the war. We were in kindergarten, and we had that room with the nice big bench. Some of us were absent during an air-raid drill practice, and the next day the teacher took us out in the hall and pointed us toward the gym. She said, "If we have a drill, you go right to the gym, but you have to get in your group based on where you live, and you walk home with that group." Some of us lived all the way over on Newcastle Road.

Sure enough, the bell rang and it was time for us to walk down

Peter and David Cole, circa 1943

to the gym. The whole school was down there getting into these groups. Well, we got into a group all right. We walked from Cherry Road School down Clover Road, but when we went to school, we always went down Granger because it was much closer to Newcastle. So here we were, little kindergartners with all the other grade levels with us, and we were walking like this, way down to Newcastle and way over to our house. We were the very last ones to get to our house. But we did it. We lived through that time even though we didn't realize what was going on and everybody else did.

One day Miss Parsons took us all out into the field to see a jet fly over. In our eyes, Cherry Road School was the hub of the war effort, and Miss Parsons was in charge; she was fearless, and it was contagious.

> We were standing at the blackboard lined up to go to fourth-grade English when Miss Parsons announced the end of the war.
> —Martha Ballard Lacy, class of 1949

We remember during the war, Miss Parsons taught the phonics classes herself. She would bring in yarn and teach us how to knit. We made nine-inch squares and then put them together to make afghans. She had the boys do it as much as the girls. She would box the blankets and send them to the troops. We can remember tearing old sweaters apart to get the yarn.

Cherry Roaders supported the war effort in all kinds of ways—by doing without, collecting and saving, planting gardens, organizing air-raid drills, and preparing for the worst. The Mothers' Club, teachers, and staff led students in numerous efforts to support the troops and one another. They were carried up in the surge of patriotism sweeping the country. They collected rubber, aluminum, and milkweed pods to help with what President Roosevelt had outlined in one of his fireside chats as war production goals. They bought bonds and stamps. The war became a theme around which the students lived and learned.

Consumer goods—tires, gasoline, and luxury items like silk—

were rationed. Mothers were asked to curtail their use of what were called foundation garments. Fathers were asked to cut back on driving to work, to take the bus or the train. Everyone pitched in, cut back and helped out. They were bound together in a shared enterprise of total war. Their efforts may or may not have been effective in the end, but they kept everyone focused on the positive they could achieve for the good of all.

Marc Terziev receives the Distinguished Flying Cross

Every Westvale family who had a son or daughter serving in the military had a small banner with one star or more hanging in the front window of their home. A gold star meant they had lost a loved one in the war. The mothers formed an organization called the Gold Star Mothers.

President Roosevelt died on April 12, 1945. The following month on May 8, with Harry Truman as president, the war ended. The nation's new leader announced over the radio to the country that General Eisenhower had informed him that the forces of Germany had surrendered to the United Nations. He added that he wished Franklin Delano Roosevelt had lived to see this day.

President Roosevelt's time in office—the only president to be elected to serve four terms—was one of the gravest in modern history. They were years of gloomy economic depression, widespread unemployment, and a world war.

After the war, most of the boys came home to Westvale, and some brought wives. For some, the ideal they had learned as kids at Cherry Road—the belief that the world is a safe, fair, and perfect place—had been left somewhere in the Pacific. But they went forward and built their lives, trying to leave behind what they'd seen overseas. They built new homes for their new families, parked cars in the driveway, bought television sets. They had babies, and soon the number of students at Cherry Road School exploded. In 1945 there were 340 Cherry Road School students; by 1953, a record 770 students were attending. Miss Parsons still knew every student by name; she knew their family, their family's circumstances, and how each child was performing in class.

The family farm changed too. It no longer held its status as the ideal way to make a living or the ideal way to live one's life. Many of the returning soldiers went to college on the GI bill.

The Mitchell Family, 1940: Leland, Jeanette, John C. Jr. (Jack), Lloyd, and Mildred (Millie)

John C. Mitchell, Sr. (father), Mildred (mother), Jeanette, Lloyd, Jack, Millie, and Leland (seated), 1940

Cherry Road Pupils Well Drilled

WITH NO SIGN OF PANIC, children of the Cherry Road School sit quietly in the corridor of the school, waiting for their escort teacher to check their group before taking them to their homes.

Air Raid Drill at School In Cherry Road Is Flawless

Quickly and easily, children of the Cherry Road School are learning what to do in case of an air raid.

They had their third air raid drill yesterday afternoon, and at its conclusion Miss Marion Parsons, principal, reported that within 20 minutes of the alert signal the 310 children had been escorted safely to their homes.

The first signal finds the youngsters putting on their hats and coats, children of the higher grades helping the kindergarten and first grade pupils.

Within five minutes a second signal sounds to call the children from their own rooms to their escort teachers. The school district has been divided graphically, each of the 10 teachers and office workers being named an escort teacher to see the boys and girls safely home.

After the escort teacher checks her group, shee takes them out of the building and to their homes. Cooperation of the parents has been sought, and at the door of their homes the children are met by one of the parents.

Sunday, October 13, 1940.   SYRACUSE HERALD-AMERICAN

NEWS OF THE SCHOOLS

Pupils Make Afghans for War Victims

A STITCH IN TIME, according to these boys and girls of Cherry Road School, will keep European war refugees warm during the winter months. Members of the Junior Red Cross, they are knitting afghans. Left to right are William Erickson, Thomas Larkin, Judy Salisbury, William Thomson, Mary Lundy, Ned Olney and Barbara Fawcett. Standing in back at right are Susan Hoehner and Richard Lindgren.

Boys Join Girl Knitters At Cherry Road School

Boys, as well as girls, at the Cherry Road School have gone in for knitting these days.

Equipped with knitting needles and a few scraps of yarn, they are turning out neat little knitted squares, which when sewn together, will make afghans for European war sufferers.

The making of afghans is a Junior Red Cross project of boys and girls in the fifth and sixth grades at the school. Two of the blankets will be made—one by the 36 pupils in the fifth grade, and other by the 74 pupils in the sixth grade.

In addition to doing the actual knitting, the children are collecting scraps of yarn and ripping out old knitted articles to begin anew on the yarn.

Fifty-six squares are needed for a single afghan, and whenever the boys and girls have completed their schoolwork and finished preparation of the next lesson, they turn to their knitting. Miss Mary Kimman, a teacher at the school, organized the knitting classes.

Miss Marion Parsons, school principal, announced that in addition to their knitting, the Junior Red Cross members at Cherry Road School are busy filling Christmas boxes for the children of other lands.

Thirty-six boxes are being prepared for shipment by Oct. 16, the boxes being filled with such articles as toys, school supplies, sewing materials, washcloths and hair ribbons.

Cherry Road School with an enrollment of 265 children, nearly all of whom are Junior Red Cross members, last spring won the Betts Memorial flag for outstanding work.

In all, approximately 1,000 Christmas boxes are being filled by Junior members of Syracuse and Onondaga County, and will be sent later this month to European refugee children, and to the children of Puerto Rico, Virgin Islands and the Canal Zone.

Chapter Twenty
A Life of Dreams

A man who carries a cat by the tail learns something he can learn in no other way.

—Mark Twain

THE MICROPHONE SHOOK in Marion's hand when she pressed the button to make the announcement on September 3, 1945–the final surrender had been yesterday. The war was over. There would be an observance in the gym. A chorus and clatter of voices swept throughout the school as she replaced the microphone.

Before heading to the gym, Marion took a few moments to gaze out the window. She watched her sister Grace heading toward the school. She was running. struggling to keep two plates heaped with something from falling over. Marion guessed, from where she stood by the window, molasses cookies—hopefully not black on the bottom.

Yesterday the whole family spent the afternoon celebrating at Ned and Emma Jerome's. They wanted to be close, rejoice in the end of the nightmare. The boys were coming home, some had already come home. The Parsons and Jerome families gathered around the radio in hopes of hearing any news. Today the children—and it looked like Grace too—were still in the mood for a party. Though not completely certain about the surrender quite yet, so much to take in after all they had been through—Marion would not quell her sister's enthusiasm. After all, Peter was scheduled to ship out to

Guam. She wondered if he had left already, or if there had been word from him. She didn't know how to read the expression on her sister's face as she bounded up the sidewalk toward the front door.

Marion wiped a thin layer of dust from the windowsill with her finger and watched her sister disappear up the front steps and through the front door.

She would allow the celebration to carry on. Why not? Fathers, husbands, brothers, nephews—all those boys, all in danger beyond words, all gone for so long—now they would be safe from harm. She cared deeply about every one—all of them. They would be coming home.

Once she got everyone in the gym settled down, she'd spend the rest of the day going from classroom to classroom, welcoming her students—her children—back for another school year, talking to them about the war and what it meant for it to be over.

The children had been instructed to bring their stamp collections for the first week of school, and they would be on display in each classroom until Parents' Night. There was so much to be done—no time to be tired or in pain. Inoculations were scheduled. They would do the annual Schick Tests—a small scratch on the skin to see if the child was susceptible to diphtheria, an upper respiratory disease—at the same time. The medic volunteers would be coming around to set up the clinic soon. She anticipated the usual number of tears and bruises and trips to the gym to retrieve ill students. Last year two, maybe three, children had fainted in the gym before they even got close to the needle. One girl had been taken to Crouse-Irving Hospital but was released with only a bump on the back of her head.

Chaos. Had the flag been raised? She shoved the big double doors open, inhaling fresh air. Mildred Coulter waved from her front porch. Marion waved back to her friend and thought, Without you, the Mothers' Club, the neighbors, my team of teachers, how would we survive times like these? So much that is unknown lies ahead.

When Marion made the decision to leave her life in the rugged territory she loved, she left behind people she loved too—perhaps someone special—three thousand miles away from Syracuse. She returned to the farm and did what needed to be done, but she vowed to return to Omak, if only for a visit. Over time, Cherry Road School became her life, but she still dreamed about the day after retirement when she and her sister Martha would drive across the country and visit the places and the people she'd left behind. She had been young when she left; she still had life in front of her. There would be other opportunities for travel, love, a family of her own, she told herself then. Today Marion felt the joy of her special relationship with every Cherry Road student. She didn't consider herself a hero.

She believed it was part of her responsibilities as a teacher and administrator to keep up to speed with educational research and instructional methodology. She often spent summers in Boston attending advanced education seminars, learning new theories in educational management and reading instruction. She would travel to Massachusetts, stay with her sister Martha, and enroll in graduate classes at Harvard or Boston University. She also took graduate studies at Syracuse University during the school year. She was hungry for information about how others were running public schools.

Like President Roosevelt, Marion believed there was no danger too great, no challenge too profound—she would provide the framework, the opportunity, and the inspiration ... the people of Westvale would do the rest. Like FDR, Marion could try everything; she could move in different directions at the same time; she could let the horses run, never doubting her ability to rein them in should they threaten to become uncontrollable.[2] By leading in this way, she allowed her students and her teachers the opportunity to reach their full potential.

After the war, on March 2, 1949, the Mothers' Club took Cherry Road students to see the Freedom Train, and fathers went along too. Other Mothers' Clubs and schoolchildren from around the city were there as well, as it was the grand opening of the train's stay in Syracuse. The Freedom Train was the idea of then-Attorney General Tom Clark. On the heels of World War II, he decided it was a good idea to remind people that even though the war was over, it was still important to keep an eye on the idea of freedom. Funded by Congress and the American Heritage Foundation, the traveling eleven-car museum had on display 150 government documents in glass-covered cases, including the original draft of the Declaration of Independence by Thomas Jefferson. Documents dating back to the Civil War provided teachers with a backdrop for dialogue with students about history and liberties—freedom of speech, a woman's right to vote. The Freedom Train toured the country from 1947 to 1949.

After the visit to the Freedom Train, the area Council of Mothers' Clubs issued a joint statement about their ideas on freedom:

- We have the freedom to serve our community.
- We have the freedom of choice in our programs and policies.
- We have the freedoms of associations with our teachers, educational leaders and other mothers and fathers.
- We enjoy freedom of participation, freedom from ignorance.
- We enjoy freedom to see, to hear and to do things in our schools with our children.

One night Marion was leafing through her journal, thinking about where the children would go on their eighth-grade trip. She landed on her journal page about the sights she had seen along the shoreline she had sailed by on the Great Lakes Steamer back in 1923. She remembered the sounds of the ship, the chill, damp air of the Great Lakes she remembered the hills adjacent to the Saint Mary's River where she could see coal, iron, and copper mining operations. She had watched, intrigued, as other ships passed, giant freighters carrying ores, wheat, coal, and lumber—so much productivity and industry. She had made careful notes about every point of interest—picturesque Mackinac Island, Arch Rock, Point Lookout, and Fort Holmes. She had enjoyed every moment of that trip on her way out West—meeting people, seeing the sights. One night she watched people dance on the deck of the large ship. That was in the Roaring Twenties—the Jazz Age with flapper fashion—and Marion was an old-fashioned girl from an old-fashioned family. Now she smiled at her younger self. She remembered feeling like she had gone to a circus.

She decided to arrange a special trip this year for her eighth-grade students. They would go on another Great Lakes Steamer. There were so many students in the school, she could hardly remember all their names. Was it four hundred students this year? She couldn't recall. There were lots of things she couldn't remember lately. Maybe it was related to her hearing impediment. She needed a new hearing aid.

≈

"Miss Parsons, it's time to open the store. I wonder if I might get the key from your desk."

"Of course, Helen. When you're finished with the store, would you please come in here and we'll finish up the financial report."

The door shut, and Marion watched her secretary Helen Wright through the window to the outer office. She didn't want to alarm the young woman about the financial report; she was such a sweet person—always there when anyone needed her. After all, what could Helen do that would make a difference now? The superintendent had made it clear. They had surpassed four hundred students this year. Classrooms were crowded. If something wasn't done soon, they'd have to divide the school and send some of the students, or even entire grades, up to Fairmount Elementary School. She couldn't bear the thought, and she knew that if word got around, everyone would pay attention to that instead of schoolwork. She would keep this problem to herself until the trustee meeting next month.

By her estimates, she and the trustees would have enough time during Christmas break to work on the beginnings of a proposal to present to parents and the Westvale Improvement Committee. It would be just enough time to do all the calculations—what was actually needed to keep the school going and the students together for the next ten years. If they failed, the school would be split down the middle—and so would the community. She couldn't let this happen. She would ask the Mothers' Club for help.

The doorbell rang sooner than Marion had expected the mothers to begin arriving. She arranged a big smile on her face on her way to the door, but when she opened it, she was genuinely happy to see Ivy Schuyler.

"Come in, come in! Don't you look lovely in that dress." She flung open the door and then her arms to the woman who still worked hard for the Mothers' Club even though her children had already moved on to Solvay. "Let me take your coat, Ivy."

Marion felt comfortable with Ivy, and the two women worked shoulder to shoulder in Marion's narrow kitchen finishing the rest of the tea and sandwiches before the doorbell rang again. This time a crowd hovered around Marion's tiny front porch. It was snowing; thick, dark clouds loomed above Cherry Road. Without sunlight on the snow, the front lawn took on a gray hue. Marion wasn't sure why this made her feel blue, but she hurried to close the door as soon as Claire Parsons—the last of this small parade—entered the foyer.

Lunch would be served in the dining room, cookies and tea in the parlor where they could discuss tactics for convincing the neighborhood about the new school addition. Marion and Judge Farnham had already met with the contractors. These additional six rooms would cost more than twice what the original school building had. Times had changed, and Marion knew that the longer they put this off, the less likely it was that they would be able to pass a measure to finance this addition.

"Ladies, we have work to do," she said, and the room fell silent. Fifteen women had managed to squeeze into Marion's cozy living room, and they waited in silence to hear what she had to say. "We need a minimum of six new classrooms. John and I have met with the builders and with the West Genesee Improvement Association, and I'll tell you right now, the numbers are high."

No one spoke. Marion cleared her throat. "In order to finance the entire cost of the addition, which we need to do, a bond measure in the amount of nearly $160,000 will have to pass. The exact amount is $156,900. I would like to—and am suggesting we take action today—form a citizens' committee of the two organizations to further study the proposal. We will have to provide a report and make it available for public record."

"Is this the third or the fourth addition?" Mrs. Stewart smiled, offering Marion a segue to flesh out the story for the rest of the women in the room. She and Marion had gone over the goals for the meeting the night before, listening to the Boston Pops Orchestra in front of the fire. An aroma of wood smoke and peppermint tea still hung in the air. They had gone over the bids and the property tax records, as they would have to be certain about the numbers before taking their case to the public.

"Well, we started with just two classrooms a little over twenty years ago. Not long after we opened the doors, we increased the size of the school to five classrooms, and then twelve classrooms. This is the fourth construction project in just over twenty years, and yet we must have at least four new classrooms. Times have changed, and the numbers are going through the roof. That is the message we must convey to the voters in Westvale."

The Mothers' Club applauded. The back of Marion's throat ached. She felt tired. She would not break down; she never did. She would not let on that for the first time she feared losing the school. "If we can't meet the minimum standards, we might lose some of our grades. They might split the district and send some of the children to Fairmount."

Allie, who had been retired from the Mothers' Club for over ten years but who deemed this meeting important enough to attend anyway, spoke up, "We are still part of the Common School District No. 1, am I right?"

No one answered because everyone knew she was right. They waited for her to continue with her point. "We have a responsibility to serve the children of this neighborhood. If my figures are correct, and I checked with the town hall yesterday, we are growing at the rate of fifty new homes a month."

"We're on the right track here," Marion said. "I'd like someone to take notes, please."

Claire raised her hand to indicate she had a notebook and pencil at work.

"These are the facts," Marion continued. When Marion spoke, everyone listened. "I never thought I'd see this day, but these calculations might even be conservative. According to a preliminary study—and we asked Bob Salisbury, George Hockensmith, Don Martin, and some others to help—the projected population growth indicates a need of twenty-six classrooms by 1960. This is on the basis of thirty pupils per classroom. Our job is to inform the community, to help them understand our needs and why it is critical to keep our school community intact."

Mrs. Ballard raised her hand. "We have an emergency on our hands. Unless anyone objects, I move we unanimously vote to form a citizens' committee effective this afternoon."

"We have less than six months to get the word out," Marion said. "The vote will take place in late February. We want to reach all eligible voters on a regular basis between now and then. That includes all our homeowners, those who pay property taxes, and all of our parents."

It was dark by the time Ivy left. The first to arrive and the last to leave, Ivy was a friend Marion could always count on. Every mother's hand had gone up when she asked who would be willing to host a neighborhood tea—so much to accomplish in the upcoming months to ensure that Cherry Road School would go on as it always had. What if they didn't have enough room by the time September rolled around? If the bond didn't pass, the school or the neighborhood would be sliced up like a pie. Her hands would be tied. Marion sighed into the darkness. What would Papa do?

She decided she would write to Jim Parsons before getting ready for bed. Young Jim had started his second year on the faculty at Berkeley and had invited her to visit. Marion was surprised when the aspiring young writer decided to pursue geography, dropping his editorial position on the school paper. His father, her beloved cousin, Dr. Jim Sr., had been gone now for many years. It hardly seemed possible. She would write to young Jim and thank him for the invitation and plead for a rain check. How many years had it been since she and the eager boy had ridden the trolley from Pasadena to

Los Angeles and journeyed on the glass-bottomed boat to Catalina Island? Even then, he had reminded her so much of his dad, full of fun and so bright. The trip would have to wait; California would still be there next summer.

Marion turned out the lights in the kitchen at 303 Cherry Road and headed up the stairs. She liked to sleep in the south bedroom where the cardinals gathered on the porch roof in the morning, searching for her daily gift of suet. She could watch them after sunrise from her writing desk. For now, sleep would not come soon enough.

Marion Parsons' house at 303 Cherry Road

Chapter Twenty-One

Farms, Families, and Baby Booms

Be tethered in native pastures.

—Henry James

By 1950 there were nearly six hundred students enrolled in the school, and an additional one hundred students were forecast for enrollment the following year. Student numbers were predicted to top eight hundred by the mid-1950s. Nationally, close to 90 percent of the new population of Baby Boom children were now enrolled in public schools.[3] At the time of the last addition to Cherry Road School, they couldn't imagine ever needing more room.

The people of Westvale were finally put to the test when they were asked to vote on a bond of $156,900 to add six more rooms to the school. Just how much were they willing to give to keep their school in concert with the times? The Mothers' Club and the West Genesee Improvement Association joined forces and conducted an extensive study of the proposal. Then they launched a diligent public relations campaign.

The bond passed by a landslide, and within the next two years, Cherry Road School had twenty-one classrooms, two kindergartens, three offices, and a new playground. A new school bus made three

Ned and Emma Jerome and their children

trips a day delivering youngsters to the school. Ready to meet the future head-on, Cherry Road had been founded to support a growing community and a world changing in ways that would have been hard to imagine just one generation earlier. The people of Westvale were earnest in their desire to keep up, to provide their children with an education for the twentieth century. Without the participation of parents and abundant community partnerships, the red-brick school might have had a different fate.

Westvale had become a new kind of place, but it still thrived on the traditions of the past. Farms gone, the new ideal was a nuclear family—different from the old days when several generations of a family, farmhands, and housekeepers might have all lived under one roof in a big farmhouse. But the priority was still community, and its heart was still the school.

In some ways, they were still a small community. If a car went by on the street, residents still ran to the window to see who it might be. Some of the families had been here for a long time now, over thirty years. The Parsons Family, the Jeromes, the Schuylers, and the Terrys had been in the area for more than one hundred years. Most of the families of Westvale still knew each other, were related, or both.

Marion hadn't been up to Myrtle Hill since early in the summer in 1951 when she, Martha, and Grace had spent the afternoon weeding and pruning the family plot. They left long stems of her mother's prize roses lying next to her headstone. Now on this October afternoon, the flowers were still there, dried and stiff. Her eighth-grade girls stood quietly by the edge of the plot, waiting for her to say something. She had volunteered to take the older scouts this year, knowing, or perhaps sensing, there might not be too many more opportunities.

"We came here today for our first Girl Scout meeting because I want to share something with you about the past, but not the past

Parsons farmhouse. Sarah Jerome Parsons grew up in this house. Francis and Sarah raised their children here, then their son, Charles F. and his wife, Vernie Drawbridge Parsons, raised their family in this house. It is gone now, a victim of vandals and fire.

Another shot of the Parsons' farmhouse with carriage barn

you might imagine. The badge we will earn for our first activity is a skill-building badge, and we will call it our artifact badge. We'll be learning about artifacts that tell us about the past." Marion pulled her hankie out of her pocket and wiped her nose. The cold air had yielded to snow, and her nose dripped faster with every degree the temperature dropped.

She climbed out of the grassy plot, slippery with wet maple leaves. Straightening her gloves, she motioned for the girls to gather round on the side of the trail that wound through the cemetery. She put her hand on Sara's shoulder, and the girl snuggled up to her side. She wanted the girls to relax and learn, and she could see they were cold but keeping quiet about their icy toes and frosty fingers.

"Listen carefully, girls, and you might hear the sound of the snow ticking through the fir trees over there."

The huddled group stood silently, like a grove of young fir trees swaying in the wind. Karen raised her hand. "All I can hear is the wind, Miss Parsons."

"That's right, Karen. And in that wind is the story of those who came before, who lived on this hill—not my parents or my grandpar-

Clockwise: Above left: Parsons and Jerome gathering. Dr. Jim Parsons on far left standing next to Marion

Above right: Sunday picnic circa 1915 at Cedarvale. Martha, Willis, Marion, Grace Parsons. Claude Cole sitting

Left: Unknown, Marion, Martha Parsons, Unknown, Claude and Grace Cole

Gloria Luce, Marion Parsons, Helen Cole, Grace Parsons Cole, Ethel (last name unknown), Peter Cole (in front)

ents, but the Indians whose land this was, once upon a time."

The girls looked over their shoulders and down the road—they looked back at Miss Parsons, waiting for the rest of the story.

"We must always remember to be respectful of the land, to be stewards of the land that belonged to others—even though our ancestors and our family are buried in it. These grave markers name my family—but what about the families who lived here thousands of years ago? Where are their markers, do you suppose? What is left to mark their passage over the land? And what were their lives like?" She looked at the girls' faces, bright red with the cold. "What do you suppose they grieved for, or hoped for?"

The new girl from Split Rock raised her hand. Then more hands started to pop up, and everyone was eager to say something. "Is this an Indian cemetery too?"

They had forgotten the cold, the light autumn snow. "That's a very good question. And people can discover answers to questions like that by finding artifacts, examining them. An artifact can be something from the past, a bowl or a tool for example, that has been left behind. An artifact tells us a story about the past. And yes, artifacts have been found in this area that could possibly indicate that people lived right on this hill, thousands of years ago, long before the white people came."

The scout troop had moved in as close as they could without knocking her over. "So we can learn about them by uncovering pieces of … artifacts."

Two girls in the back of the crowd had crouched down in the dirt and were digging on the side of the cemetery road.

"Girls, we're not going to dig here." She smiled at Jean Miller, who had come along to help and to bring some of the girls in her car.

It would be dusk soon, and Marion wanted to get her Scouts back to the school in time for the tea party they had planned for today's meeting. "Just remember, you never know what you might find that others may have overlooked for centuries. One time, out behind my father's barn, my sisters and I were digging a spot for a new vegetable garden, and we found a grave marker, a tiny headstone buried next to a blackberry thicket."

"Whose was it, Miss Parsons?"

"We aren't sure, Marilyn. It could have belonged to a family two hundred years ago or two thousand years ago. There was no writing on it; just two small symbols that looked like stick people. Each one seemed to be holding something."

The wind picked up, and Marion noticed the sun had fallen behind the hill. "Girls, by the time we are finished with our work on this badge, perhaps you will be able to hear the sound of the snow falling."

They stood still as statues, listening and waiting for their next directions from Miss Parsons.

Next week she'd take them up Jerome Hill. She would show them the old fence she and Belle discovered last week, the rusted cast-iron tool they found buried beneath rotting leaves. If the weather was right, she'd let them lie on their backs and watch snow fall out of the sky.

By the end of the war, the farming era along the Genesee Turnpike was over. But not for the Jerome Dairy—they were just getting under way. Officially established in the early 1920s by brothers Harry "Dutch" Jerome and Edwin "Ned" Jerome, the dairy had started out by selling milk to neighbors who came by with jugs to be filled with fresh raw milk. Then Ned bought a milk wagon and hitched it to one of his work horses, and they began delivering.

Van Jerome, delivering milk

He ladled fresh milk from the cans in the wagon into glass bottles for the customers. They painted Jerome Dairy on the side of the wagon in big sweeping letters. Later on, Ned stayed back at the farm, and his son Van, daughter Connie, nephew Jim, and friend Clayton Burritt delivered the milk out of the back of an old Packard, where

Ned Jerome and the Jerome Dairy Wagon

the milk cans were packed in ice. Then they expanded and added an old Studebaker to their fleet.

During the war, Ned and Clayton made deliveries from the horse and wagon again to conserve on gasoline and help the war effort. After the war, when gas rationing ended, Jerome Dairy delivered with milk vans again. As a young boy, Van had been sent up to the barn in the early morning darkness before school to herd cows. As a grown man, back from the war, he was so reliable, the people of Westvale could set their clocks by the young and energetic man strolling up to their back doors before sunrise. He'd put fresh bottles of milk into the little milk cabinets that had been installed in each customer's house—replacing empty bottles from the day before—and close the pint-size door, always unlocked. On the inside, families opened a connecting door and retrieved fresh milk in time for breakfast. Mornings were synonymous with the clanging of glass bottles and the whistling milkman. It took time, but people began to enjoy the pleasantness of life again as the strain of war faded and postwar life bloomed.

The last of Willis Parsons' farm, the big old farmhouse on the corner of Genesee Street and Parsons Drive, was sold to a dentist around 1955. Peter had been living there with his family. His wife, like many young mothers of the day, was anxious to get away from the old houses and the old ways and the old people. The dentist turned the family homestead into a medical center—painted the front door red, gutted the inside of the house, and took out the big staircase—rendering the house unrecognizable.

Jerome Dairy Farmhouse, burned to the ground by careless tenants in the 1970s

Jerome Dairy Barn

Chapter Twenty-Two
Good-bye, Miss Parsons

The end of a melody is not its goal: but nonetheless, if the melody had not reached its end it would not have reached its goal either.
—Friedrich Nietzche

THE KNOCK ON THE DOOR woke Marion. She jumped from the chair and ran to the door. Ever since the war, ever since a knock on the door could mean David or Peter or any one of her boys had been killed, she couldn't bear the sound. Though many years had passed since the war, and Peter was now married with a child of his own, a certain fear still surged with every unexpected knock.

"Telegram for Marion Parsons," the young man was cheerful and she watched him skip down the flagstone walk toward the driveway.

She sat down to read the telegram, twice, and then closed her eyes, put her head all the way back on the rocking chair, and rocked back and forth, creating a melody of the familiar creaks of the floorboards and the chair. Mrs. Kinney had died last week. Amy's message was short, but she read between the short lines of the telegram that things had been hectic and her grandchildren were coming for Thanksgiving. It would probably be the whole family.

How long had it been since she was a young woman at Mrs. Kinney's table on the other side of the world? So long she could barely remember what any of them looked like, even though she and Amy had remained close friends all these years through their regular correspondence—and so many canceled trips. She didn't blame Amy for possibly forgetting about her—busy with her children and now grandchildren coming along one after the other. And Mabel, dear cousin Mabel, had given up on her coming back to California for another summer jaunt years ago. They had had a wonderful time when she and cousin Esther came to visit Syracuse, several times now since Marion had spent the summer with them in orange country. What a summer that had been.

It was getting dark, but Marion kept rocking even though her arms felt chilly. She had a rhythm going, and like Peter's little Nancy often pointed out, it had the best creak of any rocking chair ever. She would keep on until she could go no longer. Isn't that what she always did?

Pshaw. What about this self-pity? No more of that. Tomorrow she would begin the report cards, and this year there were almost seven hundred. It hardly seemed possible there would be this many, and they were such delightful children, every one of them. What about that Ballard boy? She smiled to think how far he had come. She would miss them all, and her teachers too, when she retired at the end of the school year. Thank goodness for Fred Fuller stepping up to be the new principal. The school and the children would be in good hands with him and Jean Miller, who would serve as his vice principal.

When she opened her eyes again, the room was dark and cold. Were those morning birds singing in the Stewarts' backyard? Had she slept all night in the chair? She eased herself up and shuffled over to the stairs. One step at a time, she was careful not to slip on the polished wood Mrs. Loverock kept so clean and shiny. Without taking off her dress, she placed her hearing aid on the dresser and lay down on the bed, covering herself with the bedspread. She slept a bottomless sleep until the sun stole through her white lace curtains.

❦

It was more than just the last day of school. The year was 1952 and it would be Marion's last day as principal and supervisor of Cherry Road School. She'd be around to help Mr. Fuller get his footing over the summer months and next fall, but it wouldn't be the same.

People kept asking what she was going to do next, what about that trip out West with Martha? She had told everyone she was going, had planned on going. But now the doctor had all these things to declare, about her health, about her memory lapses. She couldn't remember exactly. So she answered by saying, "It will be an extensive trip. We'll take our time and drive across the northern region of the country. We'll visit some of the sites where I stopped on my excursion back in the twenties."

For now, there was too much going on to think about a journey. She had to get through today. She had to express her gratitude to the teachers and the staff.

Marion stood in her closet examining the row of suits and dresses. She had left her hearing aid lying on the desk, but she could still hear the phone ringing. It would have to wait, whoever it was; it was too early in the morning, and if she didn't get going, she would be late for her last day. She pulled her dressing gown tighter around her waist. It was important she settle on the right dress. She wanted to be comfortable, and she wanted to give a professional appearance. She had given up trying to look pretty, and that was fine with her. But the truth was, she did not want this day to be her last day. Her memory was just fine, no matter what the doctor said.

She paused in the vestibule where there were cupboards filled with hats and gloves, pocketbooks, and her fox stole. She pulled on a pair of light-colored cotton gloves, then took them off and tried on her brown cotton gloves with the buttons. She decided against gloves and then picked out a hat pin and adjusted her straw hat with the silk flowers, arranging the veil so it would lay even with the front of her hair. No, she'd wear the Buster Brown. The phone rang again.

"Miss Parsons, there's a dog running up and down the hallway. What should we do?"

"I'll be there in a few minutes, Helen, close the doors to each classroom if they aren't shut already."

She cleared her throat and looked around the den one more time, gazing out the dining room window at crowds of children walking up Cherry Road toward the school. She would leave by the back door. On the way out, she checked the milk box and found the extra pint of milk she had asked Van to leave for today. How could she have forgotten that David and his family were coming down from Rochester for the weekend?

The phone was ringing again as she closed the back door. Her toe caught on a basket in the middle of the step, and she almost tripped, almost fell. Marion hung on to the post for a minute to catch herself and then bent down to pick up a small wicker hamper. A tiny bouquet of forget-me-nots tied in a lavender ribbon tumbled onto the walkway. She pulled back a checkered cloth covering a pile of individually wrapped packets, each little packet tied with a string that held a note card with a child's signature.

She carried the basket and her pocketbook through the breezeway and into the garage, placing them on the backseat of her car. Today she would drive.

By the time she arrived at the front of the school, children should already have been in their classrooms, but a crowd had gathered inside the open door. A small girl in a checkered dress shouted, "It's Miss Parsons!"

She sat in the car watching children file out onto the front step. She should reprimand the girl, reprimand them all for being out in the hallway when they should be in class. She pulled herself out of the Chevrolet and closed the door. But before she could say anything, before she reached the steps, everyone was upon her at once, telling her about the big dog that had gotten into the building and that no one had been able to catch the dog until Mrs. Haskins found a rope and coaxed the shaggy creature into her classroom.

"Can we keep the dog?" The girl did not appear to be aware of her infractions. None of these children did. Mercy.

"How did the dog get into the school?" Marion asked. Peering through the window over their heads she could see Helen standing just inside the door. Why didn't she come out here and shoo these children back to their classrooms?

The Hamlin girl spoke up. "He was on the playground, Miss Parsons, and looked like he had been there all night. He was thirsty, so we brought him in to give him some water, and then he just started running up and down the hall."

She examined the growing brood of children looking at her expectantly. The bell had not been rung because she had not been there to ring it—the flag had not been raised.

Fourth grade teacher Elsie Haskins appeared at the top of the stairs. "Miss Parsons? I had a ham sandwich, and I gave it to the dog and put him on my old winter sweater on the floor in the back of the room. I broke the sandwich in pieces. Maybe the children would like to feed the dog a few more bites of the sandwich."

The crowd moved in a swarm behind Marion and then streamed up the stairs toward Mrs. Haskins' room. Marion laughed, her gay laugh, switched her pocketbook from one arm to the other, and started up the stairs toward her office. "Elsie, I'm going to let you take it from here." She was wiping tears from her eyes when she removed her hat and suit jacket and took her place behind her desk.

A pile of letters had been placed in the center.

> *May 25, 1952*
> Dear Marion,
>
> Just a friendly greeting to help you celebrate this event in your life.
>
> How pleased our fathers could be as they knew their "frail" daughters have survived and withstood.
>
> I will always be deeply thankful for assisting in your Church School Kindergarten work and the background and training you gave me. I can't seem to retire from it and had 13 today.
>
> The best in the world to you and be sure to enjoy retirement.
>
> Sincerely,
> Grace Cain

Dear Miss Parsons:

It was with great pride that the Fairfield Garden Club had planted a Schwedler maple, in your honor.

It stands in front of Cherry Road School where all who see it each day will think of you who have done so much for our school, our children and our community.

A Schwedler maple is a very popular tree in North America as a street tree, because it transplants well, and is tolerant of city conditions. It is inclined to have a low head and produces dense shade. The bark is very dark. The terminal buds in winter are fat and red. The spring leaves are deep red, changing to a dark green. The flowers are yellow-tinged with purple.

We are happy to honor you in this way,
Sincerely,
Doreen S. Graves
Recording Secretary

She spent the day going from classroom to classroom—to the janitor's office, the library, walking the halls of Cherry Road School and soaking in the sounds and smells. At the end of the day she returned to her office and shut the door behind her. Marion pulled out the top drawer of her desk and took out her address book and a packet of hearing aid batteries and placed them into a straw basket she had left under the desk for this purpose. She picked up her father's letter opener and the letters and put them in the basket. She opened a side drawer and shuffled through a pile of envelopes and files. She would leave these for now. She pulled roll after roll of school picture proofs from the bottom drawer. She had planned to take those today, just to be sure not to forget. These were her copies, her pictures of every student who had ever attended Cherry Road. She unfurled one of the rolls and smiled at some of the faces she hadn't seen in years, faces of children who were now adults, who had fought in a war. Some had come home to Westvale to raise their families; some of their children were in the school right now. Nancy, who spent so much time with Marion at her house, begging to hear stories "about the olden days" out of Marion's "think," would start kindergarten next year. It didn't seem possible.

"Miss Parsons?"

"Elsie, I'm sorry, I didn't see you there—"

"That's all right, Miss Parsons. I just want to let you know that one of my boys took the dog with him at lunchtime, took that dog home. I thought maybe he'd come back with an angry mother, but instead he came back and said, 'Mrs. Haskins, guess what? We found the owners, and they gave me a twenty-dollar reward, and my mother says I can spend it any way I like!' And that dog, he got my sandwich, and the boy got twenty dollars."

They laughed and held their stomachs. Wiping her eyes, Elsie started to walk out the door but turned and said, "You can teach a lot of compassion through an animal, Miss Parsons. Seems like stray animals always wind up in my room."

> She was the sweetest thing. All the teachers were, and Cherry Road is one of the fondest memories I have of childhood. I can remember the name of every teacher in that school. Miss Parsons was so revered. You just stood taller and walked better when she went by. When she came down the hall or into your classroom, she just commanded respect.
> —Sara Davis, class of 1953

"Wait, Elsie, I ..."

"Yes, Miss Parsons?"

"You'll come by for tea, won't you?"

"I sure will. I sure will."

She had said goodbye to everyone, but there would be more retirement festivities. Marion stood to close the windows. She was tired, but she decided to walk one more time through the empty building.

The first door she opened was the kindergarten classroom where she had taught first grade the first year here, had shared those duties with Miss Cummerford. There were toys in the play corner that she recognized from the old school. The little hutch cabinet and a table and chairs were what Cousin Herbert had made for the children when they were Tiny Tots in her father's parlor. She squatted down and rested on the miniature chair, and the years stretched out in her mind, unfolding into the past. Where had they gone? She would have to tell Martha she wouldn't be able to drive across the country. It was

---

The Merchants National Bank & Trust Company
OF SYRACUSE
TWO HUNDRED SIXTEEN SOUTH WARREN STREET
Syracuse 1, New York

Kenneth F. Barton
Trust Officer

May 7, 1952

Miss Marion Parsons
303 Cherry Road
Syracuse, New York

Dear Miss Parsons:

I consider that I personally am very fortunate to have the privilege of advising you that a resolution was unanimously passed at the annual meeting of the School Board held on May 6, 1952, expressing to you the very deep and sincere appreciation of the residents of the district for the long and faithful service which you have rendered to the School and the community and in particular, to the children of the Westvale area.

I am sorry that you were not present at the meeting so that you could have realized from the manner in which this resolution was adopted how very deep the feeling of the people was and in what esteem you are held in the community.

Sincerely,

Kenneth Barton

> As the second principal, my father was a viable part of the early years of Cherry Road, but the efforts of [Miss Parsons] were … well, she started and built the school and transitioned it from a farming community to a suburban community, which is a significant change. If we forget her legacy, somebody has dropped the ball. She was an amazing woman. —Jay Fuller, Class of 1956

becoming more difficult for her to travel. A trip of that magnitude would be out of the question. She hoped her sister wouldn't be too disappointed.

By the time Marion returned to her office for the last time, the sun had gone down. She took the bell from the desk and set it in the basket, careful not to bend the pictures. She checked to see if the windows were down in the outer office. It was then she noticed that the blackout curtains were still there. They had been there almost a decade. How could she not have noticed? They had been important safety measures during the war, a way to hide from the enemy behind darkness. She would ask Mr. Lamphere if he could take them down. They wouldn't be needing those any more. The war had been over for a long time, and it felt like a dream, all of it.

> At the time of Marion Parsons' retirement, there had been fourteen eighth-grade trips, including several trips to New York City, a trip to Buffalo, to Niagara Falls, and to Detroit. In 1940, twenty students went on an Easter trip to New York City.

The Mothers' Club would oversee the retirement festivities. The club had grown and flourished over the years, had become the steam in the engine that kept the red-brick school growing and maintaining standards of excellence, helping to make it one of the highest-ranked schools in the state.

Syracuse Post-Standard
May 24, 1952

The Mothers' Club of Cherry Road School joins with the community of Westvale to present this testimonial luncheon in honor of Miss Marion Parsons, who for twenty-six years has been principal of Cherry Road School.

Friend, confidante, and inspiration to countless children, Miss Parsons has served the community in more than a professional way. She is our well loved neighbor and friend.

Keeping constantly abreast of the latest trends in education, she has kept the standards of Cherry Road School high, giving our children fine instruction coupled with a happy school experience.

The founder of the Mothers' Club in 1927, she has been its inspiration and staunch supporter throughout its years of service, working with the mothers of our community toward the betterment of our school and closer parent-teacher relationships.

All of Westvale salutes Miss Marion Parsons—a gallant lady. We wish her much success and happiness in her retirement as she has given those whom she has served over the years.

The Westvale community loved Miss Parsons so much, they all wanted to throw her party after party for her retirement. Marion's dear friend Ivy Schuyler was no exception, and she took this special occasion to write a tribute to Miss Parsons, produced and performed by community members, teachers, and students in the school gymnasium. The place was packed.

A Tribute to Miss Marion Parsons
May 24, 1952
Tribute written by Ivy Schuyler, Directed and Narrated by Mrs. James Cooper
Music Director: Mrs. Fred Fuller
Artist: Judy Manniello

CRS Alma Mater, by John Garofalo, sung to the tune of America the Beautiful
Surrounded by the hills and dales
Beneath fair skies of blue
In Westvale, stands our school,
that's been
To all of us so true

We came to thee in infancy
For knowledge, love and truth
We learned in school—
"The Golden Rule"
To carry on through youth
And when in life, we reach our goal
We'll ask the Lord to bless
Our Alma Mater—that to us
Has brought such happiness

Chorus:	Oh, Cherry Road, we'll honor thee
As swift years hurry by
Our love for thee-eternally
Is one that shall not die.

Prologue
In the vale of Onondaga
Lies the friendly town of Geddes
Once a neighborhood of farms,
Lowing cattle, plowing horses,
And in orchards, cherry trees
White as snow with beauteous blossoms.

On a Spring day in an orchard
Walked a girl petite and lovely
Walked the daughter of the Parsons.
As the blossoms fell about her
So her thoughts flew here and there
Dreams she had of how the future
Held for her some service rare.

So to school and on to college
Many were the hours and long
Preparation for her future
On her lips a prayer and song

Happy days with many friendships
Long, sad days when health would fail
But she always held her head high
And her spirit did prevail.

Once again she walked in beauty
Cherry blossoms all about her
Marion, proud with her diploma
Friends and family all about her.

Hers the greatest gift of friendship
Hers the always winning smile
Hers the ringing sound of laughter
All that made her life worthwhile.

In the little one room schoolhouse
She their mistress, Mistress Marion
With the little ones about her
Started out upon life's mission
There she taught the ABC's
And other lessons more important
How to face life's harder moments
With a smile of strength and courage.

Now a glimpse of the little schoolhouse
Where the Parsons went to school
Andres, Neals, Jeromes and Schuylers
Trudging down the dusty turnpike
Seeking knowledge, throwing balls
Pulling hair with shrieks of laughter
But with deep respect for teacher
Dear Miss Marion whom they loved.

Plans for the New School
Years elapse, and Geddes farmland
Changes hands, new names appear

Schuyler Lawns and Parsons Drive
Westvale with its lovely homes
Where a man may plant a tree
And see it grow to maturity
Where a woman may raise a child
And see it have security.
Once cherry blossoms bloomed in Spring
Now the children laugh and sing.

So Miss Marion's dreams grew broader
As new families appear
She envisions a new building
Ministering to her children.
She invites a group of mothers
In to share her wondrous vision
And they talk as women always
Talk until their project grows
And they work at ice cream socials
Plays and parties, cards and shows.

Song of the Workmen
We are the carpenters and the masons
Hard the work and loud the noise.
We are building for the future
Generations of girls and boys.

Miss Parsons' Office After School
After another busy day
Miss Parsons pauses at her desk
She wonders if it's all worthwhile
If she has given of her best

"Oh that pounding
Another addition means more confusion
The first grade is meeting but half a day

Some of the classes are out of the building
No wonder my hair is turning gray.
New families are coming by the dozens
Today I enrolled two sets of twins
If triplets join our school tomorrow
I'll know I'm punished for my sins.

Epilogue
What shall we call this school we've builded
Out of the hopes and plans of our teacher
She the author and inspiration
Marion Parsons the little dreamer

We will name it for the orchards of Geddes
We will call it Cherry Road School.

Yes in the orchards we've builded our school
And though the trees are no longer there
We seem to see a woman reaching
To pick the ripe and luscious fruit
Not the fruit of the cherry trees
But the ripe fruit of her labors.

Our little teacher wants no praise
No spoken word or eulogies.
She doesn't need them. Every day
She'll meet them out upon the street
Or on the bus young office girls
Or those with books and cap and gown
And lads in uniform come home.
And when her lovely trip is o'er
And Westvale's hills again she'll see
She'll open wide her wide front door
To chubby lad with grubby prize
Or little girl who's skinned her knee.

Song
We are the parents of Westvale
Proud of our girls and boys
Grateful to Marion Parsons
Who shared their sorrows and joys
    We are the Cherry Road graduates
    Honoring our Principal's name
    Trying to live as she taught us
    Always to play the game.
We are the students of Cherry Road
All of us wanting to say
How much we love Miss Parsons
On this her honored day.
    We are her neighbors and friends
    All of us gathered here
    Homage to pay and our love to express
    To someone we hold dear.

Chapter Twenty-Three
My Aunt Marion

*We are made wise not by the recollection of our past,
but by the responsibility for our future.*

—George Bernard Shaw

Aunt Marion looked after my father, Peter; my Aunt Helen and Uncle David in their childhood—was their mother too. She offered the same love for their children as well, including little Nancy—me. They called her Nattie, or Nantie Marion. They loved her dearly. For my cousins and me, she was a grandmother. We called her Aunt Marion. We all love her to this day.

Aunt Marion was a small woman, but strong—the most solid woman I have ever known. One would think, cuddling up to her, that she wore the boned corsets of her mother's day. The truth is, her girth was solid muscle. She chopped kindling and fire logs, carried wood, dug in her garden, walked to and from school every day.

She smelled of sweet talcum powder. If I catch the scent of lilac, I think of her and the feel of her soft skin. She loved the small pleasures in life—always game for a fire in the fireplace, a batch of molasses cookies in the kitchen, or a ride to Marble Farms for a double-dipped ice-cream cone. Nights by the fire call to mind the click clack of her knitting needles, the smell of something baking, a heaping bowl of fresh popcorn. After she retired, we would watch slide shows of her recent travels whenever I spent the night. She and Aunt Martha often toured points of interest on the eastern seaboard—

Mother, me, Aunt Marion, 1952 (school in background)

Amish Country, the Jamestown Settlement.

I spent many overnights at Marion's, where I played dress-up in her closets, wrapped myself in a fox stole or a lamb's wool cape, topped it off with a veiled felt hat—a princess crown with feathers. If I let Aunt Marion down—told a white lie, or a bigger lie—those moments are painfully emblazoned in my memory. I try to be honest, careful of others, and true to my word, if for no other reason than to mitigate my youthful shortcomings, for the times I let her down. I know now there are others who feel the same way.

Aunt Marion taught me to have fun, sing songs, play games, live just on the edge of reckless; to be social, have tea parties, invite my friends, quarter the sandwiches on the diagonal; to feed the birds, eat ice cream, and order exotic flavors to see what they taste like. Because of her, I have a lust for what's interesting about the past, a curiosity about technologies of the future.

Mother and Marion have lunch in the backyard, circa 1947 (note milkdoor by the back door)

I never heard a complaint from her. For all the time I knew her, she wore a hearing aid. In those days, hearing aids did not hide conveniently behind one's ear. Hers was a square box fastened to the top of her slip and brassiere, the size and shape of a cell phone. From there, a wire ran up her chest, around her neck, and joined to a thimble-sized button in her ear. This earpiece was kept in place by a sort of crookneck attachment. Having watched her talk on the phone from the day I was born, it never seemed odd to me. Didn't all great aunts talk into a phone as though it were a microphone? To others, it must have seemed peculiar to see this buckshot of a woman with the receiver of a telephone at her breast, speaking with great authority into the mouthpiece. Instead of ears and eyes in the back of her head, it may have appeared as though she had ears and eyes all over the place.

I could feel Marion approaching before the sound of her jingling car keys, her laughter, and her merriment filled the room. Her face radiated cheerfulness, and her good humor was infectious. When she was angry, that spark endured but changed to a stern, dark flicker.

She loved to play games—board games, card games, and lawn games. She took her bridge and her croquet seriously. She and I would play two-deck canasta for hours. She was never too busy to spend time playing with children. Though some houses had televisions in those days, they were turned on only occasionally. She taught my cousin Barbara and me how to knit. We learned by having knitting races. We didn't need a prize—winning was enough.

> Marion took Helen and me to the World's Fair. She drove us in the car, and we stayed at a hotel. We were there for three days, and I can tell you that there were a lot of people there. We walked and walked and saw so many different things. It was amazing, the most amazing place I had ever been, the most amazing thing I had ever done. It was the first time, I think, I ever saw a television. It was at the RCA building, I believe. By the time we got back to Syracuse, we were pooped. Marion must have been pooped too, but she never said so. —Peter Cole, class of 1940

She loved to have tea parties in the backyard. In summertime, she would set up the card table and serve iced tea and bacon, lettuce, and tomato sandwiches. She'd host birthday parties, where we played serious croquet.

She never let go of her love of travel, her longing to see the world. She adjusted to her circumstances, I believe, by taking her students with her. Sometimes she took her nieces and nephews, sometimes an entire eighth-grade class. My father didn't remember as many details about those days as some of his classmates, but he did remember his magnificent excursion with his Aunt Marion and his older sister, Helen, to the World's Fair in 1939.

The 1939–40 New York World's Fair covered over 1,200 acres of Flushing Meadows-Corona Park on Long Island. At the same time, the Golden Gate International Exposition was held in San Francisco. The theme of the New York World's Fair was based on the future—its opening slogan: "Dawn of a New Day."

After Aunt Marion retired, she kept a picture of every one of her students in her bureau drawers. On rainy days after her retirement we'd lay them out on the card table and go through every one. She'd tell me each student's name and stories about them—I wanted to hear about it all, over and over again. She never tired of showing me the pictures or telling me the stories.

Marion and Cherry Road School class of 1950 on their way to New York City!

Chapter Twenty-Four
Marion

People will forget what you said, people will forget what you did, but people will never forget how you made them feel.

—Maya Angelou

Nancy flew past the den window on her two-wheeled bike. Marion heard the crunching of gravel as her niece disappeared around the back of the house, followed by the clatter of the garage door opening and closing. They'd have cream cheese and Ritz crackers. She'd want a fire. Even though it was too hot outside for a fire on this September afternoon, Marion filled the cubbyhole next to the fireplace with enough wood for a nice long fire. They would look at the slides from the trip to Amish country. Nancy had seen them before, along with the Williamsburg slides, but she didn't seem to tire of the pictures.

Later on, after the fire was set and the popcorn popped, after they had examined each and every one of the student pictures again and Marion had told Nancy all their names, Marion leaned back in her rocker. She was tired. Without warning, Nancy climbed in her lap. She had grown too big to ride on her lap, but Marion let her stay, let her six-year-old legs hang down the front of hers, let the young girl rest her head on her shoulders.

"Nattie Marion?"

She rocked the rocker until it creaked. "Yes?"

"Tell me a story out of your think ... about the olden days."

"A winter story or a summer story?"

"A winter story! One where you get snowed in! And the horse and buggy."

"Let me think …" Marion ran her fingers through the girl's hair, rubbing the back of her small neck. "It was the dead of winter, and all we children were at school. We went to a one-room schoolhouse on Terry Road. In the wintertime, boys were supposed to take turns stoking the fire in the potbellied stove. They didn't mind one bit because it gave them a chance to stretch their legs and look out the window. I remember Cousin Herbert raising his hand, offering to go out to the woodshed. No one minded, really. That wood was heavy and filled with prickly slivers and dirt. Whoever went would have to get dressed against the cold, so it was often Herbert or Ned who kept the stove going.

"That day, when it was time to go home, it was snowing and blowing so hard, we only got as far as the Jerome's. We were too cold to go all the way home. But instead of going inside the house, we cousins went in the barn and, on a dare, we all climbed up to the hayloft. Someone thought it would be more fun up there. Quite the contrary, it was cold as ice! So just as we were ready to climb back down and go into Aunt Mary's where it was warm, and where there might be a plate of molasses cookies, Cousin Guy spotted something under a bale of hay over in the corner. We all ran over to see what was inside the mysterious wooden box. Guy had the box, and he fiddled and fiddled to get it open—his fingers were probably nearly frozen. Were we surprised when what looked to be a ruby necklace fell onto the floor of the hayloft. Sure enough, it was Grandma Julia's garnet and crystal necklace, the one she wore at her wedding."

Marion paused and the creaking sounds of the old rocker filled the silence.

She went on. "We never did find out how it got up there. No one pressed the subject—everyone was just glad to have the necklace found, and our grandmother had not even known it was missing."

"They didn't find out who stole it?"

"There had been some tramps that came through the summer before, and someone thought they saw two men coming out of the barn one morning and guessed they could have been sleeping in the hayloft. They believed that when Uncle Jim went up to take his horse out for an early walk, he had rousted the men.

"Anyway, we were all mighty scared, even though the boys wouldn't admit to it. When we finally settled down with cookies and milk, Ned made up a story about a family who secretly lived in the barn and led their lives at night while the rest of us slept. By the time we were ready to go home, it was dark, and we all were too frightened to go outside. So Uncle Jim hitched up his horse and sleigh. When we rode in the sleigh on nights like that, we'd wrap ourselves in thick woolen blankets to keep from freezing, and if we were good, he'd let us jingle the sleigh bells. How Martha loved those bells; so we let her ring them all the way home because she had been terrified by the story of the family who lived in the barn in the dark of night."

Nancy had fallen asleep, and so had Marion's legs, but she kept on rocking until she could no longer feel her toes or her feet, until the fire went out and all she could hear was an occasional car drive past on Cherry Road.

After she retired, the years stretched out behind Marion like a ribbon unfurled before its time. Where had the time gone? She had told her sister they could not take this trip they had planned for so long. She had worked hard, dreaming about the trip, had held on to a faith that one day she might finally fulfill her duties. Over the years it became more and more difficult to leave, even for one day. Papa would have been proud of what had become of his dreams, of the red brick school he never got to see. When he died, the cherry orchard still covered this part of Cherry Road. Why, there was hardly any Cherry Road when he passed. It felt like a streak of summer lightning had flashed and in that short time houses had gone up all over what had been their farm, Papa's farm. Now, it was a real neighborhood. Buses went by the house day and night. Sirens blared nearby.

There was a time she used to pray silently on her way to school; sometimes out loud into the wind. She prayed her father would come back, that a letter would come from Tom, for the strength to keep going. She prayed mostly for the children—the girl who had to return to Bulgaria and live behind the Iron Curtain; the girl who had contracted polio and would now live in an iron lung; for the family whose father had to walk miles in the dark to work a second job at Crucible Steel. The years had turned all of it into a dream.

These people were her family. She wouldn't leave them even if she could. She and her sister Martha took short trips around the eastern part of the country. Martha came to live with Marion in the little house on Cherry Road after her own retirement. Together, they enjoyed the company of their cousins and visits from family and former students. Some invited, some just taking a chance, they would knock on the front door of the quaint, shingled and shuttered house, waiting to hear the jolly greeting, to feel the familiar warmth of their Aunt Marion or their Miss Parsons.

After she retired, the days were long. She cared for her roses and her peonies. She cared for the birds—cardinals and chickadees, robins—she hooked rugs and lunched with friends. But she missed having children to care for every day. She missed her teachers, the Mothers' Club; she missed meetings and social events. The stories she told herself during the day and to her nieces and nephews at bedtime were more and more about the past. Her dreams were filled with people and places she hadn't seen in thirty years. She had longed for love. When former students Sara and Mary Beth knocked on her front door one day, giggling and nervous when she invited them inside, she felt their love and affection in a new way. She had done what was asked of her by those she loved. She had been obedient, a good daughter and a good neighbor. She was rewarded with love. She had rejoiced in the successes and ached for the pains of hundreds of children. When Mrs. Kinney had read her fortune in the tea leaves all those years ago, Marion had mistaken 'someone' special to mean one person, but she had found her own true love in the life she was meant to live right there in the old cherry orchard.

Marion Parsons died on February 7, 1972. She never returned to Omak or to California.

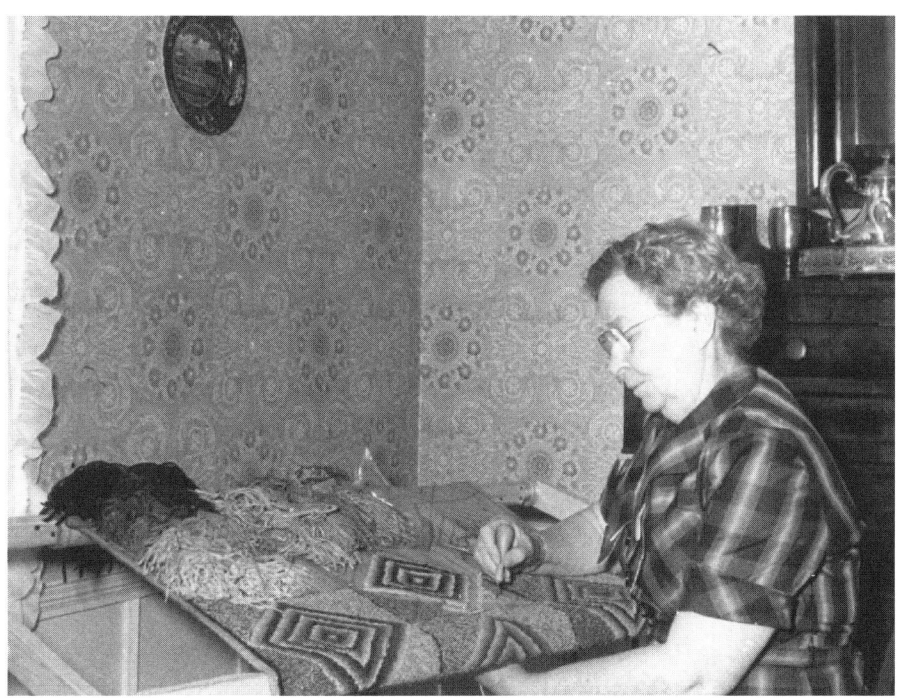

Marion hooking a rug in her dining room, circa 1958

Mrs. Sidney B. Coulter
Cherry Road
Syracuse, New York
February 21, 1972
Dear Martha,

My son Robert has written me of the death of your beloved sister.

We are saddened at the loss of such an esteemed friend. All who loved her must only be thankful that she has been released from her long illness, however.

The world is a better place because of Marion Parsons for with her gentle and wise guidance, she left her mark on the lives of so many children. We were always grateful that ours were among those fortunate ones.

My daughter Betty, whom I am visiting, joins me in sending you and all of the family our deepest sympathy,

Most Sincerely,
Mildred Coulter

February 8, 1972
Dear Martha,

Your sister was such a wonderful person that all of us who were fortunate to know her experience a real loss at her death.

Miss Parsons was the first principal under whom I taught. Her guidance and leadership were equaled only by her friendship for her teachers. What a real and wonderful person she was! Her example has been the guidelines for my own teaching career, and I feel that her influence upon me enriched my entire teaching experience.

We suffer a real loss with her passing.

In Sympathy,
Elizabeth (Tibby) Muench Dumanian

February 13, 1972

I was very sorry to hear of the death of Miss Parsons and I know that she will be missed by all who knew and loved her. She was always very firm with all of her students, but we knew she cared for us or she wouldn't have insisted on our behaving like she wanted us to. There were four of us and she saw us through grade school and I was the last one. When years go by you always wish that you'd have more time to stop and see people but it never seems to happen that way.

My family will always have fond memories of her and Cherry Road.

My sincere sympathy,
Anne Sherry

February 11, 1972,

...When all is said we have to agree that she had a good and full life and that she knew how to make the most of it both for herself and for others. One of the things that sticks in my mind somehow is the way she had her roots so deep right there in Syracuse and on Cherry Road and in the cherry orchards. Somehow I'll always remember Sunday dinners there in the old house with all of you and those tales of far off Mozambique and the cherry picking times … and such.

As ever,
Jim Parsons

Ivy K. Schuyler
115 Newcastle Road
Syracuse, New York 13219

January 13, 1972

Dear Martha:

Excuse my typing, as I am a terrible writer.

What a beautiful service in memory of Marian. It made me think of the service held in memory of Stella. You must miss both of them very much.

My girls loved Marian, Judy had her all through school and Sandy part of the time. They join with me in expressing our sympathy to you.

You will have countless letters and cards so don't try to acknowledge mine.

Just the other day I was reading the program of Marian's retirement and what fun we had composing a play about her life - I am sure you have a copy.

When I broke my wrist Marian drove me several times to work - when I had to move and could not find a house to rent or buy she drove me around - she was a real friend. I wish I had seen more of both of you in recent years.

Express my sympathy to all of your family. I will hope to see you soon .

With love
Ivy

Marion Parsons, 1888—1972

In Honor of Miss Parsons

With our deep affection and gratitude.... the Mothers' Club of Cherry Road School joins with the community of Westvale to present this testimonial luncheon in honor of Miss Marion Parsons, who for twenty-six years has been principal of Cherry Road School.

Friend, confidante, and inspiration to countless children, Miss Parsons has served the community in more than a professional way. She is our well loved neighbor and friend.

Keeping constantly abreast of the latest trends in education, she has kept the standards of Cherry Road School high, giving our children fine instruction coupled with a happy school experience.

The founder of the Mothers' Club in 1927, she has been its inspiration and staunch supporter throughout its years of service, working with the mothers of our community towards the betterment of our school and closer parent-teacher relationships.

All of Westvale salutes Miss Marion Parsons—a gallant lady. We wish her much success and happiness in her retirement as she has given those whom she has served over the years.

—The Corinthian Club, May 24, 1952

Epilogue

I have come to believe that a great teacher is a great artist and that there are as few as there are any other great artists. It might even be the greatest of the arts since the medium is the human mind and spirit.

—John Steinbeck

CHERRY ROAD SCHOOL was rich in social and human capital. It arose in a community where people came together to build a school, but in doing so, they also built enduring relationships that held the school together for years to come. It was this communal culture upon which classroom teachers thrived, and therefore so did the students.

The Cherry Road neighborhood, and the larger Westvale neighborhood, nestled in the old Town of Geddes, embodied the sort of community that comes together like the force of an army regiment to face difficult times head-on—poverty, war, snowstorms, fires, a growing population—with a we-can-get-through-this-together attitude.

Westvale became a sort of ad-hoc community without anything to hold it together but a school, a handful of churches, and a grange hall. There were no stores, no courthouses, and no street corners where kids hung out, just the red brick building in the middle of a network of streets that grew up out of cornfields and potato fields and an orchard. Eventually there was a long boulevard called Parsons Drive. Before that, it had been a dirt farm road where my great-grandfather drove a wagon filled with boxes of fruit, a plow to till a field, or a sleigh filled with children.

By the second decade of the twentieth century, family farms throughout the country were being surveyed and sold, lot by lot, parcel by parcel. Locally, farming was also becoming less and less a viable enterprise. The prices farmers could command for apples and cherries, potatoes and corn, had plummeted. The economic landscape of Central New York, like the rest of the country, was changing forever. People born and raised on farms along the Genesee Turnpike knew that however these changes played out, a solid education supported by a close-knit community would help pave the way for their children and their children's children's success. Though the city of Syracuse grew around it, Westvale remained—and remains—intact.

If you stop today and look closely, some of the farmhouses, families, a hidden tunnel from World War I, and the school are still there. The old Terry Road School has been moved and is now a residential house. The Jerome Dairy, the last of the extended family's successful agricultural operations, has been gone since the 1960s. Pastureland can be picked out beneath and around the freeways, shopping malls, and housing developments. Where now there are parking lots, you might imagine a field, a young boy running through the buttercups, fishing pole or muskrat traps in hand. Suspend disbelief and you'll see cows and a towering barn where a freeway off-ramp now intersects a highway called Genesee Street.

> Life is something extraordinarily wide and profound; it is a great mystery, a vast realm in which we function as human beings. If we merely prepare ourselves to earn a livelihood, we shall miss the whole point of life; and to understand life is much more important than merely to prepare for examinations and become very proficient in mathematics, physics, or what you will ... attention comes when you are deeply interested in something.
> —Krishnamurti

For over fifty years, Cherry Road graduates have been meeting regularly for reunions. Some are small, monthly lunch gatherings.

Some are larger-scale excursions to relive their eighth-grade trips.

Marion knew how to make people feel like they mattered, that they belonged to something important and so did their family. Dennis Owen, now in his eighties and a well-known philanthropist for children's educational programs, used to be Miss Parsons' paperboy. He is still proud of the regular conversations they had on her front porch.

Miss Parsons may be gone, and so is the ringing of her bell, but she is not forgotten, especially by those who remain in Westvale. Today, Marion is honored by the annual award given out in her name—one boy and one girl are selected from the graduating class to receive the Marion Parsons Achievement Award. They are chosen based on criteria that include character traits, citizenship development, scholastic achievement, special interests in which they excel, and general improvement in some personal barrier they have worked to overcome. Students are nominated by teachers, who select two whom they believe are worthy of the award's namesake. Several of the alumni interviewed for The Brass Bell said they were once recipients of the award and consider it one of their highest achievements.

> At Cherry Road, home values of courtesy, respect, kindness, and love of country were reinforced. A philosophy of mine, Napoleon's "L'audace, l'audace, toujours l'audace" served me well in my Marine Corps career. It may well have sprouted at Cherry Road.
>
> We were strong, healthy kids and played recess football roughneck style. Miss Parsons sometimes watched and, bless her wisdom, let us play. She was a kind, gentle lady, but inside tough as the Marines I fought with.
> —Joseph Richard Owen, class of 1938

Cherry Road School only went to the eighth grade, but students claim those years had more impact on them than their time in high school or college. Even the most unreliable and naughty students who attended Cherry Road School during the days of the Great Depression and World War II still gather with their classmates to remember. They marvel at their luck at being part of the community, at having known Miss Parsons. Some steady themselves with canes,

Peter Greene, our treasurer, saw we had money to send out mailings, and that pretty much got things going. He is no longer living. Dick and I were able to come from Pennsylvania for the fifteenth, which I chaired. Bob Salisbury and Joan Marcocia were the rest of the committee. Miss Parsons was there. I remember that she got a real kick out of Don Miner's reporting that he had six children. Most of us had only two by then.

I think we chose Christmas vacation that year when more of us came from other states to be with local families. We continued to meet every five years, and will continue as long as [at least] two of us are able to be there.

For our fiftieth reunion, we decided that instead of being in Syracuse, we would try to go back to Detroit, Michigan. We would go by way of the boat as we had then, but then we discovered [our original ship had been scrapped.] The remnants of the original ship [were] in Belle Isle. So we would take a boat to the museum, where we saw the remains of the ship called the City of Detroit III. We entered the Dossin Great Lakes Museum—95 percent of the room has original materials that have been restored. It was called the Gothic Room. It had its original grandeur—a magnificent light fixture hanging from the ceiling. It was built in 1912, and it was the largest side-wheeler in the world. Before she was scrapped in 1950, 7.5 tons of handcarved English oak beams, columns, and arches and three-paneled lead glass LaSalle windows were carefully removed and stored in a barn until 1956. We got to see all of these things. As we were going through the Gothic Room, we discovered remnants of the actual metal cups we had drank out of in our state rooms in 1949.

We thought about the fundraising events we had held to earn money for each student, about the mere cost of $25.68 per student in 1949. The ship bell was in the room. We got to see the whole thing—the doors weren't much taller than we were! We even saw the helm of the wheel room.

2014 will be our sixty-fifth year since 1949, and we will have our twelfth reunion. We have also had gatherings when anyone comes to the Syracuse area. —Martha Ballard Lacy, class of 1949

bolstering a knee surgery or hip replacement. The younger ones, in their seventies, organize the gatherings. Some show up at monthly luncheons at the old Morgan's restaurant that overlooks a slope where, as youngsters, they used to take risks on bikes and sleds. The restaurant is not too far from the cemetery where Marion, her sisters, parents, cousins, aunts, and uncles are buried.

At the top of Myrtle Hill, the Parsons, Jeromes, Schuylers, Andrews, Babcocks, and Terrys—the farm families of the nineteenth century—lie in peace. Perhaps they know that a semblance of their vision for the future came to pass. They might be shocked by the strip malls and the glut of traffic up and down West Genesee Street, sad to see that Route 695 cut a permanent and deadly swath through the Jerome Dairy Farm, taking out the glorious barn and its hayloft as well as the tenant farmhouse. The empty farmhouse, a target for vandals, had to be razed in the 1970s. From the highway, if you know what you're looking for, you can catch glimpses of Jerome Hill, still intact, hidden beneath fir trees and remnants of farm foliage, and Geddes Creek or Terry's Woods.

> I was her paperboy for years. I had one of the largest routes in the city and would collect from my customers on Saturday. At one point, I was a star on the basketball team, and we had won a game the night before. She said to me the next morning when I came to her house to collect for the paper, "That was a good win for Cherry Road School, Dennis." I never forgot that. She'd give me a piece of candy every once in a while.
> —Dennis Owen, class of 1940

Although many of Marion Parsons' students have passed on, those graduates who remain among us agree on two things: Miss Parsons was their first and greatest hero; it was because of her—because they could not bear to let her down—that they endeavored to be successful in word and deed.

The Westvale and surrounding communities gather every year to celebrate Flag Day. They meet at the old flagpole at Cherry Road School, and from there, they parade along the same path Miss Parsons had led them in school parades of the past.

Marion's journey never took her back to her beloved western country, never gave her a husband and children, but her heart's desire for family was realized in ways she never could have imagined.

Marion takes a trip via Greyhound, 1948

Afterword

Alumni gather to talk about CRS at the Solvay-Geddes Historical Society: Marilyn Marcy, Joe Owen (behind Marilyn), Jim McClennen, Jack Mitchell, Bob Salisbury, Dennis Owen

TIME HAS HAPPENED to them all. They come to the town hall to hear what I have to say about their past—to see one another. The room is full, some are standing out in the hallway, and we try to find extra chairs. Most everyone in the room has gray hair, including me.

I show them pictures on a big screen—a PowerPoint presentation, a photograph collection in sepia tones I've put together from the big box of family pictures. Some once belonged to my Aunt Marion—they had been in a velvet-covered photo album on a lamp table in her front room. As a young child, these old pictures thrilled me as much as her stories about the olden days.

The old-timers have come to hear what I know, to see if I might be able to evoke times gone by. I tell them my story about the brass bell.

When Marion retired, she took the bell with her. The bell sat on a shelf in her den, but to my dismay, the ringer was removed—hidden in an undisclosed location. The rule about the bell was this: if I was generally a good girl, I would be allowed to ring the bell. I'd hide my eyes while Aunt Marion retrieved the ringer. Then I could ring the bell two, possibly three, times. The bell is heavy, made of brass. You have to put a lot of weight behind it—you have to know what you're doing.

When the fun was over, I'd cover my eyes again, and the ringer would be returned to its hiding spot. No, I never cheated—never peeked to see in which direction she went, did not listen to her footsteps.

But mine is a small offering; I have only pictures and a few anecdotes dredged up out of my own "think," stories Aunt Marion told me fifty-some years ago. It is they who have the stories.

I can't pretend to know how Marion felt about her life, if she regretted giving up on her young dreams, her life out West, if she regretted choosing what might be construed as duty over desire. Did she lament not having a family of her own? She had nieces and nephews, two generations, who considered her a mother, a grandmother. Hundreds, if not thousands, of former students love her, admire her, and hold her as a role model. No one I know of has let her down. Perhaps she found more than her heart's desire as the matriarch of the school in the cherry orchard. She was an ordinary person, and the ordinary things she accomplished were extraordinary. She was inspired by the courage of the people she met out West who had carved a life for themselves out of the wilderness. She took this with her on her life's journey. She was inspired by the people around her, their dedication to family, and their courage during trying times.

Miss Parsons led her charges into a world that changed with its inventions, its social chaos, and its economic ups and downs. She led with a set of moral values you might say were of the Victorian era, passed to her by her parents, and those values guided Marion through the zeitgeist of the times and the places she traveled. She most often took children with her, and she always wore a hat and gloves.

After Marion died, my father, Peter, and my Uncle David were overcome one afternoon with an inspiration to honor her and the history of the school. They took the bell and headed over to the school, walking along the same path Marion would have walked every day for twenty-five years on her way to school and back again. I'm told Uncle David shed tears when he handed the bell to the current principal and asked her to keep it safe in Marion's honor. Those of us who loved Marion—her family, her students, and her friends—are all apt to shed a tear when we think of the woman who transformed a one-room schoolhouse into a public education success story.

Today the bell sits quietly on the corner of Miss Parsons' old desk at the Cherry Road School office. An artifact from the past, it evokes emotion for those who were there, who knew and loved their Miss Parsons and my Aunt Marion. It reminds us that we have the capacity to find meaning and purpose in what we do if we are willing to work together. It reminds us to stand tall, do our best, and be

Bertha, Grace, Marion (at the oars), and Martha Parsons, circa 1907

respectful of ourselves and others. Though the Cherry Road School represented in this book is in the past, the stories and remembrances of those who lived through the Great Depression and two world wars have meaning for the present.

Nostalgia has been described as a longing, or yearning, for the past. A certain smell in the air, a sound, a word, carries us in an instant to another time and place that made us happy or sad, filled us with enough emotion to evoke the memory again and again. The thing about memory is that everyone remembers incidents and places in their own way, in their own version. It may be slightly different each time it is evoked or recalled. But there is one common theme among the expressed memories of Cherry Road School and Miss Parsons: the feelings they stir up are warm and heartfelt—even the scolding, even the fear of the scolding is remembered with love.

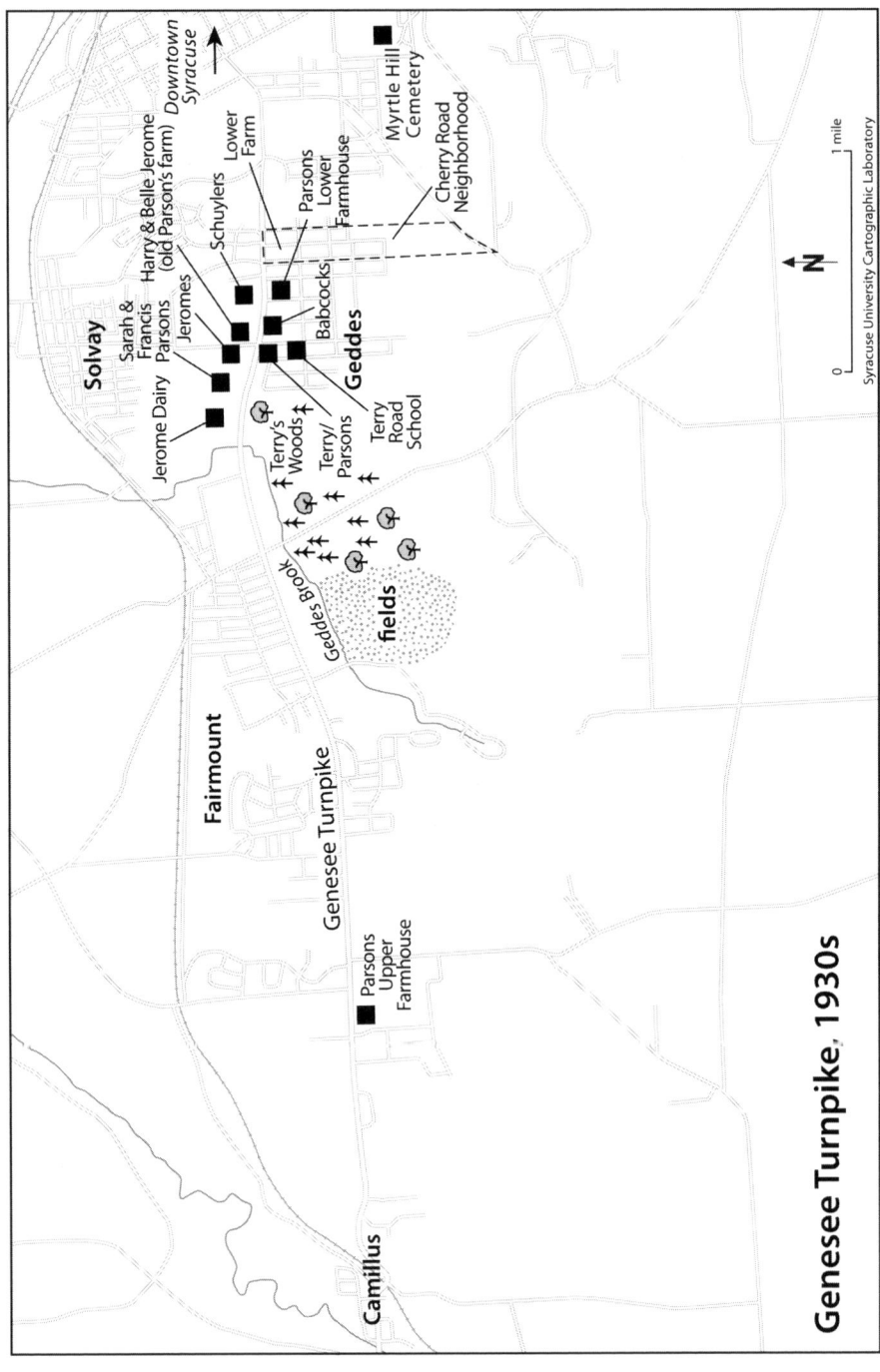

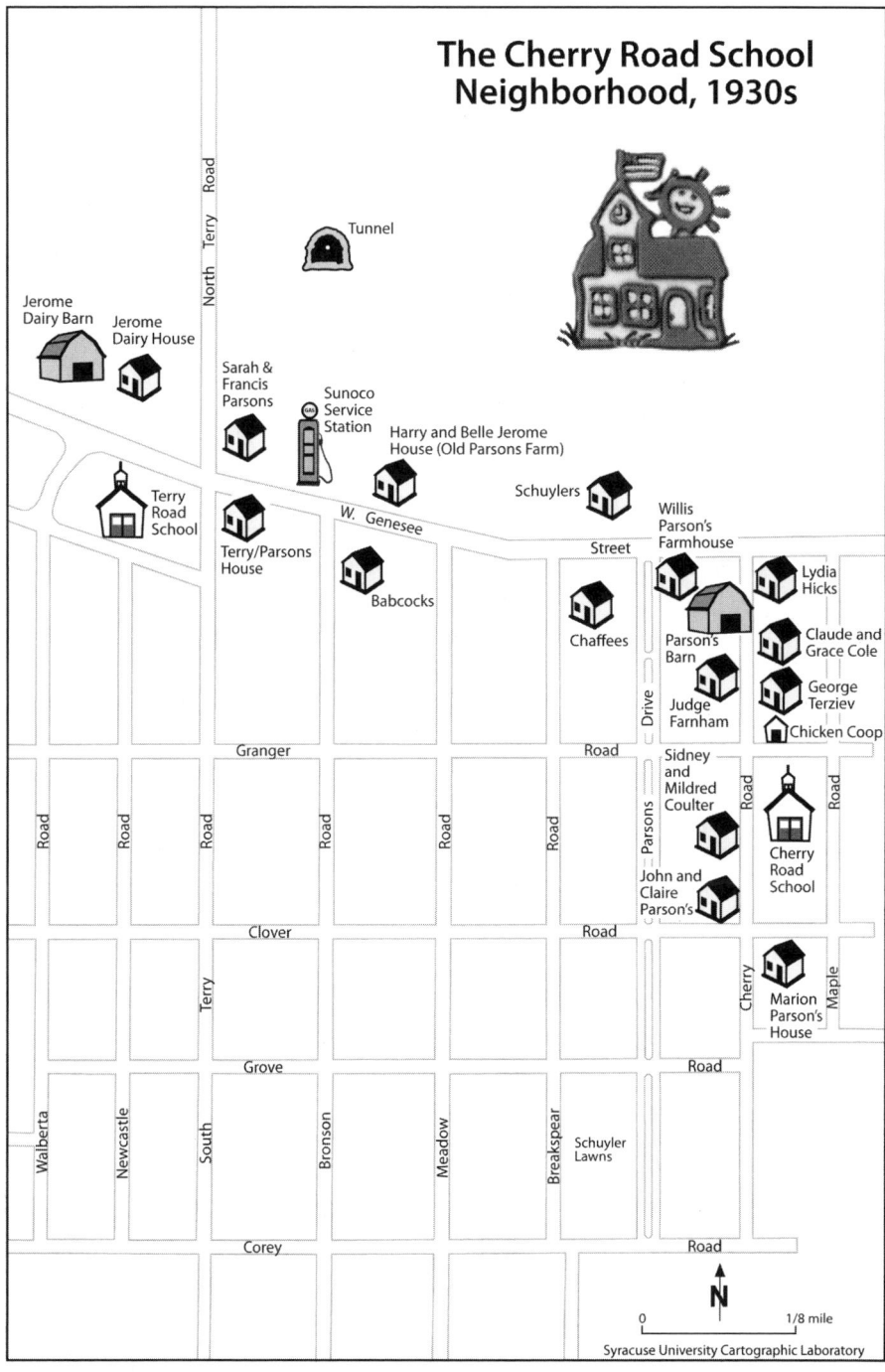

Appendix A

What became of the Cherry Road Alumni interviewed for *The Brass Bell*?

Class of 1949 reunion in 1994, 45 years after graduating eighth-grade

William "Bill" Ballard

After leaving Cherry Road School (CRS) in 1955, Bill Ballard went on to high school, and then served in the US Navy on a destroyer in 1960. In 1962 he went to work for Fulton Boiler Works in Pulaski, New York, and worked there in various capacities, including boilermaker, until he retired in 1997. Bill married Joyce Sweatland in 1964. They had two children, William Jr. and Michelle. The family lived in Williamstown, New York. Today, Bill is retired, and he and Joyce live in Pulaski, New York, on Lake Ontario.

Robert "Bob" Coulter

Bob grew up across the street from CRS, graduating from there in 1940. Immediately after high school he joined the navy and was in the first class of naval aviation cadets to have no college experience.

He later attended the universities of Georgia, South Carolina, and Colgate as a naval cadet. He went on to Pensacola to become a naval aviator and was discharged from the navy in 1945. Bob graduated from the Syracuse University College of Law in 1952 and was admitted to the New York State Bar. Bob married Joan Wood in 1949, and they have three children they raised in Phoenix, New York. He has been town attorney for townships in Central New York and was active in the Republican Party. He was the justice of the peace in the town of Lysander, and as such, a member of the Judicial Conference, New York State, 4th Department. He was an active member of the New York State Magistrates Association. In 1983 he received a citation from the North Republican Club for "Outstanding Reward for Service." He has served on education boards, is an active Mason, Shriner, and Jester in New York and Florida. He was also active in the Episcopal Church and various veterans' organizations. He is an honorary member of the Phoenix Volunteer Fire Department, having served actively for many years. A big part of Bob's life was flying his Beechcraft Bonanza airplane. He is semiretired now, and he and Joan have moved into his childhood home across from the school and are refurbishing the house with their daughter, Barbara. They divide their time between New York, Florida, and their summer home, an island cottage in Canada.

Sidney Coulter (former trustee)

Bob Coulter's father, Sidney Coulter, was active in and supportive of CRS. He was a long-time Trustee for the school. He received special posthumous recognition for his distinguished service to Onondaga Community College and the Central New York community as a founding trustee: the John H. Mulroy Founders Award, approved by the College Board of Trustees in May 2012. The award recognizes individuals whose exemplary service advances the mission of this small college where many CRS students have continued their education. His award serves as an example of the sort of friends and neighbors CRS enjoyed and thrived upon throughout the years.

Elizabeth "Tibby" Muench Dumanian (former teacher)

Students remember Miss Muench fondly. Tibby Muench Dumanian taught during two tenures at CRS, a total of twenty-one years. From 1939 to 1944, she taught the second grade; from 1961 to 1976, she taught the eighth grade and served as the librarian for the sixth, seventh, and eighth grades. She remembers having more than 40 students in her second-grade class back in the 30s. Her salary at that time was $900 a year. Tibby left CRS the first time to complete a bachelor's degree at Syracuse University, then worked as a graduate assistant to earn her master's degree in Education and Psychology. She married Barco Dumanian, had two sons, and stayed at home to raise her family for fourteen years. When she returned to CRS in the 1960s to teach language arts, she enjoyed an increase in annual salary of over $5,000. Five years later, the state of New York offered a grant to establish a special education program, and she took that job. She retired after eleven years to teach ceramics as a visiting artist at Syracuse University. She closed her personal art studio at age ninety-one due to her growing blindness. When I first interviewed Mrs. Dumanian in October 2010, she was ninety-three years old, living alone. Though she has lost her eyesight and her hearing, it was only recently that she stopped gardening. Tibby is an artist and an avid outdoorswoman. She has been an inspiration to all whose lives she has touched.

Mildred "Millie" Mitchell Dunk

Millie Mitchell Dunk, one of the five Mitchell children, was one of the original chicken-coop kids and one to whom this book is dedicated. She began first grade in the converted chicken coop with ten other children. Millie, or "Mitch" as she was fondly called by many, was active in school and church activities growing up and held leadership roles in clubs and sports. She was head cheerleader and president of her church's youth group in high school. Millie was voted most active in her class and was the first runner up for class queen during her senior year at Solvay High School. Mitch met Bill Dunk from Jordan, New York, when she was fifteen. They were married on June 6, 1942. They lived in Georgia while he was in the service. She worked for the government during World War II at Robins Field Air Force Base. Their first child, Bill, was born there, and the family returned to New York and had two more children, Barbara and Nancy. Mitch taught Sunday school at her Presbyterian Church, was a Girl Scout leader and Cub Scout den mother. She loved the field of nursing and volunteered for the Red Cross and two women's clubs while balancing her family roles. The family moved to Leesburg, Florida, in the fall of 1960 when Bill transferred with his company. Millie worked for the Florida Greeting Service and the Chamber of Commerce, and was a writer/photographer for the local newspaper. She was the first woman to be commodore of the Leesburg Boating Club, and she was named "Florida Mother of the Year" by the Lakes Business and Professional Women's Club. Millie and Bill were active in camping groups, square dancing, and the Boating Club. They were the King and Queen of the National Campers and Hikers Association. Bill passed on September 25, 1991. Millie and Bill have eight grandchildren and eleven great-grandchildren. Millie is ninety-two years old. She lived in the same house in Florida for over fifty years. She now resides in an assisted living facility in Leesburg, Florida. Her childhood memories of CRS contributed to the heart of this story.

William "Bill" Eriksson

Bill graduated from CRS in 1943 and from Solvay High School in 1947. He went to work for J.D. Taylor Construction and then for Gene Irish Construction. He eventually started his own successful construction company, Eriksson Construction. Bill married his high school sweetheart, Shirley Kuhns, in January 1949. Bill and Shirley had gone together to both the junior and senior proms at Solvay High. They have three children, two boys and a girl, three grandchildren and one great-grandchild. Bill was active in the South Onondaga, New York, community, serving on the school board for twenty years and part of his tenure as president. He was a member of the South Onondaga Fire Department. Bill died in December 2012. He shared many wonderful stories for this book, as did his lifelong pal, George Kinder.

Justice John H. Farnham (former trustee)

Judge Farnham was the first and the longest sitting trustee on the CRS board of trustees, serving in this capacity for thirty years. A close friend of Willis Parsons, Judge Farnham worked closely for many years with Marion Parsons concerning all sorts of school matters, from financial to social. Admitted to the New York State Bar in 1917 and later forming the firm of McCurn, Farnham, and Martineau, in 1959 Farnham was named a Justice of the New York Supreme Court. He served with distinction in this capacity until 1971. Prior to his Supreme Court Bench appointment, Judge Farnham served as Justice of the Peace for twenty-five years. A staunch community member, Judge Farnham was counsel to the New York State Fair Commission and later became its Chairman. He was a warden of St. Mark's Episcopal Church for thirty-five years.

Elsie Bidwell Haskins (former teacher)

Mrs. Haskins turned ninety-four this year. She lives at her home in Minoa, New York. She loves to tell stories about her days at Cherry Road School, and one of her favorites is the time she was to be married and she went to Miss Parsons and asked for permission. I guess you needed clearance in those days. Miss Parsons said she would have to put it before the Board of Trustees. Elsie is still waiting to hear back on their decision. The best part of the story is that all of her students showed up for her wedding. Elsie has two children, five grandchildren, and eight great-grandchildren. She was an active member of the Eastern Star for seventy-five years. A passionate community member until recently, when she has had to slow down, she hosted a minister's breakfast at the Baptist church for many years. She never missed a sporting event of any of her grandchildren. She was as enthusiastic a mother and grandmother as she was a fourth-grade teacher.

Betty Templar Jerome

Betty graduated from CRS in 1934 and then graduated from Solvay High School. She held a master's degree from Syracuse University and taught home economics at Solvay High School. She married Van Jerome, one of the original chicken-coop kids, and a childhood friend from Betty's days at CRS. This book is dedicated to Betty and to two of the original eleven children. Without Betty's stories, the story told in The Brass Bell would not be possible. She and Helen Cole, my aunt and Marion Parsons' niece, were best friends throughout their school days. Betty spent a lot of time with Helen at Marion's house. She considered Marion family—and they were also related through marriage. Betty worked briefly as Marion's secretary at CRS while Van was overseas during WWII. Betty and Van raised two daughters and a son at their home on Genesee Street, next to the Jerome Dairy where Van grew up, around the corner from Betty's childhood home on Bronson Road. She lived in the family home next door to her beloved nephew, Jim, and his family until her death this year. Betty had celebrated her 91st birthday in September. She is survived by her children, seven grandchildren, and twelve great-grandchildren. Van died in 2004.

George Kinder

George graduated from CRS in 1943 and Solvay High School in 1947. He worked summers during the war at Allied Chemical (Solvay Process). The summer after he graduated from Solvay he went to work at Allied and stayed on until he retired in 1987. The plant closed in 1986. George was the supervisor of maintenance. He married Ruth Webb in 1949. They have two children, a boy and a girl, six grandchildren, and three great-grandchildren. George and Ruth lived in Westvale for ten years and then built a house in Marcellus and still live in this tiny village about twelve miles west of Westvale. Today they live along the banks of Nine Mile Creek in Marcellus where they downsized from the family home. George has always been an avid woodworker, building furniture in his home shop. He and Ruth have enjoyed playing golf together for many years at Myrtle Beach and in Florida. George says this year is the first time in twenty-four years that they didn't go to Florida for the winter.

Martha Ballard Lacy

Martha graduated from CRS in 1949, from Solvay High School in 1953, and from Cornell University in 1957. She later took a master's degree at Syracuse University before returning to a career in teaching. She married Richard Lacey, whom she had met during her first year at Cornell. The mother of three children, over the years Martha taught home economics, traveled with her family and stayed home to raise her children while substitute teaching to help support the family. When her children went to college, she taught at Syracuse University to help with tuition and then returned full-time to teaching in the upper grades until she retired in 1998. She recalls "the wonderful teachers at CRS encouraged me to choose a career in teaching." Martha and Dick have three children and seven grandchildren. They have lived in Binghamton, New York; New Jersey, and Western Pennsylvania. The family returned to Central New York in 1979. Today, Martha supervises student teachers in Family & Consumer Science at SUNY Oneonta. She is a memoir consultant and CRS reunion planner, and maintains their family-oriented home in Jamesville, New York. It was the friendships and the memories from CRS, she notes, that prompted her to take charge of organizing the CRS reunions. She is active in her church, sings in the choir, and is well-known for her homemade maple syrup.

Marilyn Lewis Marcy

In 1951, Marilyn went on to Solvay High School and from there to Cortland State Teacher's College. She married Eugene Marcy in August 1958. They have three children. Marilyn began teaching in Niagara Falls a month after their marriage. She taught school off and on throughout the years, including at Walberta Park School in Westvale and for many years in Vernon, New York, as she raised her children. At one point during her career in education, she took a position with IBM to help develop an online teaching tool, Writing to Read, for kindergarten and first-grade students. Traveling around the country, she trained teachers to use the program. Marilyn loved teaching and says, "I think it was because I had such great role models at Cherry Road School." When she retired, she and her husband moved back to Westvale, buying the house she grew up in, and they live there today.

Jim McLennan

Jim graduated with the CRS class of 1949 and the Solvay High School class of 1953. He joined the Air Force where he trained as an aviation cadet. He flew jet fighters in the US Air Force and the Air National Guard for thirty years; he was deployed to bases in Canada, Europe, Africa, and the Middle East as a commander, retiring as a lieutenant colonel. He worked as a sales manager for KLM Royal Dutch Airlines and Northwest Airlines. He and his wife of fifty-six years, Robin Lutzy, both graduated from Syracuse University. They have two children and raised their family in Syracuse; Columbus, Ohio; and New Mexico, retiring in Skaneateles, New York, where they live on the lake. Jim and Robin have three grandchildren. They love to travel and have visited Europe and Africa and frequently tour the United States; they are avid fans of Syracuse University sports, enjoying season passes to football and basketball games.

John "Jack" Mitchell

Jack graduated from CRS in 1948 and went on to Solvay High School. He graduated from Syracuse University in 1956 and served with the US Air Force from 1956 to 1960. He worked in the Claims Department for Travelers Insurance from 1960 to 1988. Jack served as an Onondaga County legislator representing western Onondaga County from 1985 to 1995. He was the majority leader in the Legislature. While in the legislature, Jack served on many boards including Cornell Cooperative Extension, the Finger Lakes Board and as Legislative representative to Onondaga Community College. Jack married Anabel Cross in 1956. They have spent time doing mission work in Russia and Mexico. Jack and Anabel Mitchell have four children and five grandchildren. They have lived in Sioux City, Iowa; St. Johns, Newfoundland; and Marcellus, New York. Today they split their time between Forestport, New York, and Carlsbad, California where Jack enjoys photography, gardening and hiking. He has hiked many of the mountains in the Adirondacks and on the Appalachian Trail.

Leland Mitchell

Leland Mitchell was one of the original Cherry Road School students who attended their first year in the chicken coop in George Terziev's garden—he and his sister, Mildred (Millie), and his brother, Lloyd. I dedicated this book to Millie and Leland, and to Betty Jerome—the survivors who generously shared their stories. Without their extensive input, The Brass Bell would be a figment of my imagination. (Betty Templar was married later to Van Jerome, who together with Leland, kept the kids in the chicken coop entertained. They were best friends throughout their lives.) Leland graduated from CRS in 1934, and four years later from Solvay High School where he was captain of the basketball team. After high school, he entered the Coast Guard and served in Texas at Brownsville. German submarines had been spotted in the gulf and he was part of a Coast Guard cutter crew. He was involved in patrolling the coastline. While there, Leland married Florence Dwyer. They have six children. After the war, Leland and Florence returned to the family home on Terry Road in Westvale, as did his brother Lloyd and his sister Mildred and her husband. There were five Mitchell kids, children of John and Mildred Mitchell: Lloyd, Leland, Mildred, Jeanette, and Jack. They were a tight-knit family. Leland went to work for New York Telephone Company in 1945 where he worked as a technician. Eventually he and Florence moved to a postwar reconditioned barracks at the air based that would become Hancock Field. He organized a basketball team made up of friends—mostly veterans who often played at CRS—and organized a league. The family then moved to Mattydale, New York, where they lived for thirty-two years, and then to Camillus, New York, and lived there for twenty-seven years. These are small towns around the Central New York area. His wife, Florence, died in October 1998. Leland stayed on at the Camillus home for another fourteen years, and when he turned ninety years old last year, he moved to an assisted living facility in Baldwinsville, New York, where he remains today. He and his sister Mildred are the oldest surviving CRS students.

Dennis Owen

From paperboy to philanthropist, Denny graduated from CRS in 1940 and from Christian Brothers Academy in 1944. He attended the School of Foreign Service at Georgetown University, graduating in 1951. After living in Westvale for forty-one years, he and his wife, Eleanor Sullivan, whom he married in 1954, moved to Skaneateles Lake, one of the nearby Finger Lakes, in 1967. Eleanor died in 1982, and Dennis finished raising their eight children—five sons and three daughters—by himself. He now has twenty-one grandchildren. Denny has contributed $3 million to assist in educating the needy and deserving, helping them go to college. Currently he provides funding to cover the cost of tuition at a private school for twenty children who will all go on to college with his help. He is active in his local community, sitting on four boards of organizations that feed the homeless and provide assistance to minority and inner-city youth in need. He is proud of the fact that his children all have graduated from universities and have learned from him the importance of giving back to society. Dennis' brother Joe, and sister, Maureen, also graduated from CRS.

Richard "Joe" Owen

The older of the Owen brothers, Joe, who was known as Rickie then, graduated from Cherry Road in 1938. He went on to Solvay High School and then Christian Brothers Academy. Joe studied forestry at Syracuse University before serving with honors in the US Marine Corps. A decorated hero, Joe is the author of the book, *Colder Than Hell: A Marine Rifle Company at Chosin Reservoir*. His compelling account of the Korean War tells the story of the infamous Chosin Reservoir and how Joe's company, Baker-One-Seven, triumphed against all odds on frozen slopes in a horrific battle. Joe tours the country lecturing about his experience in World War II and the Korean War, and about military history. Joe is a combat-decorated marine (Silver Star and two Purple Hearts). He has been active in prisoner rehabilitation. He married Dorothy Litz in 1946, and they have six children. Joe entered the marketing business at General Electric in 1952, and then launched his own marketing company in 1960, working with Fortune 500 companies until he retired in 1990. He and Dorothy raised their children in Westvale. Joe retired and they moved to Skaneateles Lake in the Finger Lakes Region west of Syracuse. He currently writes and does volunteer work.

Martha Parsons Paine

Martha and her sister, Karen, and brother, Charles, lived across from the school and from their cousin, Marion Parsons. Martha graduated from Cherry Road in 1955 and then attended high school at Pebble Hill, a private school in Syracuse, and then two years at Mary A. Burnham School in Northampton, Massachusetts. She attended Endicott College, majoring in child development, and took her internship at Cherry Road School. She then taught as the assistant head teacher at the Jewish Community Center—using many of the skills she learned at Cherry Road. A move to Maine in 1963 took her to the Stepping Stones School where she taught preschool and kindergarten for three years. She married H. Wayne Dickison in 1963, and they raised their two children in North Andover, Massachusetts. Martha married Richard P. Paine in 1988 and together they have ten grandchildren. In addition to her years as an elementary school teacher, Martha has volunteered for the Boston Jr. Council Symphony, the Children's Museum, and as a fundraiser for the Junior League of Boston. She is a thirteen-year breast cancer survivor and an active fund-raiser for four cancer organizations. Martha and her husband live in Nashua, New Hampshire.

Charles Parsons

Charles (Chuck) grew up under the shadow of his relation to Marion Parsons and his family's proximity to the school. Charles' grandfather, Charles F. Parsons, and Marion were first cousins. Like everyone else, Chuck adored Marion. In 1951, Chuck left CRS for Solvay High and then completed high school at Deerfield Academy. He graduated from Dartmouth College in 1959 and then served as a first lieutenant in the US Army from 1960 through 1962, a time that included the construction of the Berlin Wall. He married Elfriede Metzner in 1962 in Bamberg, West Germany. Since then he has taken up the family business, running Parsons & Associates Insurance Agency Brokerage since 1962. The company developed a marine insurance program for charter boat operators on the Great Lakes and New York inland waters. Chuck has served as president of the Professional Insurance Agents Association of New York, the Onondaga County Insurance Agents Association, and the Syracuse Rescue Mission. Elfriede and Chuck have three children and four grandchildren. They are a tight-knit family and spend all their time together, both at the family business and while enjoying family vacations where they delight in the outdoors and boating.

Robert "Bob" Salisbury

After leaving CRS in 1949, Bob attended both the Solvay High School and the Mount Herman School. After he graduated from Williams College in 1958, he returned to Syracuse and pursued a career in banking, working in the estate, trust and investment business, starting out at First Trust and Deposit (now Key Bank), then on to Marine Midland Bank (now HSBC) in 1981, retiring in 1995 as vice president of Investment Services. Bob married Tori Salisbury in 1957, and they have three children. The family lived in Manlius, New York, for many years and moved in 1983 to Cazenovia, where he and Tori run a horse-boarding farm.

George Nicholas Terziev (former trustee)

Known to most of the CRS students as Mr. Terziev, George retired from his research laboratory job at Solvay Process Company—where he had worked for 46 years splitting molecules and reassembling the atoms into new and more useful molecules—in 1951. From then on he devoted himself to his garden and what he noted in his own journal as the, "infinite realm of horticulture, flowers, shrubs, and trees ad infinitum." He would do this on the two-acre lot he bought from Willis Parsons in 1920. George also wrote that his favorite of the plants he had surrounded himself with were the wild primrose and Daphne Mezereum. He had so thoroughly planted his property that "….even his next door neighbors (this author's grandparents) could not see what he was doing."

Helen Wright (former school secretary)

Helen worked as Marion's secretary for many years and shared fond memories of her experiences at CRS for this book. She graduated from Solvay High School on February 1, 1946. On February 4, 1946, she went to Cherry Road School as the school secretary. Her interview for the position with Miss Parsons—she would never call her anything else—took place in Marion's living room over tea. After Marion retired, Helen stayed on under Fred Fuller and then when Mr. Fuller took the job as superintendent of the district, Helen went with him. She stayed on there under Dr. Harold Longlitz and the four superintendents that followed. She retired in June 1992. Says Helen of Miss Parsons, "I will never forget her. Miss Parsons was a wonderful lady and a special day in June was dedicated in her honor at Cherry Road. You couldn't ask for anyone better."

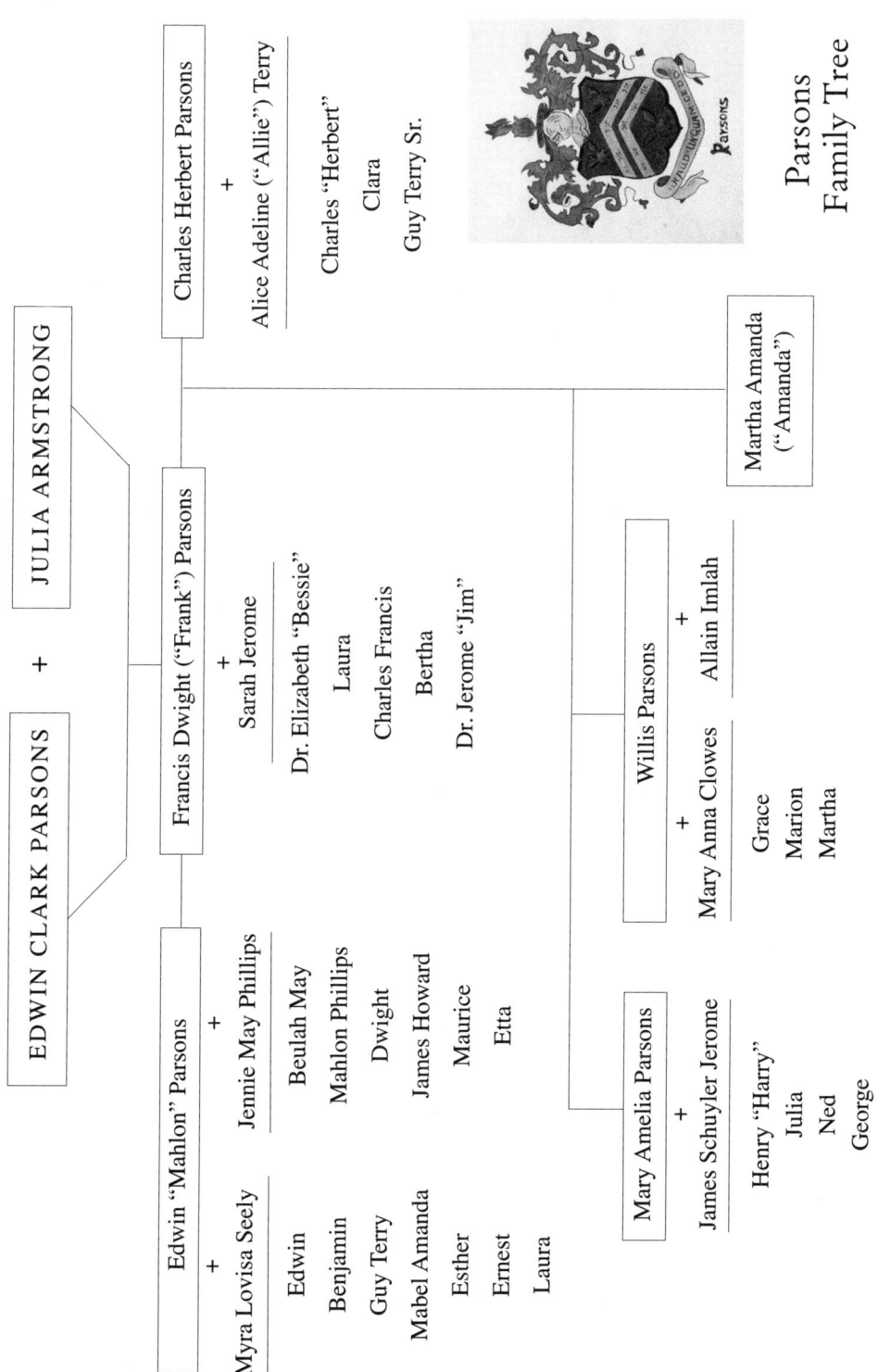

References

Notes

1. "What Happened to the Family Farm?" Public Broadcasting Service, accessed August 16, 2011, http://www.pbs.org/independentlens/realdirt/familyfarms.html.

2. Doris Kearns Goodwin, *No Ordinary Time* (New York: Simon and Schuster, 1994).

3. US Bureau of Labor Statistics, Consumer Expenditure Survey, and US Census Bureau, *Statistical Abstract of the United States*.

4. J. Krishnamurti, *Think on These Things*, ed. D. Rajagopal (New York: Harper, 1970).

Bibliography

"1932–1934 Franklin V-12." How Stuff Works. Accessed July 3, 2011. http://auto.howstuffworks.com/1932-1934-Franklin-v12.htm.

"Auburn and Syracuse Electric Railroad." Wikipedia. Last modified February 13, 2012. http://en.wikipedia.org/wiki/Auburn_and_Syracuse_Electric_Railroad.

"Balboa Park (San Diego)." Wikipedia. Last modified April 9, 2013. http://en.wikipedia.org/wiki/Balboa_Park_%28San_Diego%29.

"Eighth Graders Hit New York High Spots." *Syracuse Post-Standard*. 1935.
Eyestone, June E. "The Influence of Swedish Sloyd and Its Interpreters on American Art Education." *Studies in Art Education* 34, no. 1 (1992).

Gillespie, Harriet Sisson. "New England Bred." *Better Homes & Gardens*. March 1934.
The Great War and the Shaping of the 20th Century. Public Broadcasting Service. 2004.
"Prologue." Quotes: Jay Winter & Blaine Baggett, "The Great War, And the Shaping of the 20th Century."

"Handsome Suburban School Replaces One-Room Building." *Syracuse Herald*. February 28, 1941.

"History of Pasadena, California." Wikipedia. Last modified on April 29, 2013. https://en.wikipedia.org/wiki/History_of_Pasadena,_California.

"History: The Plunge." Belmont Park LLC. Accessed September 29, 2012. http://www.belmontpark.com/history-plunge.

Holcombe, Randall G. "Growth of the Federal Government in the 1920s." Cato Journal. Accessed August 30, 2011. http://www.cato.org/sites/cato.org/files/serials/files/cato-journal/1996/11/cj16n2-2.pdf.

"Introduction to the Great War." Public Broadcasting Service, *The Great War*. Accessed

August 17, 2011. http://www.pbs.org/greatwar/chapters/index.html.

"Mission Beach, San Diego." Wikipedia. Last modified April 1, 2013. http://en.wikipedia.org/wiki/Mission_Beach,_San_Diego.

Omak Stampede. Accessed September 30, 2012. http://omakstampede.org.
"On the Water: Major Rowing Regatta in Marine Stadium." *Gazettes*. Accessed September 28, 2012. http://www.gazettes.com/lifestyle/lighter_living/on-the-water-major-rowing-regatta-in-marine-stadium/article_e51d16ac-8905-11e1-9465-001a4bcf887a.html.

"Panama—California Exposition." Wikipedia. Last modified April 20, 2013. http://en.wikipedia.org/wiki/Panama%E2%80%93California_Exposition.

"The Pike." Wikipedia. Last modified March 20, 2013. http://en.wikipedia.org/wiki/The_Pike. "Post World War II Suburbs in Pennsylvania." Pennsylvania Historical & Museum Commission. Accessed August 20, 2011. http://pa.gov/portal/server.pt/community/post-war_suburbs_1945-1965/18881.

"Pupils Make Afghans for War Victims." *Syracuse Herald American*. October 13, 1940.
"Rocky Mountain Mission—Northwest." Society of Jesus, Oregon Province. Accessed September 29, 2012. http://www.rockymtnmission.org/index.php?page=omak-wa.

"Sept. 9, 1926: Radio Sets Up a National Broadcasting Craze." *Wired*. Accessed September 30, 2012. http://www.wired.com/thisdayintech/2010/09/0909rca-creates-nbc/.

Sims, Ralph. "Parsons Farm Subdivision Explained." *The Advocate*. September 13, 2000.
———. "The Roads of Camillus." The Advocate. December 6, 2000.

Sutton, Bettye. "1930–1939." Lone Star College-Kingwood Library, *American Cultural History*. Last modified June 2008. http://wwwappskc.lonestar.edu/popculture/decade30.html.

"Timeline of the Great Depression." Oregon Public Broadcasting, *American Experience*. Accessed December 16, 2012. http://www.pbs.org/wgbh/americanexperience/features/timeline/rails-timeline/.

Town of Geddes, 1776–1976, pamphlet prepare by The Bicentennial Committee, 1976.
Whitley, Peggy. "1920–1929." Lone Star College-Kingwood Library, *American Cultural History*. Last modified November 2008. http://wwwappskc.lonestar.edu/popculture/decade20.html.

PHOTOGRAPHIC CREDITS

Cover: Clockwise from upper right-hand corner: Terry Road School, circa 1916: Courtesy of Betty Jerome; Terry Road School, 1897; West Hill School District, Hill & Vale, 1974; Papa puttering down the turnpike: Courtesy of the Parsons-Cole Family Archives; Terry Road School, 1925: Courtesy of Betty Jerome; Marion Parsons: Courtesy of Marilyn Lewis Marcy; Cherry Road School, class of 1940: Courtesy of J. Richard Owen; Cherry Road School, early 1930s: Courtesy of Donald Cole; Center: Marion Parsons, February 28, 1941: Courtesy of the Post Standard, Syracuse, New York.

Dedication page:
• Millie Mitchell Dunk, Courtesy of the Mitchell Family Archives; Betty Templar Jerome, Courtesy of the Jerome Family Archives; Leland Mitchell, also Courtesy of the Mitchell Family Archives

Introduction
• Terry Road School, 1897; West Hill School District, Hill & Vale, January 1974

Chapter One
• Yellowstone Park, 1923: Marion Parsons' Travel Journal, Courtesy of the Cole Family Archives
• The Kinneys, 1924: Marion Parsons' Travel Journal, Courtesy of the Cole Family Archives
• A page in Marion's diary: Marion Parsons' Travel Journal, Courtesy of the Cole Family Archives
• Papa and Mother visit: Marion Parsons' Travel Journal, Courtesy of the Cole Family Archives
• Omak teachers: Marion Parsons' Travel Journal, Courtesy of the Cole Family Archives

Chapter Two
• Omak School: Courtesy Okanagan County Historical Society.
• Willis and his grandchildren: Courtesy of the Cole Family Archives

Chapter Three
• Parsons cousins: Marion Parsons' Travel Journal, Courtesy of the Cole Family Archives

Chapter Four
• Terry Road School, 1908: Courtesy Spike Brigati
• Martha, Grace, Marion Parsons, 1909: Courtesy the Parsons-Cole Family Archives
• Terry Road School Building: Used with Permission of an Authorized Representative of the Parsons' Family Archives
• Willis Parsons, Grace, Marion, Anna, Martha: Courtesy of the Parsons-Cole Family Archives
• Willis Parsons' farm: Courtesy of the Solvay Geddes Historical Society
• Martha Parsons, 1897: Courtesy of the Parsons-Cole Family Archives
• Claude Cole, 1909: Courtesy of the Parsons-Cole Family Archives

Chapter Five
• Marion Parsons, circa 1908: Courtesy of the Parsons-Cole Family Archives
• Mary Anna Clowes Parsons: Courtesy of the Parsons-Cole Family Archives

- Julia Armstrong Parsons: Courtesy of the Parsons-Cole Family Archives
- Mary Anna and her brother, Viniah Clowes: Courtesy of the Parsons-Cole Family Archives
- Papa puttering down the turnpike: Courtesy the Parsons-Cole Family Archives
- Fishing party in Nyasaland, Africa: Courtesy Max Docherty
- Allain Imlah Parsons' brother-in-law: Courtesy of the Society of Malawi
- Martha, Grace, John, circa 1915: Courtesy of the Parsons-Cole Family Archives
- Cousin "Jim" Jerome Parsons: Syracuse Herald-American, April 29, 1918
- July 4, 1916: Courtesy the Parsons-Cole Family Archives
- Terry Road School, circa 1916: Courtesy of Betty Jerome
- Terry Road School, 1925: Courtesy of Betty Jerome

Chapter Six
- The Tots, circa 1926: Courtesy of the Parsons-Cole Family Archives
- Parsons family picnic: Courtesy of the Parsons-Cole Family Archives
- Willis examines his prize apples: Courtesy of the Parsons-Cole Family Archives
- Willis and grandson, John Parsons Cole: Courtesy of the Parsons-Cole Family Archives
- Sunday picnic: Courtesy of the Parsons-Cole Family Archives
- Willis, Helen, Grace, David, Allain, Marion: Courtesy of the Parsons-Cole Family Archives
- The Parsons and Jeromes bring in the hay: Courtesy of the Parsons-Cole Family Archives
- Willis Armstrong Parsons: Courtesy of the Parsons-Cole Family Archives
- James Schuyler Jerome: Courtesy of the Parsons-Cole Family Archives

Chapter Seven
- Willis Parsons' Cherry Orchard: Courtesy of the Terziev Family
- George Terziev and his children: Courtesy of the Terziev Family
- The Terziev House: Courtesy of the Terziev Family
- Helen and David Cole, the twins: Courtesy of the Terziev Family
- George N. Terziev: Courtesy of the Terziev Family

Chapter Eight
- Halloween on Cherry Road: Courtesy of the Parsons-Cole Family Archives

Chapter Nine
- The New Cherry Road School: Courtesy of Donald Cole
- The Coulters, Mildred and children: Courtesy of the Coulter Family
- Claude and Grace Cole and Family: Courtesy of the Parsons-Cole Family Archives
- Cherry Road School teachers, 1938: Courtesy of the Parsons Family Archives

Chapter Ten
- Peter Cole and his older brother, David: Courtesy of the Parsons-Cole Family Archives
- David, Peter, Helen Cole: Courtesy of the Parsons-Cole Family Archives
- Cherry Road School, early 1930s: Courtesy of Donald Cole
- Cherry Road teachers, June 19, 1936: Courtesy of the Parsons-Cole Family Archives
- Cherry Road School mothers: Courtesy of the Parsons-Cole Family Archives
- Seventh and eighth grade girls, Cherry Road School, 1934: Courtesy of Betty Jerome
- Marion and Cherry Road School Students: Courtesy of the Terziev Family
- Fall, 1934, Cherry Road School students: Courtesy of Betty Jerome
- Frances Terziev, Penny, David Cole: Courtesy of the Terziev Family

- Boys in Mrs. Amedro's eighth-grade class, 1938: Courtesy of J. Richard Owen

Chapter Eleven
- Miss Costello, Miss Kendell, Miss Parsons: Courtesy of Donald Cole
- Cherry Road School, class of 1940: Courtesy of J. Richard Owen
- Marion Parsons in her backyard: Courtesy of the Parsons-Cole Family Archives
- Miss Parsons, Miss Costello, Miss Robinson, Miss Hannigan, Miss Bidwell, Mrs. Miller: Courtesy of the Parsons-Cole Family Archives
- Marion Parsons: Courtesy of the Parsons-Cole Family Archives

Chapter Twelve
- Old coal furnace: Courtesy of the Parsons-Cole Family Archives
- Rooms for rent at 3012 W. Genesee Turnpike: Courtesy of Solvay-Geddes Historical Society
- Cherry Road School, 1944: Courtesy of Donald Cole
- Miss Parsons and Miss Robinson: Courtesy of the Parsons-Cole Family Archives
- 303 Cherry Road, Marion's house: Courtesy of the Parsons-Cole Family Archives
- Marion's living room: Courtesy of the Parsons-Cole Family Archives

Chapter Thirteen
- Cherry Road School teachers, 1940: Courtesy of Donald Cole
- Eighth-grade graduating class: Courtesy of Donald Cole

Chapter Fifteen
- Cherry Road School band: Courtesy of William Ballard

Chapter Sixteen
- McArdell's Gas Station: Postcard created by McArdell Family

Chapter Seventeen
- Fred Fuller, Jean Miller, Marion Parsons, John Garafalo: Courtesy of Marilyn Lewis Marcy

Chapter Eighteen
- Marion's hearth: Drawing made for Marion by roomer E. Goetchuiss, Courtesy of the Parsons-Cole Family Archives
- Cherry Road School basketball team; Courtesy of Marilyn Lewis Marcy
- Marion poses at her hearth: Courtesy of the Parsons-Cole Family Archives

Chapter Nineteen
- Martha Parsons, Peter Cole, Marion Parsons: Courtesy of the Parsons-Cole Family Archives
- Frances Terziev, Navy Wave, 1945: Courtesy of the Terziev Family
- David Cole, John Farnham, Marc Terziev: Courtesy of the Terziev Family
- Marine Lieutenant J. Richard Owen takes a helmet: Courtesy of J. Richard Owen
- Peter and David Cole: Courtesy of the Parsons-Cole Family Archives
- Marc Terziev: Courtesy of the Terziev Family
- Mitchell Family: Courtesy of the Mitchell Family
- Mitchell Family: Courtesy of the Mitchell Family

Chapter Twenty
• Marion Parsons' house: Drawing by H. Newlove, Courtesy of the John Peter Cole family

Chapter Twenty-One
• Ned and Emma Jerome and their children: Courtesy of the Jerome Family
• Parsons farmhouse: Used with Permission of an Authorized Representative of the Parsons' Family Archives
• Parsons' farmhouse: Used with Permission of an Authorized Representative of the Parsons' Family Archives
• Parsons and Jerome gathering: Courtesy of the Parsons-Cole Family Archives
Sunday picnic circa 1915: Courtesy of the Parsons-Cole Family Archives
• Marion, Martha Parsons, Claude and Grace Cole: Courtesy of the Parsons-Cole Family Archives
• Gloria Luce, Marion Parsons, etc.: Courtesy of the Parsons-Cole Family Archives
• Van Jerome, delivering milk: Courtesy of Betty Jerome
• Ned Jerome and the Jerome Dairy Wagon: Courtesy of Betty Jerome
• Jerome Dairy Farmhouse: Courtesy of Betty Jerome
• Jerome Dairy Barn: Courtesy of Betty Jerome

Chapter Twenty-three
• Mother, me, Aunt Marion: Courtesy of the Parsons-Cole Family Archives
• Mother and Marion: Courtesy of the Parsons-Cole Family Archives
• Marion and Cherry Road School class of 1950: Courtesy of the Parsons-Cole Family Archives

Chapter Twenty-four
• Marion hooking a rug: Courtesy of the Parsons-Cole Family Archives
• Marion Parsons, 1888–1972: Courtesy of the Parsons-Cole Family Archives

Afterword
• Alumni gather: Picture taken by Author
• Bertha, Grace, Marion and Martha: Courtesy of the Parsons-Cole Family Archives

Appendix A
• Class of 1949 reunion in 1994, Picture taken by Dick Lacy, Courtesy of Martha and Dick Lacy

About the Author
• Nancy "Camille" Cole: Picture taken by Rachel Hadiashar, photographer, Portland, Oregon

About the Author

Nancy "Camille" Cole is a retired educator who works as an educational program development consultant, educational grant writer, and freelance writer of fiction and nonfiction. She has worked both at the ground level in the classroom and at the state level at the Oregon Department of Education, where she oversaw the deployment and implementation of a statewide distance-learning network and served as a school improvement specialist.

She is the coauthor of *Videoconferencing for K–12 Classrooms*, published by the International Society for Technology in Education (ISTE) in 2004 and again in 2009, and the author of *Connecting Students to S.T.E.M. Careers, Social Networking Strategies*, 2011, also published by ISTE—a professional society for educators and one of the largest publishers of K–12 education books.

Camille lives in Portland, Oregon. Her fiction and nonfiction works have been published in various literary journals, city magazines, and education journals.

Photo by Rachel Hadiashar